MOUNT MORIAH

"KILL A MAN—
START A CEMETERY"

By Helen Rezatto

Art by Rose Mary Goodson

Modern Photography by Al Gunther

FENWYN PRESS
Rapid City, South Dakota 57701

9th Printing

QUOTATIONS FROM THE FOLLOWING WORKS ARE USED BY PERMISSION OF
THE PUBLISHERS

Old Deadwood Days, Estelline Bennett, Copyright 1935, Charles Scribner's Sons; *The Black Hills or Last Hunting Grounds of the Dakotahs,* Annie D. Tallent, Copyright 1974, Brevet Press; *The Black Hills and Their Incredible Characters,* Robert Casey, Copyright 1949, The Bobbs-Merrill Company; *Pioneer Years in the Black Hills,* Richard B. Hughes, Copyright 1957, Arthur H. Clark Company; *Theodore Roosevelt—An Autobiography,* Copyright 1913, Charles Scribner's Sons; *My Life on the Plains,* General George Custer, University of Nebraska Press, Copyright 1966, R. R. Donnelly & Sons; *Following the Guidon,* Elizabeth B. Custer, Copyright 1890, Harper and Row; "An Account of Deadwood and the Northern Black Hills in 1876," Seth Bullock, Copyright 1924, *South Dakota Historical Collections; Bury My Heart at Wounded Knee,* Dee Brown, Copyright 1970, Holt, Rinehart, and Winston; *The Cheyenne and Black Hills Stage and Express Routes,* Agnes Wright Spring, Copyright 1948, University of Nebraska Press; "Wild Bill Hickok and Calamity Jane," Clarence S. Paine. Reprinted from *The Black Hills* edited by Roderick Peattie by permission of the publisher, Vanguard Press, Inc. Copyright 1952 by Roderick Peattie, Copyright © renewed 1980 by Mrs. Ruth Peattie; "Trip to and from the Hills," by J. Bryan and C. Hollenback. The material first appeared in Clyde C. Walton, ed., *An Illinois Gold Hunter in the Black Hills: The Diary of Jerry Bryan, March 13 to August 20, 1876* (Springfield: Illinois State Historical Society, 1960), pp. 35-36.

QUOTATIONS FROM THE FOLLOWING WORKS ARE USED BY PERMISSION OF
THE AUTHOR OR THE EDITOR:

The Black Hills, Peattie, ed. "History Catches Up," Leland D. Case, Copyright 1952, Vanguard Press; *South Dakota,* John R. Milton, Copyright 1977, W. W. Norton & Co. Inc.; *Silver is the Fortune,* Mildred Fielder, Copyright 1978, North Plains Press; *Potato Creek Johnny,* Mildred Fielder, Copyright 1973, Bonanza Trails Publications; *Historical Cooking of the Black Hills,* Riordan, ed. Copyright 1971, Mountain Co., Inc.; *Gold Gals Guns Guts,* Bob Lee, ed. Copyright 1976, Deadwood-Lead '76 Centennial, Inc.; *Gold in the Black Hills,* Watson Parker, Copyright 1966, University of Oklahoma Press; *Black Hills Booktrails,* J. Leonard Jennewein, Copyright 1962, Dakota Territorial Commission (by permission of Mrs. J. Leonard Jennewein); *Calamity Jane of the Western Trails,* J. Leonard Jennewein, Copyright 1953, Dakota Books, (by permission of Mrs. J. Leonard Jennewein); *Deadwood—The Historic City,* Don Clowser, Copyright 1969, Fenwyn Press Books; *Here Comes Calamity Jane,* Irma H. Klock, Copyright 1979, Dakota Graphics; *Deadwood Gulch—The Last Chinatown,* Joe Sulentic, Copyright 1975.

AUTHOR'S NOTE

The day after I became a resident of Deadwood, SD, in June, 1976, I took an early-morning hike up to Mount Moriah Cemetery which I had visited several times before. Since my last visit as a tourist, nothing had changed. The cemetery was just as picturesque and beautiful as I remembered it; the panoramic views of the northern Black Hills were spectacular as ever; and the informative signs still pointed the way to the graves of the celebrities whom I call The Big Four: Wild Bill Hickok, Calamity Jane, Potato Creek Johnny, and Preacher Smith. The first three especially have received much publicity, mostly of a promotional nature.

Many questions came to my mind. How did Mount Moriah get its start as a burial ground? Was it during the Black Hills Gold Rush of 1876-1877 or was it later? Weren't there colorful denizens more illustrious than Wild Bill and Calamity Jane buried here?

These were the questions that intrigued me and stimulated my historical curiosity. I decided to write a pamphlet about Mount Moriah and some of its inhabitants. Then I began researching the Record Book of the Deadwood Cemetery Association, in libraries and museums, and in Mount Moriah itself. I began interviewing pioneers, historians, and knowledgeable residents of Deadwood and the area. I gathered so much information that I was forced to write a book instead of a pamphlet.

I haven't found all the answers to the enigmas of century-old Mount Moriah, and it would take volumes to write about the over 3,500 inhabitants of the cemetery, known and unknown. Of course, I had to write my own interpretations of the lives of the Big Four. I have also written 40 additional vignettes about a representative group of pioneers and notables.

Yes, there are more than 40 inhabitants of the "city of the dead" who are deserving of recognition. However, in making the final selection of subjects for the vignettes, I have chosen particular ones not only because they were prominent or flamboyant but also because there was considerable information about them in the newspaper files, in regional histories, and in the memories of Black Hillers who were willing to share their reminiscences with me.

Certainly I, a Johnny-Come-Lately, needed all the help I could get to absorb and understand and appreciate the history of the Black Hills, and especially of Deadwood, the locale where the pioneers of 1876 and their descendants have maintained a rivalry about who was first to arrive in the Hills during that memorable year. Even a few days difference in arrival time has become a semi-serious status symbol. Although I had a 100-year difference to overcome, I have met many friendly and helpful natives along the historic trails.

In the book itself I have used informal footnotes—or footsies—at the bottom of many pages to provide side-lights and additions to the main subject matter. These footsies are quotes from newspapers, from Black Hills' histories, from recollections of old-timers, and from comments of Black Hillers. I hope the reader enjoys the footsies and the photographs and the maps and the sketches and the epitaphs. I hope the reader enjoys the entire book.

DEDICATION

TO THE MEMORY OF THE PIONEERS AND THE COME-LATELY'S, THE FAMOUS AND THE INFAMOUS, THE KNOWN AND THE UNKNOWN, TO ALL THOSE WHO SLEEP IN THE GRAVES—MARKED OR LOST—OF MOUNT MORIAH CEMETERY.

Photo courtesy of Deadwood Chamber of Commerce.

"The Christian cemetery is a memorial and a record. It is not a mere field in which the dead are stowed away unknown; it is a touching and beautiful history, written in family burial plots, in mounded graves, in sculptured and inscribed monuments. It tells the story of the past—not of its institutions, or its wars, or its ideas, but of its individual lives—of its men and women and children, and of its household. It is silent, but eloquent; it is common, but it is unique. We find no such history elsewhere: there are no records in all the wide world in which we can discover so much that is suggestive, so much that is pathetic and impressive." Joseph Anderson

TABLE OF CONTENTS

AN APPRECIATION

One of the pleasures of working on this book was exploring Mount Moriah with artist Rose Mary Goodson and with photographer Al Gunther.

Watching Rose Mary draw graves and cemetery roads and lilac bushes on a map was fascinating. It was even more fun to see the picturesque quality of old tombstones take shape on her magic paper. She also made beautiful grave-stone rubbings which unfortunately could not be effectively reproduced for this book. The ever-present visitors in Mount Moriah always gathered around this artist and map-maker with the sketch pad and charcoal pencils.

Such good exercise it was trying to keep up with photographer Al Gunther on his explorations throughout Mount Moriah. Carrying cameras and tri-pod, we searched in vain in the rocky Chinese section for a wooden headboard with a Chinese inscription. How I wish I had snapped agile Al's picture when he shinnied up a tall ponderosa in search of a better camera angle. Or when he lay on his stomach in the April snow to achieve that towering-monument look for the photograph of the George Ayres' marker.

Another pleasure was walking through Deadwood's main street (rightly called historic) with Don Clowser, an expert on the location of the sites of 19th century Deadwood. He made me see the gold camp as it used to be: Chinatown and the opera houses, the Gem Theater and the log cabin where **The Black Hills Pioneer,** the first newspaper, was published. When Don explained, "Over there was the bull flat turn-around," I could almost hear the crack of the whips and the cussing of the bullwhackers.

Many are the rewards of pursuing historic trails with creative people.

The Author

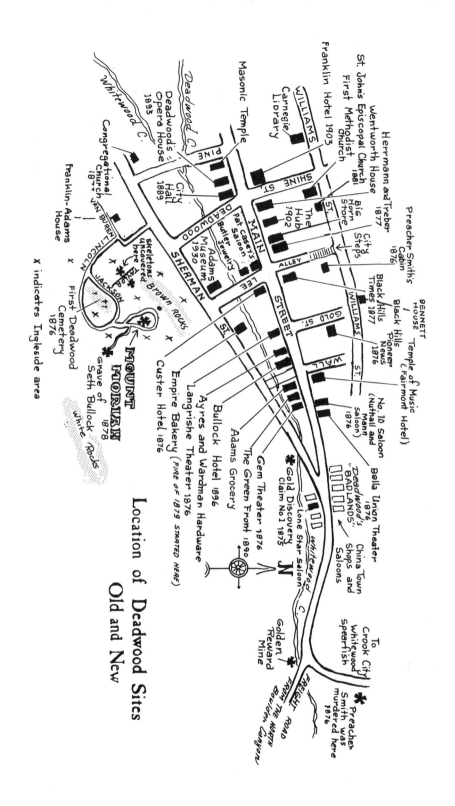

Location of Deadwood Sites
Old and New

I
HISTORY OF DEADWOOD AND ITS TWO BOOT HILLS

"The climate in the Black Hills is so damn healthy that you have to kill a man to start a cemetery."

So said George Ayres, an early pioneer of Deadwood, Dakota Territory, who helped found the gold camp in 1876 and became a prominent hardware merchant and civic leader known for his wit.

Deadwood Gulch

Even though the climate didn't always cooperate to provide permanent residents for the first haphazard boot hill, there were plenty of deaths—and many were violent—in brawling, lawless Deadwood Gulch. A murder a day was common in the early days of the rambunctious gold camp, and every prospector was technically a trespasser in country where the United States government had specifically forbidden him to go.

The Deadwood area was the magic lodestone where the richest placer deposits in the world were discovered during the Black Hills Gold Rush of 1876, the last gold stampede in the Wild West. Thus, to Deadwood, Dakota Territory, led the trails for stage-coaches, oxen and mule teams and

Photo courtesy of South Dakota Historical Society.

Long wagon trains pulled by oxen, horses, mules, and burros converged on Deadwood Gulch from every direction. Many pioneers or pilgrims walked beside the wagons loaded with a variety of supplies and equipment: beer, flour, chamber pots, mining tools, pianos, saw mills, the first narrow-gauge locomotive—even a wagon-load of cats.

wagons, horsemen, and walkers. The trails—dusty, muddy, rocky—began
at the closest railroad stations in Sidney, Nebraska; in Cheyenne, Wyoming; in Bismarck, Dakota Territory; and at the Missouri River docks in
Fort Pierre, Dakota Territory. These rutted pathways through the wilder-

Photo courtesy of W. H. Over Museum.

**Deadwood looking North, 1876. The scene for the murder of Wild Bill Hickok. Historians
dispute whether the assassin Jack McCall was caught in the Senate Saloon or the city meat market, both visible on this picture. Note the General Custer Hotel on right.**

ness converged on the muddy, crowded main street of Deadwood Gulch,
fiesty with gold fever. It soon became the metropolis of the Black Hills, and
eventually the government gave up trying to keep its citizens out of the forbidden Indian country.

Gold was the magnet that attracted miners, dance hall girls, gun slingers, gamblers, suppliers, saloon-keepers, journalists, doctors, lawyers, adventurers, hoboes, lawmen, visionaries—a colorful cast bursting with drama. These gold-seekers staked their claims, established businesses, threw together crude shelters of canvas and evergreen branches in the narrow, twisting gulch, surrounded by the pine-forested mountains of the Black Hills, which, according to the Laramie Treaty of 1868, belonged exclusively to the Sioux Indians, gold or no gold.

Photo courtesy of Centennial Archives, Deadwood Public Library.

The first boot hill at Ingleside where Wild Bill was buried after he was murdered. The fences were to keep out roaming cattle and horses. In 1879 Wild Bill's body was moved up the hill to the new Mount Moriah Cemetery just visible at the upper left.

Ingleside, the First Boot Hill

The first people, including Wild Bill Hickok, who died with their boots on were buried in Whitewood Gulch, later known as the Ingleside area of Deadwood. The gold camp in 1876-1877 sprouted so rapidly with false-

(Dick Costello, the Deadwood Chief of Police (1924-1935) often explained local history to the tourists.) He said that when Deadwood was founded, they thought it necessary to lay out a cemetery. This was done and it was discovered that a cemetery without any occupancy was not a cemetery. They, therefore, waited and waited for somebody to die, but the climate was so fine that nobody did. This was finally solved by going out and killing a man and burying him in the cemetery. Thus, the cemetery became a cemetery. **Deadwood Doctor,** F. S. Howe, M.D

Deadwood, like every big mining town that has yet been located in the West, was full of rough characters, cut-throats, gamblers, and the devil's agents generally. Night and day the wild orgies of depraved humanity continued . . . the arbiter of all disputes was either a knife or pistol and the graveyard soon started with a steady run of victims. **Heroes of the Plains,** Buel

fronted buildings, shacks, log cabins, tents, and dugouts crowding up and down the gulch that more room was needed for actual living space. The founders decided that more level land was needed for building expansion for the living instead of providing burial ground for the dead.

Mount Moriah Established

A group of pioneers, many of them Masons, laid out a new cemetery higher up the hillside on a rough mountain top. This craggy plateau with the Brown Rocks outcropping was not designated as the official cemetery until 1877, according to John McClintock, prominent Deadwood historian and author; or until 1878, according to the Secretary's Report of the Deadwood Cemetery Association of Jan. 15, 1924, published in the **Deadwood Pioneer-Times** of that date. This discrepancy in dates is typical of Deadwood's history, for seldom do two sources agree on when something actually happened, let alone exactly what happened. The new cemetery was named "Mount Moriah."

Photo courtesy Adams Memorial Hall Museum.

A funeral procession to Mount Moriah on the old road winding along-side the mountain. The band leads the way, followed by horse-drawn hearse and mourners walking. Ladies in rear. The figure of a man is on the banner. No Date.

"The land of Moriah" is mentioned in the Bible, Genesis 22. Presumably, the name "Moriah" was chosen because this mountain-top cemetery was laid out by Masons, and in the Masonic ritual is a line "Bury him on the hill west of Mount Moriah." A cemetery map drawn in 1895 identifies various streets, and these names are related to Masonic ritual: Jerusalem,

David, Darius, Solomon, Mary, Boaz, Paul, Hiram, Jabez, John, Jachin, Calvary, and Moriah.

Photo courtesy of Al Gunther.

Not all of the writing in the historic Record Book is as legible as on this title page. Rufus Wilsey was an old prospector who the *Black Hills Daily Times* reported had once been wealthy from his mining claims but died poor. "He was taken with a cramp in his right side. He groaned once or twice. He could not speak but gasped a couple times. His jaw dropped and the man was dead."

The Superintendent keeps records of deaths with dates and cause of death and is to issue orders for burial of all persons upon presentation of a proper certificate of the cause of death made by the attending physicians and verified by oath of two responsible persons. The sexton is required to have such order from the superintendent before digging or allowing any ground to be dug. Record Book of Deadwood Cemetery Association, Feb. 24, 1879

My father, Col. W. J. Thornby, a Mason and Shrine Potentate, was very proud that he had helped lay out Mount Moriah. Although he bought a lot there, he often told my mother he wanted to be buried in Troy, New York, where he was born. Because no new lots were available, several family friends are buried in the Thornby lot in Mount Moriah. Recollection of Katherine Thornby, daughter of Black Hills Pioneer of 1877; curator of the Adams Museum, 1961-1978.

Record Book of the Deadwood Cemetery Association

When most of Deadwood burned in the great fire of 1879, many valuable records were lost forever, but somehow the Record Book of the Deadwood Cemetery Association escaped the flames which destroyed the city offices. Several modern historians believe that this Record Book was probably kept in the home of the sexton or superintendent of Mount Moriah; and if these homes survived the various fires in Deadwood's history, then so did this historic book.

The most interesting explanation is that during the fire of 1879, a city official buried the Record Book in the old Ingleside cemetery where it was later exhumed intact. The book has been rebound but otherwise authorities believe it is the original. It is now kept in the city finance office, and names of people who die and are buried in the old family lots in Mount Moriah are still recorded.

The major portion of the Record Book provides columns for the name of the deceased, date of death, nativity, residence, cause of death, information about section and lot number, and remarks. In some instances, causes of death have been certified by a doctor or midwife. For some entries complete information is given; for others, nothing except the name and date.

The first burial listed is Rufus Wilsey, January 14, 1878, and is the only entry on that page. The first listing alphabetically under "A" is Viola Alden, July, 1878. The cause of death is not given but she is buried in Potter's Field, No. 209. However, the **Black Hills Daily Times,** June 1, 1878, reported that "The first mound in the new cemetery covers the mortal remains of James DeLong, the miner who was killed in the Pecacho tunnel." Mr. DeLong's name cannot be found in the Record Book. Such are the confusions and contradictions of history.

In the first part of the Record Book, 14 people are listed as being interred in Mount Moriah, but there is no date of death or other information provided about them.

Usually, those who recorded the information in the Record Book kept the names of the dead listed alphabetically and by date; but when the pages for a certain letter were filled, then names beginning with that particular let-

In 1952 when fire destroyed the City Hall where many important documents and records were kept, Dick Curtis, the water and street commissioner, had the Record Book of the Cemetery Association in his safe in another building. "Boy, are we lucky!" he said to me, holding up the book jubilantly. Recollection of A. H. Shostrom, retired city employee and Deadwood historian.

About a hundred times a year and almost every day during the tourist season, someone comes in to ask for help in locating the grave of a relative buried in Mount Moriah. We check the Record Book to see if the name is listed, then the lot and section; next we try to locate position of the lot in a general area on the old map, then wish the searcher good luck and send him on up to Mount Moriah. Searchers are about 40% successful in finding a particular grave. Comment by Jo Brotsky, City Finance Officer and Cemetery Sexton.

ter were begun again on subsequent pages under a specific letter of the alphabet. Much of the writing is difficult to read or completely illegible.

Thus, because of the casual and inconsistent way the cemetery records were kept with many omissions, errors, and discrepancies made by a series of unidentified people, the Record Book cannot be considered a totally accurate roster of the dead in Mount Moriah. But certainly it is a fascinating historical document.

Historians, Newspapers, and Eyewitnesses

Additional information about the lives and deaths of those buried in Mount Moriah is preserved in the various newspaper accounts and the first

Photo courtesy of South Dakota Historical Society.

Annie Tallent, first white woman in the Black Hills. She was with the illegal Russell-Collins party who invaded the sacred Paha Sapa of the Sioux Indians in 1874. Later, she wrote the first history of the region, *The Black Hills* **or** *Last Hunting Grounds of the Dakotahs.*

history books about the region. Although there are often contradictions, these published writings by reporters and historians who actually lived in the days they wrote about and were often eye-witnesses to significant events are the most reliable sources for a modern historian.

The Bible of the histories is **The Black Hills** or **Last Hunting Ground of**

Numerous deaths have occurred recently, attributed to changes of water. Undertaker Smith had four bodies on hand, two were recently taken up to Mount Moriah. **Black Hills Daily Times,** Jan. 7, 1881

the Dakotahs by Annie Tallent, the first white woman to enter the Hills. She finished writing her history 25 years after her illegal entry with the Gordon Party or the Russell-Collins Party, as it is variously titled.

An old standby is **Black Hills Trails** by Jesse Brown and Capt. A. M. Willard, written in 1920 when these adventurous pioneers were old men. Willard died before the book was completed and is buried in Mount Moriah.

Richard Hughes, the first newspaper reporter in the Hills, wrote for the **Black Hills Pioneer** and covered the first murder trial, that of John Carty for the murder of Jack Hinch. He did not write his history, **Pioneer Years in the Black Hills** until he was elderly and crippled with arthritis.

Estelline Bennett, the daughter of the first federal judge in the Hills,

Photo courtesy Adams Memorial Hall Museum.

Estelline Bennett, author of *Old Deadwood Days,* **a personal reminiscence about the stage-coach days in Deadwood, 1876-1890. Picture taken in Chicago when she was Society Editor for a Chicago newspaper. Her father was Judge G. G. Bennett, first federal judge for the Black Hills.**

published her charming reminiscence **Old Deadwood Days** about the stage-coach era 35 years after it ended with the arrival of the railroads.

Then there is John McClintock, whose name is high on the honor roll

Photo courtesy of Centennial Archives, Deadwood Public Library.

John McClintock, Black Hills Pioneer of 1876, usually had a front row seat when history exploded in Deadwood Gulch. His first break as a future historian was that he saw Wild Bill's assassin run down the street with a smoking gun.

of Black Hills historians. He completed writing his **Pioneer Days in the Black Hills** when he was 92 years old, and half a century after many of the events occurred, which he often witnessed from a ringside seat. McClintock, who was usually where the action was, now sleeps in Mount Moriah.

Obviously, in the Black Hills, old-timers and especially aging authors had long, long memories.

For years the copyright to John McClintock's book was believed lost . . . Mrs. D. B. McGahey finally located the missing copyright as it had been placed in charge of her husband, the late D. B. McGahey, former curator of the Adams Museum. At his death no one knew where the copyright was located. Lois Miller, "McClintock's Book Gives Final Word on Hills History," **Rapid City Journal,** Jan. 13, 1953

Murders, etc.

In his book, McClintock documented 97 murders in the first three years (1876-1879) of the settlement of the Northern Hills. Although Indians were often blamed for many murders, the white gold-seekers were efficient at killing each other off, some of this slaying performed by vigilantes who hanged horse thieves and stage-coach robbers.

County Undertaker B. F. Smith compiled a report which endeavored to explain why the Black Hills had such a reputation for fostering short and unhealthy lives. Smith's report in the **Black Hills Times,** Jan. 1, 1879, states: "A wrong impression has gone out in regard to the health of this country, based on the number of deaths in August, September and October, 1877, which was caused by the way men lived here that spring and summer, and from changes of climate which is always attended with more or less sickness." For the year 1878, Smith listed 16 murders "from the little gun," six suicides, and eight accidents.

Undertaker Smith declared that all the statistics and comparisons with other cities proved "our Black Hills as healthy as any other locality in the world." This conclusion, an unusual one for the man in charge of the corpses, might have provoked a laugh from George Ayres and Police Chief Dick Costello, both men having had a reputation for telling hair-raising tales about why Mount Moriah filled up so quickly.

First Murder

The first murder victim in the Deadwood area was Jack Hinch of Gayville, a mining camp just up the gulch from Deadwood. This memorable first is reported by the **Black Hills Pioneer,** July 9, 1876; and also by authors John McClintock, Annie Tallent, and Richard Hughes—and each tells a slightly different version.

The story goes that Hinch, while kibitzing at a poker game, accused two players of cheating. Later, these two men stabbed and shot Hinch until he was dead. Hinch was buried at Ingleside, which was then simply called Whitewood Gulch.

Although the suspected murderers escaped into Wyoming Territory, they were soon followed by a posse of Hinch's outraged friends. With the

Nobody got shot yesterday or last night. It's getting dull. "Gulch Hash," **Black Hills Daily Times,** May 4, 1878

A German who died and was buried in the old cemetery on the hills two years ago was disinterred, boiled down to his bones and sent back to friends in the old country. The job of reducing him was performed by a couple of men inexperienced in that kind of business, and the trouble they had doing the work is fearful to relate. They consumed an even gallon of whiskey before they got through. **Black Hills Daily Times,** Jan. 6, 1879

Murder is becoming too fashionable in this gulch. Before the body of one man becomes cold in his grave, the coroner is summoned to sit on the remains of another. There have been as high as two inquests during one day in this gulch the present spring. This is a terrible, fearful state of affairs and something must be done to put a check on it. "Another Bloody Murder— C. E. Lee Brutally Murdered and Robbed", **Black Hills Daily Times,** May 13, 1878

help of a United States marshal, the avengers captured Carty, one of the suspects, and brought him back to the Hills to stand trial even though the entire region had no legal status or jurisdiction. The miners were in an uproar over Hinch's murder, and the outdoor trial took place in the midst of a near riot on the main street of Gayville. The jury found the accused guilty only of assault and battery. This lenient jury set a precedent for another more famous trial held a few days later that August of 1876, the trial of Jack McCall for the murder of Wild Bill Hickok.

The Pioneer on August 5, 1876, published this item under "Local News": "Should it ever be our misfortune to kill a man, which we pray God it may not, we would simply ask that our trial take place in some of the mining camps of these Black Hills."

Murder of Wild Bill Hickok

Photo courtesy of Devereaux Library, South Dakota School of Mines and Technology.

Jack McCall shooting Wild Bill Hickok in the back. An old woodcut. This is the most famous event in Deadwood history even though Wild Bill made no contributions to the development of Deadwood except to die there and thus become a valuable commercial property.

The most famous occupant of Mount Moriah is Wild Bill Hickok. He was one of the first murder victims that violent summer of 1876, the summer of Custer's Last Stand, the year Deadwood was founded and the centennial year when the nation celebrated 100 years of progress. Hickok's assassination by Jack McCall is briefly noted as a cause of death in the Rec-

It is the fashion now with the ladies of Deadwood to sport hip pockets in their wearing apparel and since the reign of terror within the gulch, a few carry guns in them. "Gulch Hash," **Black Hills Daily Times,** June 1, 1878

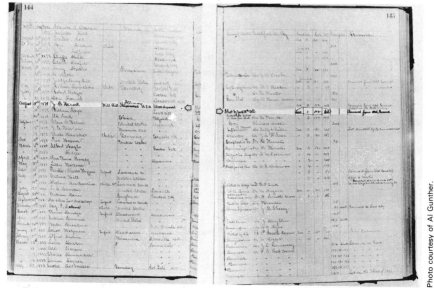

Photo courtesy of Al Gunther.

This page from the Record Book notes that J. B. Hickok (Wild Bill) was "removed from old ground" in 1879, three years after his murder. At the bottom of the page are listed four victims of the Brownsville fire whose last names began with "H". They are buried in the mass grave at Mount Moriah.

ord Book, but not until three years later, in 1879, when John McClintock and others moved Wild Bill's body from Ingleside where he was first buried to its present resting place in Mount Moriah.

Deadwood brought immortality—not wealth—to Wild Bill Hickok. To some gold-seekers, the Deadwood placer deposits provided great riches. But gold nuggets were not found glittering in the streets as many naive fortune-hunters, or "pilgrims" as they were often called, had believed when they began the perilous journey to the gold camps in Indian territory.

Stage-coach Hold-ups

Gold, and the age-old greed for gold, caused many crimes in the early days, including hold-ups of the treasure coach. The Deadwood treasure coach, with armed guards riding shotgun on the high seats at either end of the coach, and with outriders patrolling the trail, carried the gold bullion from the productive mines of the Black Hills on the first lap of the journey to the United States mint. The stage headed for the nearest railroads at Cheyenne, Wyoming, or Sidney, Nebraska.

The only successful assault on the treasure coach was a daring holdup known as the Canyon Springs robbery, which occurred about 40 miles south of Deadwood in 1878. Five men, including one desperado from Deadwood who had previously stolen John McClintock's Winchester rifle, held up Old Ironsides.

When the shooting began, the gunmen knocked off Hugh Campbell, a telegraph operator who was sitting beside the driver. The road agents

Wells-Fargo Express Co., Deadwood. Treasure wagon and guards with $250,000 gold bullion from the great Homestake Mine. Grabill photo, 1890.

wounded the driver and two messengers. Then they ripped open the iron safe full of gold bricks worth $40,000 and loaded them into a rickety old wagon. They galloped off, taking one of their wounded and leaving behind the body of their dead partner, Big-Nose George. The wagon broke down; the robbers had to hide the gold bricks in a hurry and flee for their lives. Eventually, all of these "knights of the road" were rounded up and most of the gold was recovered. But Black Hillers still search for gold hidden by stage-coach robbers, often called "fairy gold."

Hugh Campbell, who was killed instantly in the fight, was an employee of the Black Hills Telegraph Company, and he had been permitted to ride on Old Ironsides from Deadwood to his new assignment at Jenney Stockade. His body was taken to Deadwood where his funeral was conducted by the Masonic Lodge. He is buried in Mount Moriah in the Masonic Circle, and his name is inscribed on the Masonic lectern and duly recorded in the Record Book: "Hugh Campbell, Sept. 29, 1878, shot by stage robbers, Canyon Springs."

When highway robbers attacked the treasure coach, there were always gunfights and usually killings, scenes straight out of a western movie. But

Special telegram to the **Leader:** The treasure coach leaving tomorrow takes $250,000 bullion from the Hills. Item in Cheyenne, Wyo. **Leader,** Sept. 18, 1878

$2,500 REWARD

Will be paid for the return of the money and valuables and the capture (upon conviction) of the five men who robbed our coach on the 26th day of September 1878, at Canyon Springs (Whiskey Gap), Wyo., Terr., of twenty-seven thousand dollars, consisting mainly of gold bullion. Pro rate of the above will be paid for the capture of either of the robbers and proportionate part of the property. (POSTER) Luke Voorhees, Supt. Cheyenne and Black Hills Stage Co., Cheyenne, Wyo., Sept. 28, 1878

Photo courtesy of Al Gunther.

In the Record Book four murder victims are recorded on this page, including Hugh Campbell who was "shot by stage robbers, Canyon Springs." He is buried in the Masonic Circle at Mount Moriah.

during the gold rush days when the stage-coach rumbled over the trails, the good guys and the bad guys were real—and so was the gold.

The early newspapers were most efficient at providing their readers with accounts of holdups and other crimes, juicy scandals, romantic intrigues, and the gory details of violent deaths, the murders and suicides that were common in Deadwood. "The silent city" in Mount Moriah continued to grow.

Murder of Yellow Doll

Although the murder of Wild Bill Hickok is the best known homicide, there were many others. Another sensational murder whose story has become a legend and a well-preserved page of Deadwood lore took place in Chinatown, which was located in lower Deadwood. An unknown axe-wielding assailant hacked to bits the beautiful Yellow Doll, an Oriental charmer who lived a mysterious life of luxury. Chinatown leaders would reveal nothing about her but gave her an especially ceremonious funeral and kept her burial place a secret. Whether or not she was buried in the Chinese section of Mount Moriah is unknown. Her name is not in the Record Book. Each year for the "Days of '76" parade, the young girls of Deadwood vie for the honor of being chosen to represent Yellow Doll, the murdered Chinese beauty.

The remains of Mrs. Lovell, who was shot and killed while attempting to murder Johnny Rogers were consigned to the grave this afternoon. **Black Hills Times,** Oct. 15, 1878

Suicides

Suicides were common throughout Deadwood's history, and particularly among the group the newspapers labeled "the sporting fraternity," those who worked in gambling dives, theaters, saloons, and houses of prostitution, variously called The Green Front, Bella Union, Melodeon, Gem Theater. Sometimes a "resort" combined gambling, prostitution, dancing, and drinking under one roof, as did the Gem Theater.

"Soiled doves" who worked in the oldest profession were often innocent young girls who had been trapped into a life of depravity. They and the gamblers and disillusioned fortune-hunters were often desperate enough to try suicide, and if by poison, the doctors often saved them from "crossing the dark river by use of the stomach pump." Dr. F. S. Howe, who did not

Photo courtesy of Centennial Archives, Deadwood Public Library.

Dr. F. S. Howe, popular physician in the 20th century. In *Deadwood Doctor* he described his varied experiences in caring for patients. Many were victims of poison just as they were in the early days.

practice in Deadwood until the 20th century wrote in his book: "I took care of every poison known to man at this time, including potassium cyanide, carbolic acid, strychnine, bichloride of mercury, iodine, morphine, lysol and chloroform."

Epidemics

Diseases, especially diseases for which there were no vaccines nor effective remedies known in the late 19th century and early 20th took a heavy toll. Pneumonia, smallpox, scarlet fever, and especially diphtheria were the scourge of the mining camp.

━━

Dr. Babcock's old horse Goldie died Thursday night, presumably of stoppage of the bowels. The doctor drove her to the Hills in the early days, and she has taken him hundreds of miles about the country to see patients. It will not be easy to replace Goldie. **Black Hills Daily Times,** March 17, 1893

Funeral services for Frank Weaver who died from the effects of carbolic acid which he drank after he stabbed his wife Virginia to death. She will be buried at the same time in Mount Moriah. **Black Hills Daily Times,** July 7, 1923

Pneumonia is the most prevalent disease of the Hills country. There are three cases of smallpox in the city, besides a number in the pest house. **Black Hills Daily Times,** August, 1877

Photo courtesy of Al Gunther.

This wooden cross for Baby Dower is one of the few legible markers in the Children's Section in Mount Moriah, mostly victims of epidemics—diphtheria, smallpox and scarlet fever.

Deaths of Children

In 1878-1880, Deadwood and other mining camps were struck with diphtheria and scarlet fever epidemics which killed many children. Some of these victims are buried in a special children's section in Mount Moriah, identified by a sign near the area where little wooden crosses and weathered

Several new cases of diphtheria are said to have broke out within the past 24 hours in South Deadwood. This fatal disease has been reinforced by scarlet fever and it is feared if the proper precautions are not taken at once, that the two scourges will play sad havoc among the little ones of the camp. **Black Hills Daily Times,** Oct. 18, 1880

Little Laura Dague died this a.m. after awful suffering. Darrell is very low, too, with diphtheria and they did not think he would live through the night. Little Miriam has it also. June 1, 1890, Diary of Irene Cushman

artificial flowers mark the tiny graves. According to a count in the Record Book, there are at least 350 infants and children buried in Mount Moriah. Many of their grave-markers are gone, especially of those in Potter's Field where innumerable paupers were buried on the surrounding slopes of the main part of the cemetery.

Undertaker Smith, in his 1881 mortuary report, states that the children's mortality rate was more than double that of adults. He claimed that the local rate was the same as the national rate of children's deaths at that time. Obituaries often included the phrase, "a child winged its flight to heaven."

Photo courtesy of Centennial Archives, Deadwood Public Library.

Devastation in Deadwood after the great fire of Sept. 26, 1879, when 300 buildings were destroyed but only one life was lost. Residents sat on steep hillsides watching helplessly as flames and dynamite explosions destroyed much of the three-year-old town. The fire started in the Empire Bakery when a woman upset a kerosene lamp.

Flaming Disasters

Disasters, whether caused by man or nature or by a combination of the two are frequently called "Acts of God," but perhaps it would make more sense if they were labeled "Acts of the Devil." The arch-enemy of all the new mining camps was fire.

On September 26, 1879, the most meaningful date in Deadwood his-

A child named Wetcher is very low at Whitewood, where the child lies in quarantine, and every precaution is taken to prevent spread of the awful disease, the public schools have been closed. **Black Hills Daily Times,** April 18, 1893

Feb. 27, 1881—Ada—Joseph Brinkworth's daughter—Fountain City—Diphtheria
March 3, 1881—Albert—Joseph Brinkworth's son—Fountain City—Diphtheria
March 3, 1881—Minnie—J. Brinkworth's daughter—Fountain City—Diphtheria
The Record Book of the Deadwood Cemetery Association

tory, the dreaded flames erupted when a kerosene lamp was upset in the Empire bakery. Like wildfire the flames spread through the wooden buildings crowded together in the business section and then leaped through the houses stacked like match boxes on the terraced streets of Forest Hill and Williams. The fire ignited supplies of blasting powder stored in hardware stores, and the explosions shook the gulch from one end to the other, showering blazing embers over all.

Annie Tallent reported on the calamity in her history: "It spread with the rapidity of a race horse over nearly the entire business section of the town, leaving nothing in the wide pathway but heaps of ashes and masses of smoking ruins. The destruction was speedy and complete."

And this may have been the fire during which some enterprising citizen carried the Record Book to the old cemetery ground at Ingleside and buried it for safekeeping. Even if the story is unsubstantiated, it's a good basis for a legend.

Miraculously, this disastrous fire of 1879 caused only one death; the victim was a deaf Englishman called Casino Jack. His death is recorded in the Record Book, but the location of his grave is unknown, his wooded marker in Potter's Field having long since disappeared along with the hundreds of other markers.

Mass Grave for Eleven Victims of Fire

Fire was responsible in March, 1883, for the death of 11 men who worked for a sawmill at Allenton, a stop on the narrow-gauge railroad

WHAT SHALL WE DO TO PREVENT FIRE? Ex-sheriff Seth Bullock is not meeting with the success it was expected he would in obtaining subscriptions for a steam fire engine fund for Deadwood. **Black Hills Daily Times,** April 20, 1878

The community would rise, phoenix-like, out of the ashes with a new nickname for Deadwood, 'City of Sin and Ashes.' The sin had been present from the beginning; the ashes symbolized the burned-out passions of the undisciplined gold-seekers. The disastrous fire was the gold camp's first major tragedy. Others would follow. **Gold—Gals—Guns—Guts,** Bob Lee, editor

south of Deadwood, now called Brownsville. When fire broke out in a boardinghouse, men on the second floor were trapped but four managed to escape. Like so many who died in the late 1880's, little was known about the deceased except their names.

Eleven of these fire victims are buried in a mass grave at Mount Moriah. Seventy-six years after the tragedy, in August, 1959, the marker for the mass grave was dedicated at the cemetery.

Flood Disasters

Another Act of the Devil caused by nature going berserk was a flood, especially in a region of steep hills and narrow valleys. Damaging floods occurred at least six times in Deadwood's history: 1878, 1883, 1890, 1904, 1909, and 1964—and were caused mainly from the furious merging of three mountain streams: Deadwood, Whitewood, and City creeks. These streams which usually rollicked harmlessly through Deadwood often went on a spring rampage when the snow melted and rain poured down simultaneously.

After Deadwood had rebuilt from the 1879 fire, then came the Great Flood of 1883 which literally drowned out the town. This flood caused over

Photo courtesy of Centennial Archives, Deadwood Public Library.

After the 1883 flood. Deadwood was damaged by floods in 1878, 1883, 1890, 1904, 1909, and 1964. Deadwood, Whitewood, and City Creeks merge within the city limits; and before flood controls were devised, these creeks overflowed their banks from dangerous combinations of spring rains and the thawing of mountain snows.

$300,000 damage and killed several people at the toll gate below Gold Run Gulch coming down from Lead. Buildings toppled, bridges collapsed, the Methodist Church and the schoolhouse were washed away in the torrent.

The 1883 flood and the 1879 fire were rated as the worst disasters Deadwood suffered. But Deadwood was tough in more ways than one, and

G. W. Chandler, wife, and hired man Holthausen were seen to set down to dinner, and moments afterwards the house and contents went into the flood and disappeared. **Black Hills Daily Times,** May 18, 1883

the pioneers began rebuilding their town after each disaster, which inevitably provided several new residents for the "city of the dead."

Weather-Related Deaths

The various claims about the healthful climate in the Black Hills may be exaggerated; for many weather-related deaths have been recorded through the years both in the newspapers and in the Record Book. Listed under causes of death are frozen to death, died in blizzard, died from exposure, drowned in flood—enough casualties to indicate that the extremes of weather and catastrophes of nature were both hard on the population explosion in Deadwood Gulch.

Accidents

Accidents, often as the result of contact with animals or from a combination of horses and drivers, were often listed as causes of death in the Rec-

Feed Floor—Golden Reward Smelter showing mouth of blast furnace where the ore was melted. Early mining conditions were primitive. In the Record Book accidents in mines are often listed as causes of death: fall in mine, caught in machinery, crushed by timbers or cave-ins.

ord Book: trampled by a horse, kicked by a horse, run over by stage-coach, mauled by a bear, gored by a buffalo.

Accidents in the mines of the area brought death to many; causes were listed in the Record Book as these: fall in mine, killed by machinery, crushed by timbers. Early mining conditions were primitive; safety mea-

A most deplorable accident occurred at Golden Reward which caused the instant death of Ferdinand Bockleman and the terrible mutilation of his body . . . the back of his head was crushed, his left arm and right leg were torn off from the body, and a number of ribs broken . . . Anyone knowing the address of any relatives of deceased, please notify the coroner. He will be buried in Mount Moriah by friends. **Black Hills Daily Times,** April, 1893

sures were practically unknown; and the business of burrowing underground for gold and other metals was fraught with constant danger.

Dr. F. S. Howe, author of **Deadwood Doctor,** wrote that it was nothing unusual to be called out five or six times in one night for various emergencies. He recalled, "Part of the time I was at the doctor's age-old trade of bringing babies into the world, part of the time I was patching up the knifings, the gunshot wounds, and mine accidents of our lively community."

Variety Among Causes of Death

In the early days when the mortality rate of both mothers and newborn infants was high, mother and baby were often buried in the same casket with "died in childbirth" noted in the Record Book.

Alcoholism was a frequent cause of death; sometimes it was listed as "bad whiskey." Opium was listed as a cause in the Record Book for whites as well as for Chinese.

Other causes of death listed and signed by doctors and midwives were these:

catarrh	teething
dropsy of the heart	old age
summer complaint	hobnail liver
softening of the brain	broken thumb
inflammation of the bowels	struck with bar glass
want of vitality	hanged by vigilantes
God Knows	from eating 14 hard-boiled
killed by Indians	eggs

Removal of Bodies from Ingleside

John Hinch, the name of the first murder victim, is not listed in the Record Book until August 27, 1892, 16 years after his murder. If this is the same Jack Hinch who was murdered in Gayville in August, 1876, it is likely that his body probably underwent a transfer in 1892 from Ingleside to Mount Moriah, as happened to many others.

In the late 1800's and early 1900's appeared several notations in the Record Book and items in the newspapers about undertakers being hired to remove the bodies which had been buried in the Ingleside area during the first two years of the gold camp's existence and before Mount Moriah was established in 1878. Eventually, over 50 unidentified bodies were removed from Ingleside and buried in Potter's Field in Mount Moriah.

However, all of the bodies were not removed as Mrs. Helen Scotvold of Taylor Avenue in the old Ingleside site in Deadwood can testify. In 1941, when the Scotvolds began excavating to build their house, the workmen

Undertaker Robinson in 15 days has removed 35 bodies from Taylor St. to Mount Moriah. All records are lost and there is no identification. One of the bodies was buried in a buffalo robe, one in a metallic casket, the others in ordinary coffins. It is surmised that there are about 10 more to be removed but in all likelihood more will be found as work progresses.
Black Hills Daily Times, July 5, 1895

with the first scoopful of dirt uncovered a skeleton. Eight skeletons were uncovered, but there was no sign of any wooden caskets except for the metal casket handles. Mrs. Scotvold continues to find casket handles in her garden.

Across the street from the Scotvold residence are two Forest Service houses which were built upon the site of an early schoolhouse. Workmen removed 13 skeletons from this area when they built the two houses. In this Ingleside area on Taylor Avenue, excavators found five skeletons arranged in a circle with their skulls pointed toward the middle. The police and others who took charge of all the skeletons wondered if these five might have been Indians who had been buried long before the white man invaded the Black Hills.

Destruction of Historic Statues and Graves

One of the worst problems in Mount Moriah for over a century has been the destruction of historic statues and monuments, particularly at the graves of Wild Bill Hickok, Calamity Jane, and Preacher Smith.

Even before Wild Bill's body was taken from Ingleside and reburied in Mount Moriah in 1879, souvenir hunters had been busy hacking and chipping and stealing. Vandals have stolen four wooden markers from Wild Bill's grave; they have hacked at and carved on and mutilated two large statues until these had to be removed.

I remember when I was a boy and the fourth ward school stood on the site of the Ingleside Cemetery where the Forest Service houses were later built. The kids often played with human bones they found in that school yard. Then the teachers would call them 'grave-robbers.' But that wasn't true because the bones, probably dug up from building and road construction, were near the surface and protruded through the ground. Recollection of George Hunter, son of John Hunter, Black Hills Pioneer of 1877

Mount Moriah Cemetery is in a deplorable state of neglect and ruin. There is only one road that is badly washed out; it is dangerous to go there with a team and necessitates running over some graves. The headboard on Wild Bill's grave has been disfigured by a sentimental relic hunter. One side is sadly hacked and disfigured by a vandal who wished to prove he had visited the tomb of the redoubtable Wild Bill. It is a good thing for these vandals that Bill's spirit does not partake of his former aggressive nature. **Black Hills Daily Times,** 1886

Photo courtesy of Centennial Archives, Deadwood Public Library.

The sculptor Riordan beside his huge bust of Wild Bill whose epitaph was "Custer was lonely without him". Vandals eventually destroyed this first monument to the frontier marshal.

The first monument, called the Riordan bust, was nine feet tall. Erected at Wild Bill's grave-site in 1891, it was decorated with crossed pistols and a large scroll with an inscription.

Henry Robinson and son, undertakers, completed enclosing the grave of Wild Bill with a handsome stone wall surrounded by an iron fence. It will be difficult to scale by visiting vandals. The money to do the work was realized by a lecture and poetry recitation presented by Capt. Jack Crawford, poet-scout, and a firm friend of Bill's. **Black Hills Daily Times,** May 1893

The second large statue of Wild Bill Hickok which vandals hacked to pieces. Even the spiky iron fence failed to protect the grave from determined souvenir hunters.

In 1893, the **Times** carried a feature deploring the destruction of the statues of both Wild Bill and Preacher Smith. The reporter commented: "It would not be surprising if some enterprising Yankee were to resurrect Wild Bill's grave and take it east for exhibition." Everyone was urged to become a cemetery detective to catch the vandals so they could be severely dealt with.

In 1902, the city fathers tried again. This time they erected a life-size

Yesterday a reporter of the **Times** visited the old cemetery to note the progress of the contemplated improvements inaugurated by the city commissioners . . . The unsightly piles of manure have been removed . . . A great many graves have stakes and boards that have been marked, but time and the elements have obliterated them . . . We found a grave with a beautiful Italian marble headstone with engraving but the marble footstone is gone—stolen by some vandal. There is little doubt that this stone was taken before the fire and was used in the Empire bakery to roll candy on. **Black Hills Daily Times,** April 23, 1880

We visited the old graveyard and spent some time looking around its melancholy confines, now utterly forlorn and desolate . . . Many bodies have been removed to Mount Moriah, but still quite a few remain within the old enclosure . . . Decency requires that the graves should be marked or numbered so that if occasion should require it, they could be identified . . . Unlike other far western camps we did not have to kill a man to start a graveyard. A little child was this city's first gift to the great hereafter, but after that—disease, violence, and suicide soon made a goodly colony. **Black Hills Daily Times,** Nov. 21, 1881

statue made of sandstone and enclosed in a spiky iron fence and a wire cage. But nothing stopped the vandals and souvenir hunters. By 1946, this huge statue sculpted by Alvin Smith was headless and one-legged from persistent dismemberment. It now lies unburied and broken in a basement store-room

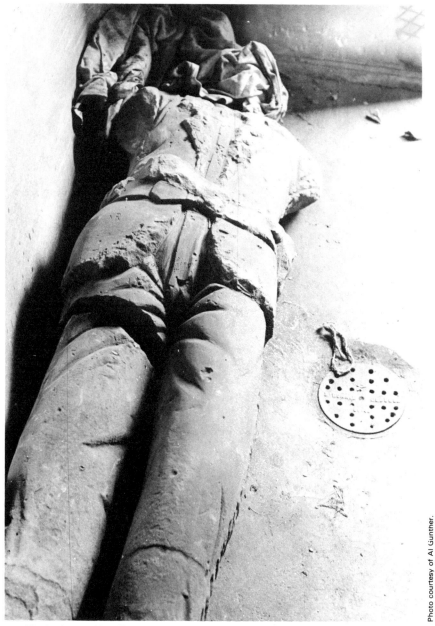

Photo courtesy of Al Gunther.

The broken and headless statue of Wild Bill in the basement of the Adams Museum. It is not on display.

in the Adams Museum.

Statues at other historic graves fared no better. In 1891, the same year that the sculptor Riordan fashioned a statue of Wild Bill, he also sculpted a life-size statue of Preacher Smith. It, too, was attacked and finally bit the

Photo courtesy of Deadwood Chamber of Commerce.

Statue of Preacher Smith in Mount Moriah. One arm and part of the beard has been hacked away. Eventually, vandals destroyed the entire statue. Only the base remains.

dust in 1933, when a tourist reportedly climbed onto the shoulders of the statue which then tumbled to the ground and broke into pieces. Today, there are no surviving statues of celebrities in Mount Moriah.

At one time a large decorative urn marked the grave of Calamity Jane, which had been presented by Calamity's friend, Madam Dora DuFran. It has long since disappeared.

Grave-sites of Wild Bill and Calamity Jane before vandals destroyed both the statue of Wild Bill and the decorative urn on Calamity's side. The urn was donated by Madam Dora DuFran.

Management of Mount Moriah

From the very beginning of Mount Moriah in 1878, when the first sexton was fired for drunkenness and neglect of duty, the citizens who had responsibility for the cemetery and for "the silent majority" were plagued with a variety of problems especially lack of finances.

The Deadwood Cemetery Association was organized in 1892; and the minutes were often published in the newspapers and preserved in the Record Book which had probably been in use for many years before 1892. These accounts of the meetings were deadly serious, as befitted their subject matter.

The first group to purchase burial ground for its members was the Hebrew Society in July, 1890, for $200. After the cemetery association was formed, other organizations reserved special burial lots for their members: the Masons, the Society of Black Hills Pioneers, Firemen, Old Soldiers, and the Chinese.

Despite troubles with finances through the years, the association managed to make yearly improvements: planting trees, repairing fences, building roads, erecting gates and stone walls.

In 1904, the group hired workmen to fix up the faded wooden headboards in Potter's Field "to restore legibility" to the inscriptions under the traditional "Rest in Peace" heading. By 1924, the Association estimated

Photo courtesy of Al Gunther.

Probably the last wooden headboard in Mount Moriah. No writing is visible. Since this picture was taken in April, 1979, this board has splintered and will soon disappear entirely.

that over 800 persons were buried in Potter's Field. Today, there is no sign of these graves of paupers on the slopes, overgrown with vegetation, which surround the visible main section of Mount Moriah with its granite and stone tombstones.

According to the last page of minutes in the Record Book, the Deadwood Cemetery Association, on Nov. 30, 1938, drew up a resolution stating that it no longer had sufficient funds to continue managing Mount Moriah. The group requested that the City Council take over the cemetery, adding it

Photo courtesy of Deadwood Chamber of Commerce.

Looking down a Potter's Field slope into the main part of Mount Moriah. Hundreds of graves have disappeared in the Potter's Field areas.

to the City Park System, and "assuming responsibility for maintaining and caring for said Mount Moriah Cemetery."

In response, the City Council of Deadwood on Dec. 5, 1938, drew up a resolution recorded in Council Proceedings, No. 7, City of Deadwood, and accepted the transfer of funds and the deed to all the grounds included in Mount Moriah cemetery. The council also recommended that a resolution of thanks be sent to the Cemetery Association "for the excellent job in maintaining the cemetery over the past several years with the limited funds available."

In 1979, Mount Moriah is currently maintained and operated as a municipal cemetery. Although it is one of the leading tourist attractions in Deadwood, there is no charge to the thousands of people who visit it every year.

Photo courtesy of Deadwood Chamber of Commerce.

A view of Deadwood from Brown Rocks. Franklin Hotel dominates main street and Denver Ave. climbs uphill with the road winding its way three miles to Mt. Roosevelt.

Brown Rocks Overlook and the Flag

The overlook near the flag pole at the edge of the Brown Rocks outcropping provides a panoramic view of Deadwood and of the Black Hills. On ancient Brown Rocks many hikers have rested; zealous ministers who hoped to reform Deadwood have stood there with megaphones exhorting the wicked to give up their evil ways. Speakers for historic celebrations have orated to the audience on the street below. The Deadwood Band has played from this natural stage, their music echoing over the gulches and hills.

The Deadwood Band, from the lofty Brown Rocks above the city, serenaded the residents of not only this gulch, but the miners in their lowly cabins over in Spruce or Two Bit gulches. The music produced at this elevation sounded very harmonious and sweet. **Black Hills Daily Times,** May 9, 1893

When William Jennings Bryan gave a political speech in Deadwood, August 24, 1899, the Deadwood band played a lively air from the cemetery hill directly above the depot, and a salute of giant powder was fired, which fairly shook the city. **Gold—Gals—Guns—Guts,** Bob Lee, ed.

The Deadwood Band has prepared head and footstones for the graves of band musicians who have died and been buried in the cemetery here, and will on Decoration Day set the monuments and decorate the graves of their dead comrades. **Black Hills Daily Times,** April 20, 1895

The Deadwood Band which often played for funeral processions and led the way to Mount Moriah. They played for other occasions too, sometimes from Brown Rocks. Jeweler George Butler has the long black beard. Picture taken at Custer, 1891.

One of the most memorable performances from Brown Rocks was presented on Christmas Day, 1877, when Jack Langrishe, popular actor in Deadwood theatrical productions, surprised the homesick pioneers by playing Christmas carols on steel chimes which rang out beautifully over the snowy gulch. He had hauled the chimes up the steep hill by sled.

Near the explanatory sign is the tall flag pole which flies the Stars and Stripes 24 hours a day. Camille Yuill, in her "Backlog" column in the **Deadwood Pioneer-Times,** has often explained about the flag on Mount Moriah: "The flag was flown for the first time on June 6, 1917 . . . Congress enacted special legislation permitting the flag to fly over Deadwood day and night." Every few weeks the city has to provide a new flag because of wind damage.

Visitors may look across the rolling park-like terrain of Mount Moriah and contemplate the lives of the over 3,500 people buried there, not only in the well-kept area with its impressive and picturesque markers, but also down the tangled and wooded slopes of surrounding Potter's Field where an unknown number of unmarked paupers' graves are lost. Always fascinating are the mysteries of the Chinese section.

Near the overlook is the grave of one of the most illustrious men in the

This lichen-covered statue marks the graves of Thomas Green, born in Barenton, England, died May 19, 1881; and M. G. Green, born 1880, died 1881, age 9 mos., 28 days.

Photo courtesy of Al Gunther.

The Chinese section about 1904. The larger structure was probably for burning ceremonial papers and incense. The smaller oven was for roasting pigs and other food in preparation for the elaborate burial services. These ovens have disappeared as have many of the bodies whose bones were shipped back to China. White Rocks in the background.

cemetery, Major A. J. Simmons; not far off is the grave of a Black Hills Pioneer of 1876, witty George Ayres. Across the cemetery up in the Jewish section is the grave of Blanche Colman, the first woman lawyer in South Dakota. Beyond the flagstone steps and terrace where Wild Bill Hickok, Calamity Jane, and Potato Creek Johnny are buried lies Irene Cushman Wilson, who wrote in her delightful diary about visiting the ghosts in Mount Moriah and witnessing a dramatic 1890 funeral procession. Far above the cemetery gleam the White Rocks pinnacles; and on the trail to this soaring landmark is the lonely grave of Seth Bullock, first sheriff of Deadwood.

Traditionally, Wild Bill Hickok and Calamity Jane have been the most popular graves to visit, but there are many other colorful inhabitants of the

Photo courtesy of Al Gunther.

The graves of Wild Bill Hickok, Calamity Jane, and Potato Creek Johnny are the most frequently visited in Mount Moriah. Their granite markers are now imbedded safely in rock walls—so far.

"city of the dead" who contributed much more to Deadwood and the Black Hills than did these two legends of the Wild West.

It is time to re-appraise the old favorites and to become acquainted with some of the neglected immortals.

End of Part I

My hobby is genealogy . . . A couple of years ago in Mount Moriah, I copied all the headstone inscriptions comprising about 1500 names so there are definitely a large number of unmarked graves in the cemetery . . . I also did some research in the **Black Hills Pioneer** and the **Black Hills Daily** and **Weekly Times** for the years 1876 through 1881 and extracted all of the births, marriages, and death and burial information . . . I know that I missed many articles because they are sometimes in such obscure corners of the newspapers, but I did manage to record 121 births, 169 marriages, and 401 deaths and burials.
Recollections of Donald D. Toms, Lead, SD, genealogist

I watched the pathetic funeral of a young miner killed in the Terra. It was nearly dark when the long procession wound up into the cemetery, and a scene not easily forgotten to see the setting sun shine on the glass windows of the hearse and swords of the marching men . . . The band played a dirge at the grave, and when the carriages came down, it was so dark as to make it necessary to light the carriage lamps. Diary of Irene Cushman

When my wife and I were honeymooning in 1947, we spent considerable time wandering around in Mount Moriah. We were particularly intrigued with the Chinese section. At that time there were still many wooden markers with Chinese inscriptions.
Recollection of Bob Lee, author and Sturgis, SD, newspaper editor

Many tourists and strangers stop in to ask if they can still buy lots in Mount Moriah because they are attracted by the magnificent view or the historic associations. There are no new lots for sale in Mount Moriah, but occasionally people sell their family lots. Because one lady decided to move her husband's body to the Black Hills National Cemetery, she sold her lot to an appreciative tourist from Illinois who wants to be buried in famous Mount Moriah.
Comments by Undertaker David Ruth

II

VIGNETTES
OF THE BIG FOUR

Wild Bill Hickok
Careless Gunfighter

The number one hero of shoot-'em-up in the tall tales of the Wild West is Wild Bill Hickok. A legend he was, is, and will be forevermore as long as western history and fiction survive—and often it's hard to tell the difference between the two.

Photo courtesy of Fiedler Collection, Devereaux Library, South Dakota School of Mines and Technology, Rapid City, So. Dak.

Wild Bill drawing in Adams Memorial Museum, Deadwood, SD. No matter where you stand, the guns are said to be pointing at you. (By N. C. Wyeth—artist.) (Courtesy of Fiedler Collection, Devereaux Library, South Dakota School of Mines & Technology, Rapid City, SD.)

Estimates on the number of men this "Prince of Pistoleers" reportedly shot and killed range from 15 to 100, not counting Civil War Rebels and Indians. Some writers claim he gunned men down only in the name of law and order or in self-defense. Others insist that he often shot his victims because he was an instinctive killer or happened to be in a bad temper. Was he a ruthless desperado or the personification of a just lawman? Or a mixture of the two? Contradictory interpretations and conflicting "facts" are legion about his life and actions. The true story is lost in the myths of western folklore.

James Butler Hickok was born in 1838, in Troy Grove, Illinois—that much is sure. During his boyhood he began learning how to use guns effectively.

When he was a young man operating a relay station for the Overland stage in Nebraska, he got into his famous and controversial fight with the McCanles horse-stealing gang. He single-handedly gunned down nine people; some say six were outlaws and three were innocent bystanders. Wild Bill was tried for murder and acquitted on the grounds of self-defense, a verdict typical of the frontier.

With the McCanles fight adding nine legitimate notches to his gun, Wild Bill received much publicity. Probably this is the time when he was nicknamed "Wild Bill" and the legend began.

During the Civil War Wild Bill served as both scout and sharpshooter for the Union Army. After the war, he tried homesteading, bullwhacking, stage-coach driving, scouting, and gambling.

Hickok scouted for General George Custer in Kansas, and the two

Photo courtesy of South Dakota Historical Society.

Wild Bill as he dressed while scouting for Custer in Kansas Territory, 1867. In Custer's book *My Life on the Plains*, the General wrote: "Wild Bill always carried two handsome ivory-handled revolvers of the large size; he was never seen without them . . . and every man openly carries a knife."

became close friends, Custer calling the gunman, "the most famous scout on the plains."

The dangerous challenges of the frontier were what Wild Bill relished. By the time he was appointed deputy United States marshal to clean up the lawless Kansas towns of Hays City and Abilene, the name "Wild Bill" was attached forever to James Butler Hickok whose shooting prowess and exploits were spectacular—the one "fact" agreed upon by all historians and by those who actually knew him.

Wild Bill Hickok was a handsome, well-dressed man with charming manners, contemporaries agree. Rumor has it that he bathed frequently in the public bath houses of the dirty frontier towns.

Photo courtesy of Deadwood Chamber of Commerce.

According to reliable biographers, he could hit a dime tossed into the air nine out of ten times; he could knock an apple from a tree with one shot and then hit the apple with another bullet before it struck the ground; he could drill bullets into the cork of a bottle without hitting the glass—and all at 25 paces or more. Many eye-witnesses reported that he never appeared to aim; yet he could handle two guns, firing simultaneously from the hips and never miss, whether in target practice or in life-or-death situations.

Wild Bill was a handsome six-footer with a handle-bar mustache and

He probably was the most accurate and deadly pistol shot the world has ever seen. **Wild Bill Hickok—Prince of Pistoleers,** Senn

He was not quarrelsome but was absolutely fearless. **Black Hills Trails,** Brown and Willard

long curling hair, but there is disagreement over whether his hair was blonde or dark-colored. Many of his contemporaries commented on his refined manners and cat-like grace. Always clean and well-groomed, he was said to have been addicted to bathing frequently in the public bath-houses of the rough, unsanitary frontier towns.

Although many women openly pursued him, Wild Bill, in March, 1876, married a rather unattractive widow; she was a daring circus acrobat

Photo courtesy of Al Gunther.

Wild Bill married widow Agnes Lake Thatcher, eleven years older than he. On July 17, 1876, he wrote a rough-hewn letter to "My own darling wife Agnes I have but a few moments left before this letter starts . . . Just got in from prospecting . . . I now my Agnes and only live to lov her never mind Pet we will have a home yet then we will be so happy I am all most shure I will do well . . . Good by dear wife.

J. B. Hickok   Wild Bill

and equestrienne 11 years his senior named Alice Lake Thatcher. After a two-week honeymoon, he left his bride in Cincinnati and traveled on the Union Pacific to Cheyenne, Wyoming, where he began planning a trip to the Black Hills.

Thus, in June, 1876, Wild Bill joined the Black Hills Gold Rush and made it to Deadwood Gulch, the lawless and riotous gold camp which was springing up within the domain of the Sioux Indians. Honest John McClintock, the trusted Deadwood historian, was usually in the right place at the right time: and of course he was there on Deadwood's only street a day in

In all Wild Bill stories true or imaginative, there are three points on which there is general agreement: that he was very handsome, that his manners were pleasing, and that he was a thoroughly honest man. **Wild Bill Hickok, the Prince of Pistoleers,** Wilstach

June when Wild Bill and Calamity Jane were galloping outriders for the long Colorado Charlie Utter wagon train as it rumbled up the gold-crazed gulch.

In Deadwood Gulch, which was estimated to have reached a population of 10,000—and some say 25,000—the first summer, where almost everyone was delirious with gold fever, Wild Bill played it cool. The already legendary lawman and gunfighter maintained a low profile, spending most of his time occupied with his greatest obsession, gambling. Not even McClintock caught him panning gold or working a sluicebox like the common rabble. The controversial marshal found time to write loving letters to his bride Alice implying that he soon hoped to strike it rich in Deadwood so they could be reunited.

On August 2, 1876, a day that will live in infamy in Black Hills history, Wild Bill was playing poker with his cronies in the Number 10 saloon; he

Photo courtesy of Centennial Archives, Deadwood Public Library.

An artist's conception of Jack McCall's shooting Wild Bill in the back of the head while the gambling Kansas marshal was holding aces and eights, "the Deadman's Hand." The bullet entered the arm of Capt. Massie who, legend says, never had it removed. The rest of his life Massie made grand entrances, saying, "Here comes the bullet that killed Wild Bill."

was sitting with his back to the door, an unusual position for a former lawman with many enemies. That was his fatal mistake. Jack McCall, a common gunslinger, burst into the saloon and shot Wild Bill in the back of the head at close range. The super-star of the Wild West died instantly. He was holding black aces and eights, known forever after as the "dead man's hand."

Jack McCall ran out of the saloon just across the street from where

John McClintock happened to be standing. Whether or not he recorded the scene in a notebook, the future historian recorded it all in his mind's eye: McCall's smoking gun and the outraged citizens chasing the assassin shouting "Wild Bill is dead! Wild Bill's been shot!"

The angry crowd, without Calamity Jane's help, as she later insisted, caught the assassin either in Shoudy's meat market or in some other building in a much-disputed location in old Deadwood.

Jack McCall was tried the next morning in the Bella Union theater, leased by actor Jack Langrishe. The miner's court which tried McCall was not a legal court; Deadwood in 1876 had no jurisdiction and no legal right to be alive, let alone pretend that a gold camp could create an official, duly constituted body to try accused criminals.

The judge, the jury, and the attorneys—if not the accused—were well aware of their make-believe status, and they all performed as though they were playing games before an unruly, packed house overflowing onto the street. Jack McCall testified that he had shot Wild Bill because he was seeking revenge for the death of his brother by Wild Bill's gun. Judge W. Y. Kuykendall and the jury accepted the eye-for-an-eye story of primitive justice and acquitted McCall, to no one's surprise except posterity's which did not understand all the circumstances.

The trial of Jack McCall was a miscarriage of justice typical of the frontier and much like the lesser-known trial of Carty for the killing of Jack Hinch, the first murder victim in the gulch. The Carty trial took place up the gulch in Gayville the day before Wild Bill was shot, and Carty was set free on the very day Wild Bill was murdered.

Other exciting happenings that day included a man found dead from drinking poor whiskey as the crowd was debating whether or not to hang Jack McCall when reports came in that the Indians had surrounded Crook City and that help was wanted pronto.

When at sundown on that August 2nd a Mexican horseman galloped in carrying the head of an Indian on a stick with long black hair flying, Illinois miner Jerry Bryan wrote in his diary: "This caped the climax, Wild Bill and everything else was thrown in the Shade." It had been a day of thrills for blood-thirsty Deadwood Gulch.

Taking his time, McCall left town. Later that month, he was arrested in

This verdict was not a surprise to those cognizant of the way in which the jury was chosen. While there were a few members of the jury who were supposed to be square men, a number of them were associates of the gang suspected of hiring McCall to murder Wild Bill. "An Account of Deadwood and the Northern Black Hills in 1876." Seth Bullock, **South Dakota Historical Collections.**

Most biographers relate that McCall was hired to do the killing by gamblers who feared that Hickok would be made city marshal. All pioneers of 1876 and other early residents who have been questioned derided this story. **Wild Bill Hickok—Prince of Pistoleers,** Senn

It is getting to dangerous here to be healthy. A man is liable to be shot here any time by some drunken desperado and it is not very safe to go out but we have decided to go morrow. **An Illinois Gold Hunter in the Black Hills,** Bryan

Wyoming, where he was rash enough to boast of having killed Wild Bill. He was eventually tried in Yankton, the capital of Dakota Territory; in this second trial, this time in a federal court, Jack McCall was convicted. He was hanged on March 1, 1877, for the murder of Wild Bill Hickok and buried with the rope around his neck.

Colorado Charlie and Steve Utter buried Wild Bill in his first grave at Ingleside and erected a wooden headboard which didn't last long. The inscription is famous in western history.

After the murder Colorado Charlie Utter and his brother Steve carried Wild Bill's body to their tent which was under the surveillance of John McClintock. A barber named Doc Pierce acted as undertaker and pronounced Wild Bill, "the prettiest corpse I have ever seen." Preacher Smith, the only minister in sinful Deadwood, said a prayer for the marshal who had so often broken the third commandment, "Thou shalt not kill." The prospectors, the merchants, the prostitutes of Deadwood, including a wailing Calamity Jane, tramped through the tent for a last look at the gunman they had thought invincible.

It is known that Captain Jack Crawford and Wild Bill were close friends. It is also true that in Cheyenne, in 1876, Hickok, before entering the Black Hills, told Captain Jack that he had never met Calamity Jane. "Wild Bill and Calamity Jane," Paine, **The Black Hills,** Peattie, ed.

The Utter brothers buried Wild Bill in Ingleside, the first boot hill in Deadwood, and placed a wooden marker above his grave with an inscription.*

The Utter brothers had taken charge of Wild Bill's body after he was slain; they had buried him the first time; and three years later, in 1879, they decided to rebury their illustrious friend in the new cemetery, Mount Moriah.

Thus, Colorado Charlie and Steve Utter, in company with a Lewis Schoenfield, and of course with John McClintock, the man who was on hand for every historic occasion either as an observer or as a participant, dug up Wild Bill's crude coffin and struggled up Moriah hill carrying it to its final resting place.

In his history book of pioneer days, McClintock reported opening the casket and finding that Wild Bill's carbine was in the casket intact and so was the gunman's corpse which was exposed down to the hips. The clothes were decomposed and off to one side of the body and to the amazement of the grave-movers, the white body appeared to be perfectly preserved and covered with a coat of lime. McClintock described how he took a stick the size of a cane and tapped many places on the body, face, and head, discovering no soft places anywhere.

McClintock, writing over half a century after that memorable exhuming, explained that these conditions of Wild Bill's corpse were the result of percolating water embalming the body tissues.

━━

Madame Lake Hickok, the widow of the late Wild Bill, accompanied by Buckskin Charley and wife, and George Carson, arrived in the city . . . The widow visited Bill's grave, and proposed, as soon as it is definitely settled that the graveyard will not be disturbed to erect a fenced monument to his memory, in which kind action Buffalo Bill, Texas Jack, and Buckskin Charley will assist her. **Black Hills Daily Times,** Sept. 4, 1877

*Wild Bill
J. B. Hickok
Killed by the assassin Jack McCall
Deadwood, Black Hills
August 2, 1876

Pard we will meet again in the
Happy Hunting Grounds to part no more
Good bye
Colorado Charlie, C. H. Utter

Old John McClintock stopped by to investigate when we were building our home on Taylor Avenue in 1941. He said that right where the workmen removed a stump to build our fireplace was the exact spot where Wild Bill Hickok had been buried at Ingleside in 1876. Recollection of Mrs. Helen Scotvold, long-time Deadwood resident.

"Wild Bill Petrified," was the headline in the **Black Hills Daily Times,** August 9, 1879, and the news story included most of the same details that McClintock later verified. **The Times** implied that the god-like status of the deceased may have been responsible for the unusual state of preservation of Wild Bill's corpse.

Photo courtesy of South Dakota Historical Society.

A bust of Wild Bill chiseled from gold-flecked granite by Korczak Ziolkowski was presented to Deadwood on "Wild Bill Day" in 1951 by George Hunter. So far it has withstood vandals, the weather, and photographers. Located on Sherman Street near the spot where Wild Bill and the Utter brothers had their tent in 1876 and right below Mount Moriah.

If the McClintock and the **Times** accounts are to be taken seriously, then one can say that the body of Wild Bill withstood the years much better than did the grave-markers and statues to his memory which did not last because of determined vandals hacking and chipping at them until they were all eventually destroyed.

Possessing a remarkably clear and accurate memory, Mr. McClintock has written an account of the history of Deadwood and the Black Hills. He is regarded as an authentic historian and his word is accepted as final on many controversial points of Deadwood history. **Deadwood Pioneer-Times,** Jan. 16, 1937

The County Commissioners advised a Lead undertaker to resurrect the body of Vinegar Bill some months ago, insisting that he clothe his nakedness and place him in a coffin that permitted him taking his rest in a comfortable position. **Deadwood Pioneer-Times,** May 1, 1908

At last, 76 years after Wild Bill's death, a sculptor carved a statue of Wild Bill that neither vandals nor the elements could destroy. On Sherman Street, right below Brown Rocks and the Mount Moriah lookout is a bust of Wild Bill by Korczak Ziolkowski, the sculptor of the Crazy Horse memorial near Custer. The statue, chiseled from a two-ton section of granite, is full of gold flecks and is said to be on the actual site where Wild Bill and the Utter brothers had pitched their tents in June, 1876.

On June 21, 1951, Deadwood celebrated Wild Bill Day and unveiled the bust, presented to the city by George Hunter, a Deadwood businessman and philanthropist, whose father John Hunter was a Black Hills Pioneer of 1877. In the evening an impressive ceremony took place; spotlights shone upon the natural stage of Brown Rocks above the crowd and a narrator read a poem about Will Bill into a microphone.*

A number of mementoes, photographs, and possessions of Wild Bill's are displayed at the Adams Museum. These include two guns, his razor, the pipe he was smoking when shot, a stone found in his boot the day he was murdered, and a leaf from his grave. The marriage license of James Butler Hickok to Mrs. Agnes L. Thatcher is also exhibited as is the affectionate letter he wrote to his bride before his death.

Wild Bill Hickok, as has been pointed out by many authors and observers, did nothing for Deadwood except to die there—but that event has turned out to be a bonanza for Deadwood which has adopted the careless gunman as its patron saint of business. However, many Deadwoodites as well as other people have objected to the extensive publicity and adulation promoted for Wild Bill who was a scout on the Kansas-Nebraska frontier, a quick-on-the-trigger marshal for Abilene and Hays City, a gambler from Cheyenne. Yet his name is inextricably linked with that of Deadwood, his last stomping ground in the border country and where he lived quietly in his tent and spent much of his time gambling until he was shot. All the books, articles, and poetry written about him, past and present, including this biography, only serve to solidify his posthumous reputation which is a mixed bag of gold dust, rubbish, and notches on a gun.

What was Wild Bill really like? Why did this man's colorful life, both real and imaginary, contribute so much to the romantic concept of the Wild West? Apparently, he had what the 1970's have labeled ''charisma,'' the power to attract others with an indefinable charm and magnetism.

General George Custer, a controversial character himself, greatly admired Wild Bill who often scouted for the general in Kansas during the 1860's. Custer praised Wild Bill's character and said that his killings were invariably justified. Custer wrote in his only book, **My Life on the Plains,** that Wild Bill was ''one of the most perfect types of physical manhood I ever saw . . . He was entirely free from bluster or bravado.''

Custer and Hickok were never in the Black Hills at the same time. The Custer Expedition of 1874 discovered gold in the Black Hills. Newspapers throughout the nation publicized the gold discoveries and thus precipitated

Photo courtesy of South Dakota Historical Society.

General George Custer, a great admirer of Wild Bill. In Custer's only book he wrote: "Wild Bill was a strange character, just the one which a novelist might gloat over . . . Add to this powerful figure a costume blending the immaculate neatness of the dandy with the extravagant taste and style of the frontiersman, and you have Wild Bill, the most famous scout on the Plains."

Photo courtesy of South Dakota Historical Society.

An Illingworth photo of the Custer Expedition of 1874 enroute to the Black Hills. Custer and his men found gold at French Creek. The extensive newspaper publicity about Custer's gold discoveries precipitated the Black Hills Gold Rush which Wild Bill joined.

Authoress Elizabeth Custer wrote glowingly about Wild Bill: "Tall, lithe, and free in every motion, he rode and walked as if every muscle was perfection, and the careless swing of his body as he moved seemed perfectly in keeping with the man, the country, the time in which he lived . . . 'He was the mildest manner'd man that ever scuttled ship or cut a throat.' "

the Black Hills Gold Rush of 1876 which lured Wild Bill Hickok to the Hills.

Elizabeth Custer, the General's beautiful wife, joined in the accolades for Wild Bill. In **Following the Guidon,** one of her three books, she wrote: "Physically, he was a delight to look upon . . . The frank, manly expression of his fearless eyes and his courteous manner gave one a feeling of confidence in his word and in his undaunted courage."

Another woman writer, Annie Tallent, described Wild Bill as a "rather heavily-built individual in ordinary citizen's clothes." She was not as overwhelmingly complimentary as were the Custers, saying that he could have

passed for a Quaker minister when she had a conversation with him on the street in Cheyenne, Wyoming. She concluded that Wild Bill was not all bad.

Yes, Wild Bill's life and death had all the makings for a legendary character of the Wild West, even bearing some resemblance to the noble heroes of classic Greek tragedy who met tragic fates because of a fatal flaw.

What if Wild Bill had not been assassinated, had instead lived to become a successful professional gambler in Deadwood? What if he had built a Victorian house and a circus ring for his darling Agnes and her horses on exclusive Forest Hill? What if he had settled down to a respectable life into his old age—what then? Who knows whether he would have been fulfilled and happy?

If he had lived to be 87 years old, in 1924, he might have waxed his iron-gray moustache and dressed up in his Prince Albert frock-coat and sombrero smelling of moth balls. Then, while riding a dignified horse and shooting blanks in the air faster than lightning, he would have led the Society of Black Hills Pioneers in the very first "Days of '76" parade. Afterwards he could have regaled the tourists at the rebuilt No. 10 saloon with lurid, true tales of the gold camp and gunfights on the frontier.

What if he had done all this—had lived to become the grand old marshal of Deadwood? Would he have become the legend he is today?

No, absolutely not!

Death—a violent death surrounded with dramatic irony—of an already notorious Prince of Pistoleers deified the legend and conferred immortality on Wild Bill Hickok, just as it had done to his friend Custer in that savage summer of 1876. Thus, his villainous murder at the age of 39 may have been necessary to complete the grand design of a Wild West saga.

Wild Bill had been resting in peace for 27 years when Calamity Jane finally caught up with him in Mount Moriah. One old-timer shook his head, "Poor Wild Bill! Now he'll be pitching and tossing until Judgment Day having that disgraceful Calamity right behind him."

From all the lurid tales of the early days in Deadwood one would think the population was entirely composed of Wild Bill Hickok, Jack McCall, Calamity Jane, Poker Alice, and their like. The good, sturdy, often well-educated pioneer is seldom mentioned. Memoirs of Charlotte Cushman Clark.

One of the questions most frequently asked by visitors of Deadwood is:
Question: Was Wild Bill Hickok a good guy or a bad guy?
Answer: He was a good guy.
Question: How can a guy who killed all those guys be a good guy?
Answer: He was on the Union side during the Civil War. He was a United States scout during the Indian Wars, a Lawman and a Deputy U.S. Marshal. **Deadwood—the Historic City,** Clowser

Wild Bill's greatest contributions had been made on the earlier frontiers. There were others who contributed more directly to the development of the Black Hills; yet his death and burial in Deadwood and the legends of his earlier deeds have forever associated him with the Hills. "Wild Bill and Calamity Jane," Paine, **The Black Hills,** Peattie, ed.

75 years of wind and rain and sunny days
Have swept thru Deadwood Gulch
And high on Mount Moriah hill
The night is still
Where the moon's glow touches
The stone of old "Wild Bill'
        (first verse)
For there a craftsman will affix
A lasting mark of '76
Wrenched from gold-flecked granite
The spirit of my kind.
I've returned to Deadwood's camp!
I've left Moriah hill
The spirit of the "gunmen" breed
Is here in old Wild Bill
        (last lines)

"Deadwood Gold Camp, Dakota Territory," by Dean Naumann (entire poem reprinted on large poster in Adams Museum. Read from Brown Rocks on June 21, 1951, when the Wild Bill bust was dedicated).

Dedicated to the late Gary Cooper (1901-1961) whose portrayal of Wild Bill Hickok in "The Plainsman" inspired research that led to this book. **They Called Him Wild Bill, the Life and Adventures of James Butler Hickok,** Rosa

The Burial of Wild Bill
By Captain Jack Crawford

Under the sod in the land of gold
    We have laid the fearless Bill;
We called him wild, yet a little child
    Could bend his iron will
With generous heart he freely gave
    To the poorly clad—unshod.
Think of it, pards, of his noble traits
    While you cover him with the sod. (last verse)

Epitaph
By Captain Jack Crawford

Sleep on, brave heart, in peaceful slumber,
    Bravest scout in all the West;
Lightning eyes and voice of thunder
    Closed and hushed in quiet rest.
Lightning eyes and voice of thunder
    May we meet again in heaven.
Rest in peace! **Poets and Poetry—Literature of SD**

(Captain Jack Crawford, the uneducated poet-scout, who presented a program of poetry and reminiscence in Deadwood in 1893 to raise money to improve Wild Bill's grave, had earlier written several poems about his friend. He wrote them while sitting on Wild Bill's grave, first at Ingleside, then later at Mount Moriah.)

Photo courtesy of South Dakota Historical Society.

Captain Jack Crawford, the poet-scout, wrote poems to Wild Bill while sitting on his grave. Captain Jack also gave readings to raise money to improve Wild Bill's grave.

Deadwood in 1876: It was a strange year in a strange place. Poetry and murder lived side by side on this island of rock and forest while the surrounding plains echoed with the sounds of war. **South Dakota,** Milton

Calamity Jane
Queen of the Wild West

Once upon a time a baby girl named Martha Canary (or Cannary) was born, somewhere around the year 1850, and probably in Princeton, Mo., although it could have been in Fort Laramie, Wyo., or Burlington, Iowa, or Salt Lake City. However, conflicting accounts of her birth agree that she came west with her parents some time around the year 1865; and while still in her early teens, Martha began roving the Wild West of Montana, Utah, Colorado, Kansas, Wyoming, and Dakota Territory.

No, Martha of the fanciful, once-upon-a-time beginnings did not grow up to be a fairy tale princess; she became Calamity Jane, Heroine of the Plains. She said so herself. She could ride, shoot, cuss, pan gold, wield a whip, chew tobacco, and drink better than most men. She was a liberated woman—Wild West style.

Documented information about Calamity Jane is hard to come by, even more so than about Wild Bill Hickok. But one fact is sure: she and Wild Bill were not lovers, even though Calamity, a red-hot publicity hound, did everything she could to convince people they were, especially after he was dead and couldn't defend himself.

Calamity Jane was a prostitute with the proverbial heart of gold. She was a Good Samaritan. She was also a scout, a bullwhacker, a teamster, and a home nurse. Whatever she was, she was always a show-off. Often she dressed like a man and passed herself off as one, especially when she wanted a job traditionally reserved for men. One perceptive biographer has suggested that her fondness for playing both feminine and masculine roles indicated hermaphroditic tendencies.

Writers have described her as beautiful and ugly, tall and short, with reddish coppery hair and with sweeping raven tresses. Some say she resembled "a busted bale of hay"; others say she was "extremely pretty." Even in the same book, **Black Hills Trails** the two authors Brown and Willard describe her in contradictory terms: "roughest-looking human that I ever saw," and "she was of splendid form, clear complexion and uncommonly good-looking." One can look at her early pictures and see that she was pretty in her youth.

"Beauty and bravery were Calamity Jane's best assets," said the renowned Dr. L. F. Babcock, the first coroner of Deadwood and the doctor with whom Calamity worked as a nurse during the small-pox epidemic of 1878, according to Estelline Bennett, whose **Old Deadwood Days** provides many colorful sketches of Deadwood characters.

━━━

In our society, the role of those maladjusted individuals who are neither completely man nor woman is difficult . . . whether or not Calamity was such an individual cannot, of course, be proven; nevertheless, the mere fact of her affectation of men's clothes and mannish ways may well have brought her safety and respect among the Indians which she might not have had otherwise. "Wild Bill Hickok and Calamity Jane," Paine, **The Black Hills**, Peattie, ed.

Photo courtesy of W. H. Over Museum.

A rare photograph of Calamity Jane when she was young and pretty. A rough life and excessive drinking caused her to age quickly.

Calamity Jane may have been a pretty girl, but she aged quickly from excessive drinking and from the rough outdoor life she led, and probably from an increasing lack of interest in her appearance. She soon looked much older than her years.

Both famous and infamous, good and bad, saint and sinner—that was Calamity's roller coaster reputation. She trampled on respectability, thumbed her nose at social conventions, and flaunted her sexual duality—sometimes so outrageously that mothers whisked their children inside to protect them from this noisy harlot. On the other hand, she nursed the sick; she shared whatever she had; she fought against the mistreatment of humans, oxen, and horses; friendly and big-hearted, she liked children and was loyal to her friends. Such a mixed bag of good and bad she was that she fascinated everybody.

Calamity Jane first entered the Black Hills in 1875 as an unauthorized member of the government-sponsored Jenney-Newton party, a scientific expedition escorted by the Dodge military command. The expedition made topographical surveys and checked up on the gold discoveries made by the Custer Expedition and publicized since the previous year of 1874.

Calamity, dressed as a man, smuggled herself into this scientific group and probably got herself hired as a teamster driving a supply wagon. Then somebody discovered that she was a female invading male territory and squealed on her. Officials told her to get lost, to hit the trail back to Fort Laramie.

Historians believe that despite her banishment, she sneaked back and therefore did enter the Hills with the Jenney-Newton expedition. Thus, Calamity Jane was the third non-Indian woman to enter the Black Hills; the first was Aunt Sally Campbell, a Negro cook with the Custer expedition of 1874; and the second was Annie Tallent with the illegal Gordon or Russell-Collins party.

Calamity's activities while masquerading as a man on government expeditions are open to speculation. Did she work both as a teamster and a prostitute among the soldiers?

When she signed up as a scout under her own name, she sometimes got by with being a woman in a man's world. And there is no reason she wouldn't have been an excellent scout. She was reported to have been at every town, camp, and fort on the frontier; she had ridden horseback or tramped over many western trails as a bullwhacker or teamster. An expert shot with both rifle and pistol, she could stand the hardships of the

Considerable is said in favor of not saying anything about Calamity. She was a disreputable old harridan, a disgrace to womankind. **Calamity Jane of the Western Trails,** Jennewein.

While in Custer City, a government outfit came in and Calamity Jane was driving one of the teams . . . The first place that attracted her attention was a saloon, where she was soon made blind as a bat from looking through the bottom of a glass. **Black Hills Trails,** Brown and Willard.

Photo courtesy of W. H. Over Museum.

Calamity Jane dressed as a scout for General Crook. In her ghost-written autobiography she commented on her habit of dressing like a man: "It was a bit awkward at first but I soon got to be perfectly at home in men's clothes."

wilderness as well as any man.

But Calamity was a liar, especially about her scouting. She lied when anyone would listen. She lied in her counterfeit autobiography about being a scout for Custer. She lied about being a scout for General George Crook in 1875 when his assignment was to clear the illegal miners out of the Black Hills.

Once in a while she told the truth. Despite debunkers who scoff at all claims of Calamity's being a scout, the name "Calamity Jane" is listed by Frank Gourard, the chief of scouts for General Crook at Fort Fetterman in May, 1876. She is also mentioned in the diaries of two of Crook's soldiers. So she did scout for General Crook on at least one expedition.

Calamity Jane pranced into Deadwood Gulch in June, 1876, and rein-

Calamity Jane has arrived. **Cheyenne Leader** will insert. **Black Hills Pioneer,** July 15, 1876

After the battle of the Rose Bud in June, 1876, Crook ordered his extra wagon trains to be sent to Fort Fetterman with the sick and wounded and I know Calamity Jane was with it for I saw her. Rancher John Hunton, as quoted in **The Cheyenne and Black Hills Stage and Express Routes,** Spring

ed up her horse right in the middle of the gold rush. Deadwood was where all the action was; and from that time on, Calamity was the raucous tomboy who kept already topsy-turvy Deadwood reeling and spinning.

By piecing together the eye-witness accounts of ubiquitous John McClintock and of reporter Richard Hughes, one can visualize Calamity's grand entrance with Wild Bill Hickok when both were outriders for the wagon train.

The two super-stars of the Wild West galloped up the gulch dressed in buckskins "with sufficient fringe to make a considerable buckskin rope," and both wearing white stetsons and clean boots. Youthful, gun-toting Calamity looked right pretty, "an Amazonian woman of the frontier," Hughes said, "and clad in complete male habiliments and riding astride."* Yelling and whooping, she waved her fancy stetson at all the cheering men jammed into the crooked, narrow main street of Deadwood Gulch.

Calamity and Wild Bill led the way for the Colorado Charlie Utter wagon train, which had originated in Cheyenne, Wyo., and was reportedly composed of about 190 people. No wonder it stopped the traffic in the gold camp where the motley gang was still working at clearing away the jumble of dead wood and working the open placer claims in the jam-packed street, noisy with animals and humans and pounding hammers, the aura of gold dust over all.

And there were the first "girls" riding like queens in the wagons, laughing and waving at the royal welcome the prospectors gave them. McClintock labeled Calamity and beautiful Kitty Arnold as "two female sports." There were also two experienced madams, both faro dealers, Madam Mustachio and Madam Dirty Em, who soon set up a thriving red-light district in the gulch.

The long wagon train wound its way below Brown Rocks and the high hill that was to become Mount Moriah cemetery, the final resting place of the two flamboyant outriders. Were there any watching who knew that Wild Bill Hickok was a marked man?

McClintock wrote that during that summer, Calamity followed Wild Bill in and out of the gambling dens like an adoring puppy, but he was a lonesome, letter-writing bridegroom and wanted nothing to do with her.

Even if he had not been a faithful husband, it is doubtful that coarse, foul-mouthed Calamity would have attracted elegant Wild Bill. There was no love affair between them, and their romance flourished only in fiction and later in the movies—and in 1876, undoubtedly in Calamity's imagination.

*Reprinted by permission of the Publishers, the Arthur H. Clark Company, from **Pioneer Years in the Black Hills,** by Richard B. Hughes

There were several women who at one time or another adopted the alias "Calamity Jane." There are extant photographs of at least three and possibly four women that have come down to us labeled by contemporaries as Calamity Jane. "Wild Bill Hickok and Calamity Jane," Paine, **The Black Hills,** Peattie, ed.

Photo courtesy of Centennial Archives, Deadwood Public Library.

A wagon train pulled by oxen. In the 1870's and 1880's the main street of Deadwood was often blocked with wagons and animals. Bullwhackers, including Calamity Jane, cracked their whips and cussed magnificently to keep the oxen under control. The muddy streets and the stench were terrible. Note the sign for "Cold Baths."

During the first four years of the booming gold camp, from 1876-1880, Calamity made Deadwood her headquarters. Like many others, she did some prospecting but never made a big strike. When she couldn't earn enough gold dust to live on from being a prostitute or a prospector or a bull-whacker, she went from saloon to hurdy-gurdy house begging for free booze, telling the bartender "fill her up and slop it over the brim." In the hurdy-gurdy dance halls she often danced with the "girls" like a man. No information is available on how successful she was as a prostitute, a mannish-looking one dressed in buckskin pants and a cowboy hat.

However, she had a spectacular reputation as a bullwhacker, and often

"I met her in '79," said a Black Hills pioneer. "Our wagons camped together the first night out of Pierre. I said, "Who is that loud-mouthed man?" and the boss said, "That's no man—that's Calamity Jane." She stood in the middle of a big circle and cracked the bullwhip like nobody else could. I never heard anything like it. When she made a right good crack, they whooped and hollered and she stopped for a drink. They just plain raised the devil around that whip." **Calamity Jane of the Western Trails,** Jennewein

crossed and re-crossed the rutted trails of the west doing this male work, wielding a 20-foot-long whip and snapping it over the backs of the plodding oxen pulling the heavy freight wagons. The art came in not actually touching the oxen with the whip, but in snaking it out to make a popping sound or crack.

Calamity also had another skill that the oxen apparently understood; she could swear, as the saying goes, "like a trooper." She was once awarded the title, "Champion Swearer of the Hills." Today, lenient publishers might permit her magnificent working vocabulary to appear in print. But, according to all reports, the list of blankety-blanks would take up too much space. Thus, modern readers who miss the obscenities and standard four-letter words will have to fill in the _____ themselves.

"The Hills reverberated to the wild howling of Calamity Jane, the untamed woman of the wild, wild west," wrote D. Dee in **Low Down on Calamity Jane.** D. Dee was the pseudonym for Dora DuFran, a noted madam of brothels in Deadwood, Lead, Belle Fourche, and Rapid City. Her rare booklet is full of historical errors, but her tales about Calamity whom she met in 1886 are probably true and support the interpretation of her personality made by more reliable sources. At least, she knew Calamity well; whether or not Calamity worked for Madam DuFran as a prostitute is unknown, but an aging Calamity did work as a laundress in the DuFran establishments.

According to Madam DuFran, Calamity had even "a band of coyotes beaten to a frazzle for sustained howling," especially when she was drunk and that was most of the time.

Estelline Bennett, in her book about Deadwood, writes about Calamity's howls and yells awakening her from sound slumber in her bed. The wild cat's caterwauling echoed up and down the terraced streets of Deadwood. Estelline, Judge Bennett's daughter, concluded, "I know she was specially privileged because other people did get run in for drinking too loud."

In Calamity's spurious autobiography, she described how, during an Indian ambush, her comrade, a Captain Egan, was injured in the fight. But she says she was able to gallop up beside him, lift him onto her own horse, and race for the fort holding the wounded captain in front of the saddle. Later, she claimed the grateful officer said, "I name you Calamity Jane, the Heroine of the Plains." And that's as good a story as any about how she acquired her name.

When she was drunk, which was often, she loved to regale an ever-

It is reported from Sturgis City that Calamity Jane walloped two women at that place yesterday. Calamity can get away with half a dozen ordinary pugilistic women when she turns loose, but she never fights unless she is in the right, and then she is not backward to tackle even a masculine shoulder hitter. **Black Hills Daily Times,** Feb. 8, 1879

Many stories are told about how she got her name, but the most likely is that her paramours were generally visited by some venereal "calamity." **Gold in the Black Hills,** Parker

present saloon audience with tales of Indian fights, stage-coach robberies—all kinds of escapades in which she claimed to have played a renegade male role. She must have been a likable liar even though her fabrications were often no more fantastic than her actual life.

In 1879, when ex-sheriff Seth Bullock conducted Territorial Senator R.F. Pettigrew on a grand tour of Deadwood, they visited "The Bad Lands," the lower section of town which included Chinatown and the red light district. When the two men stopped in a saloon, a boisterous young man in buckskins elbowed his way through the crowd to buy the two men a drink. After the encounter, Senator Pettigrew asked Seth Bullock about the man's identity. Bullock laughed, "That's no man—that's Calamity Jane!"

Photo courtesy of Centennial Archives, Deadwood Public Library.

A middle-aged Calamity Jane dressed as a scout. Often photographed with a rifle, she was an excellent markswoman with all kinds of guns. Throughout the frontier she was famous for shooting out mirrors and kerosene lamps in saloons.

And that must have been an oft-heard exclamation in Calamity Jane country.

But there was another side to Calamity Jane, a kind and gentle side, the motherly, nurturing side. Her contemporaries revered her as an angel of

If anyone was sick in camp, it was 'send for Jane'; where Calamity was there was Jane; and so she was christened Calamity Jane. **Lowdown on Calamity Jane,** D. Dee (DuFran)

mercy, a sort of combination Florence Nightingale, Clara Barton, and Joan of Arc. At least three authors who knew her relate how she nursed the sick during the smallpox epidemic of 1878 when no other woman would go near the contagious patients. No wonder Dr. Babcock described her as "beautiful and brave."

Photo courtesy of South Dakota Historical Society.

An aging Calamity Jane wearing a dress in Whitewood. The story goes that the man who took this picture promised to buy her a drink if she'd pose for him. Calamity couldn't pass up a chance like that.

Then there's the tale of penniless Calamity pulling a gun on a grocery clerk to obtain food for the sick. A lady Robin Hood, Wild West style.

In about 1880, Calamity left Deadwood, and according to the western newspapers who often mentioned her whereabouts, she lived during the next 15 years in many towns throughout Montana, Colorado, and Wyoming. How she earned a living during her nomadic life on the shrinking frontier, no one is sure.

Back to Deadwood she came in 1895, and instead of the "denizens of

Day and night she went among the sick and dying, and for week after week ministered to their wants. It made no difference to her that she knew them not, or that no gold would be there to repay her for the labor, the sacrifice, the danger. **Black Hills Trails**, Brown and Willard

Another time, while waiting tables in Pierre, she heard of a family in destitute circumstances and sick with Black Diphtheria. Jane had saved $20 in gold. She proceeded to a grocery store, purchased $15 worth of food and medicine and nursed the family until the sickness was over. "Calamity Jane," as remembered by Percy Russell in **Deadwood—The Historic City**, Clowser

As soon as a mining camp became a town and the town began trying to be respectable Calamity would move . . . A more daring and eccentric woman I have never known. She is one of the old frontier types and she has all of their merits and most of their faults. "Reminiscence of Calamity Jane by Buffalo Bill Cody," **Black Hills Daily Times**, Jan. 22, 1878

the Bad Lands" surrounding her, she was welcomed back by the elite of the town, including ex-Sheriff Seth Bullock, Dr. L.F. Babcock, George Ayres, and the editors of the two main newspapers.

According to author Estelline Bennett, who herself belonged to the elite because her father was a judge, these respectable pioneers of '76 enjoyed a special kinship with each other and with Calamity. And they respected her unforgettable role as the only brave nurse during the epidemic. This roustabout Good Samaritan was symbolic of old Deadwood, of the glorious days of '76, which these pioneers revered as an "excited little scrap of heaven."

Plain and shabby and old for her age at this homecoming, Calamity had a little girl with her, claiming it was hers, although most Deadwood-ites did not believe it. She said she was married to a Clinton Burke who drove a Deadwood hack. No one ever found a record of their marriage then or in the ensuing years.

On the night that Calamity returned to Deadwood, her old friends among the sporting fraternity arranged a benefit dance for the education of Calamity's child whom she said she wanted to place in a convent. The jamboree was held at the dive called Green Front. Estelline Bennett reported that although considerable gold was raised, Calamity got roaring drunk and blew all the money buying drinks for the old gang.

Then she got a break, a paying job where she could be the center of attention. In January, 1896, **The Black Hills Daily Times** reported that Calamity was going on tour with the amusement company of Kohl and Middleton and that she had been practicing her "splendid shooting" with a Winchester rifle.

In appraising her career, **The Times** commented on her reputation as an expert marksman with rifle, shotgun, or six-shooter during the turbulent days when life depended on the skillful use of a gun and "the most desperate outlaw feared her." Proudly, **The Times** predicted she would be a stellar attraction in the East.

Today Calamity Jane has been giving a drunken exhibition on the streets . . . It was a disgrace to our city that she was permitted to run things in such a high-handed, wild west style . . . 'The notorious ruin' as the **Lead Call** refers to her, should be given to understand Hot Springs is governed in a different manner than was Deadwood of '76. She should have been locked in the cooler. **Hot Springs Star**, Nov. 16, 1895

We are inclined to doubt that Calamity Jane was ever legally married to anybody, **Calamity Jane of the Western Trails**, Jennewein

Because of Calamity's dissolute habits, the girl was taken by authorities and placed in a convent school at Sturgis, her alleged identity and subsequent whereabouts being concealed thereafter. D. Dee states that she was a stepdaughter of Clinton Burke, which is probably true. **Deadwood Dick and Calamity Jane**, Senn

Calamity could shoot with both guns at once and hit her mark. At a turkey shoot, using a small 22 rifle she won all the turkeys and gave them to bystanders who had no luck. **Lowdown on Calamity Jane**, D. Dee (DuFran)

No reviews are available on how well "The Famous Woman Scout of the Wild West and Heroine of a Thousand Thrilling Adventures," (as she was billed) was received in Minneapolis, Chicago, and New York. Clinton Burke accompanied her and also worked for her employers. According to Madam Dora DuFran, Kohl and Middleton soon became exasperated with her excessive drinking and "her language was too much for the tenderfeet of Chicago." She was fired.

In addition to the "husband" who was never proven to be her legal mate and to her "daughter" who was never proven to be her natural offspring, Calamity's life was full of make-believe and deceit.

Calamity Jane wearing a red dress while visiting Wild Bill's grave in Mount Moriah. Both before and after Wild Bill died, Calamity did her darndest to convince people that the two were lovers—but few ever believed it.

Although there is no proof that Calamity could read or write, an autobiography appeared, entitled "The Life and Adventures of Calamity Jane" by Herself. Written by a ghost writer about 1896 when Calamity was on her eastern tour, she peddled the pamphlet on the street and in saloons. It is full of historical errors and downright lies except for at least one truthful statement: "In fact, I was at all times along with the men where there was excitement or adventure to be had."

In 1903, the last year of her life, Calamity returned to the Black Hills and wore out her welcome in Deadwood, Lead, and Spearfish. Then her friend Madam DuFran gave the aging prostitute a job as a cook and laundress in her brothel in Belle Fourche. Calamity could stay sober only a few weeks at a time, and as she grew older, her sober periods lasted only a few

days. Madam DuFran recalled how Calamity rode out of Belle Fourche behind a cowboy enroute for Spearfish. "I can still remember the wild yells she gave as she topped the hill," wrote the Madam.

Skidding downhill fast from her years of dissipation, Calamity returned to Deadwood again, the Sin City where she apparently felt most at home even though the old gold camp was doing its best to find a respectable niche in the twentieth century. Nearing the end of the trail, a worn-out Calamity lashed out at the people who tried to reform her or capitalize on her outlandish reputation: "Why don't the sons of bitches leave me alone and let me go to hell my own route?"

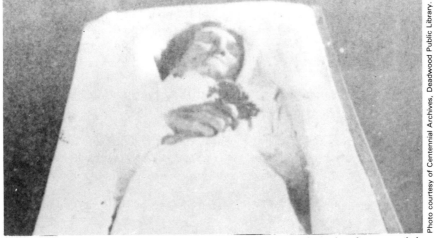

Photo courtesy of Centennial Archives, Deadwood Public Library.

Calamity Jane in her coffin. Several mourners who visited the funeral parlor to pay their last respects cut off locks of her hair. To protect the corpse, a bullwhacker friend fixed a wire cage over her head.

Sick and alone, she rode on the ore train to Terry, a mining village near Deadwood and went into seclusion in the Calloway Hotel there, saying she was going to "cash in her chips." She was right.

Calamity Jane died in Terry on August 1, 1903, aged about 53 years. Although the immediate cause of her death was variously listed as inflammation of the bowels and pneumonia, alcohol was the real villain.

Many curious people crowded into the undertaking parlor to view the remains of this woman whose legendary qualities death seemed to heighten. Souvenir hunters kept cutting off pieces of her hair until one of her old bull-

$4 came between me and fame . . . I was called to see Calamity Jane, but little knowing at the time that she was later to become nationally and internationally known, I thought of the livery bill—$4 for each trip to Terry . . . Besides that, I had an obstetric case pending, so this was one of the few calls I ever turned down. Another doctor was called. **Deadwood Doctor, F. S. Howe, M.D.**

I was just a little girl when Calamity died. I remember going with the other school kids to peer over the edge of the casket at her. Somebody had put a six-shooter in each hand so she'd look natural. I know she was a prominent person but I didn't know why. Recollection of Mayme (Mrs. George) Hunter, life-long resident of Deadwood.

whacking friends fixed up a protective wire fence to place over her head.

Both leading Deadwood newspapers carried front page stories about her death. **The Times** called her a "famous border character" and "former consort of Wild Bill Hickok," with a married daughter in North Dakota.

The Pioneer described her funeral at the First Methodist Church in Deadwood with the sermon delivered by Rev. C. B. Clark who praised her good deeds, ignored the bad, and emphasized her nursing activities. Ex-sheriff Seth Bullock remarked that at least half of the male mourners claimed they had been married to Calamity at one time or another.

Although Calamity was not an official member of the exclusive Society of Black Hills Pioneers whose original membership requirement was that the person must have arrived in the Hills before January 1, 1877, this group arranged for her funeral and paid the expenses. Big-hearted Jack Gray, manager of the Wasp No. 2 mine and a prominent Pioneer, was rumored to have paid for her expenses at Terry. Official or not, Calamity was certainly a pioneer; she had beaten most of the official Pioneers into the Black Hills in 1875 when she had smuggled herself in with the Jenney-Newton expedition.

In front of the horse-drawn hearse, the Deadwood band led the way up to Mount Moriah, followed by carriages, people on horseback, and a crowd on foot. Calamity's funeral was said to have been one of the largest ever held in Deadwood.

Undertaker C.H. Robinson was in charge of the funeral and burial.

Photo courtesy of Centennial Archives, Deadwood Public Library.

Burying Calamity Jane. Hard-to-see No. 6 is 26-year-old George Leeman, the youngest pall-bearer, who had been the first patient in the Deadwood pest house for contagious diseases. He later gained fame as the "best bartender in the Black Hills." He was a great favorite of the deceased. No. 8 with the long white beard is James W. Allen, Black Hills Pioneer of 1876.

Robinson was a brother of a dying little girl whom Calamity had nursed during the smallpox epidemic, and the eternally grateful undertaker was reported to have "laid her gently away and sealed her tomb."

Calamity's dying request has long since passed into folklore: "Bury me beside Wild Bill, the only man I ever loved." So she was. Thus, she achieved a closeness in death to her hero that she had never achieved in life.

Photo courtesy of Al Gunther.

"Bury me beside Wild Bill," was Calamity Jane's dying request. And she is buried right behind her hero—and some grave-watchers claim that Wild Bill has never stopped rolling in his grave since she caught up with him.

Author Estelline Bennett of Deadwood who actually knew Calamity Jane wrote a sympathetic chapter about her. Estelline concluded: "Her virtues were of the enduring sort. Her vices were the wide-open sins of a wide-

It is easy for a woman to be good who has been brought up with every protection from evils of the world and with good associates. Calamity was a product of the wild and wooly west. She was not immoral—she was unmoral. **Lowdown on Calamity Jane,** D. Dee (DuFran)

open country—the sort that never carry a hurt.''

Many visitors to Mount Moriah have been surprised to learn that Calamity Jane was a real person; others assume that because the graves of Wild Bill and Calamity are adjacent that they were lovers. And some say that through the years they have observed a spinning and rolling movement at the grave of Wild Bill since she moved in beside him, their graves being the most popular tourist attraction in Deadwood. Deadwood honored her claim of being married to Clinton Burke, and her most recent tombstone identifies her as Mrs. Burke.

Although Calamity once told Madam DuFran that ''I don't know anybody who would even plant a cactus on my grave,'' Madam DuFran went all out and many years later erected a large urn mounted on a pedestal for Calamity's grave. Long ago vandals destroyed the urn and pedestal.

Why did Calamity Jane achieve national fame? Willard and Brown, two historians of the Black Hills who did not live long enough into the 20th century to see how famous she actually became, asked the same question in 1924. Their answer was the ''other view of her double-sided life—nursing in the smallpox epidemic.''

Another reason for her fame lies in the fact that her deeds and misdeeds were always performed with showmanship and flair. With her mannish clothes, crude manners, and unusual occupations, she was different enough that people remembered her; and they gossiped about her through the years, handing down from generation to generation tales of her good and bad behavior. Word of mouth is a powerful tool in the preservation of history, not all of it accurate. And Calamity had a big mouth.

Early historians like John McClintock, Willard and Brown, Hughes, Estelline Bennett—all contemporaries of Calamity who knew her when, included her in their books. Many amateur writers preserved anecdotes about her in their personal diaries and informal sketches.

Probably the chief reason she achieved fame was that the Calamity Jane legend was adopted and embellished by the media. She became a heroine of dime novels and magazine stories with western settings. Two typical dime novels, authored in 1885, by Edward Wheeler were **The Minor Sport** and **Deadwood Dick on Deck** or **Calamity Jane, the Heroine of Whoop-Up.** These stories, over 80 of them featuring Calamity, Captain Jack Crawford, Custer, and other western characters had little recognizable basis of truth. But the books sold well; thus names were popularized and ''Calamity Jane'' was the sobriquet chosen for a well-known character who delighted millions of readers of romantic western fiction.

''Who are you?'' Bessie asked.

''I am Bumblebee Bob. . . .''

''You are a woman in male disguise!'' Bessie asserted.

The wounded person gave a start. ''I supposed my disguise was inpenetrable, was the reply . . . I am a woman. I am Calamity Jane, the wife of Deadwood Dick.'' **The Minor Sport,** Wheeler

Then in the 20th century, the motion picture industry discovered Calamity Jane and her picturesque appeal. Movies featuring glamorous cowgirl heroines named Calamity Jane were "The Plainsman," "Wild Bill Hickok," "The Paleface," "Calamity Jane and Sam Bass," "Texas Meets Calamity Jane," and others. Beauteous actresses whom Calamity never did resemble even when she was a pretty young girl portrayed her on the screen: Jean Arthur, Jane Russell, Yvonne de Carlo, Doris Day.

No wonder Calamity Jane became famous—and that's what she wanted all along. People told and re-told stories about her to their children and grandchildren; writers published both true and fanciful tales about her; Hollywood glamorized her. Today Calamity Jane is the unquestioned Queen of the Wild West, even if hers was no fairy tale beginning—or ending.

Yes, in her relatively short life, the real Calamity Jane did more than rattle the pages of history; she shot some lop-sided holes in the footnotes.

Calamity Creek (Lawrence County) a tributary of Spearfish Creek in the western part of the county, was named in honor of Martha Jane Canary Burke, better known as Calamity Jane, who is said to have once lived in a cabin along the banks of this creek. There is also a Calamity Gulch. **South Dakota Place Names**

Recipe for Calamity Jane's Chicken Broth: white stock consisting of old veal bones or any bones, cleaned feet of chicken, carrots, celery, herbs, cloves; raccoon or rabbit or porcupine, sorrel, leeks, chervil. **Historical Cooking of the Black Hills**, Riordan, ed.

Calamity Peak (Custer County) rising 1,200 feet from the valley of French Creek, two miles east of Custer, was named for Calamity Jane. Tradition says that Calamity climbed this peak as the result of a bet made with a soldier, but like so many other legends concerning this famous woman, there appears to be little foundation for the story. **South Dakota Place Names**

Calamity Jane's fame derives more from her unique position in that age than from the facts of her deeds or misdeeds. She was neither a woman among men nor a man among men, but rather both. She cannot be fairly judged by the standards of men and women. "Wild Bill and Calamity Jane," Paine, **The Black Hills**, Peattie, ed.

Like it or not, Calamity Jane is here to stay; she has crept into the folklore of the times and is subject to modification but not eradication. **Calamity Jane of the Western Trails**, Jennewein

Whether she is now sailing on a damp cloud playing on a harp, or hunting buffalo on Ghost Creek, is immaterial, as she will always be kindly remembered on what was the old frontier as an examplification of the old couplet:
> Life is like a mighty river
> Rolling on from day to day
> Men are vessels launched upon it
> Sometimes wrecked and cast away.
"Calamity Jane," McGillicuddy, **Rapid City Journal**

The ancients believed iron could be transmuted into gold. This woman of iron was needed in the structure of the West. Her heart was of pure precious gold. Her deeds have earned her the right to walk the Golden Streets. **Lowdown on Calamity Jane**, D. Dee (DuFran)

The clay remains—on Mt. Moriah
Perhaps we need to reach higher
For the Spirit of Calamity.
Last verse of "The Spirit of Calamity Jane," **Deadwood—The Historic City,** Clowser

I was considered the most reckless and daring rider and one of the best shots in the western country. **The Life and Adventures of Calamity Jane,** by Herself

Preacher Smith
Martyred Sky Pilot

Henry Weston Smith, known as Preacher Smith, was the first mission-

Photo courtesy of South Dakota Historical Society.

Rev. Henry Weston Smith, known as Preacher Smith. The first minister in the Black Hills, he was murdered while walking from Deadwood to Crook City to preach a sermon in the streets.

ary in the Black Hills; and his murder on August 20, 1876, a few miles from Deadwood, conferred on him the crown of immortality reserved for a religious martyr. He is honored as the first minister or sky pilot in the Hills.

Preacher Smith is undoubtedly the most famous good guy buried in Mount Moriah. The mixture of fact and fiction about him has grown into a production almost as well-known as the folk tales about Wild Bill Hickok and Calamity Jane. Certainly, he is by far the most admirable of the three.

Photo courtesy of South Dakota Historical Society.

Annie—Mrs. Henry Weston Smith. Many years after her husband was killed, presumably by Indians, she wrote an historical novel which condemned the whites and sympathized with the Indians for the racial strife.

And if a human being, either gradually or in one dramatic flash, becomes a legend, then what? Who cares about the facts that beget a legend? Most historical writers do, but they learn to keep their fingers crossed when stating an indisputable fact. So here goes.

Henry Weston Smith was born in Ellington, Conn., in January, 1827. When he was 23 years old, he was licensed as a Methodist minister and began preaching in several Connecticut towns. His first wife Ruth and their

The inscription on his monument (in Mount Moriah) gives tne year of his birth as 1827. This is erroneous as his daughter later stated that he was born in 1828. **Preacher Smith, Martyr of the Cross,** Senn

History is only a confused heap of facts, Lord Chesterfield

infant son died and were buried in the same grave. Either in 1853 or in 1858, he married the beautiful Annie Joslin.

During the Civil War he enlisted in the Massachusetts Infantry; and after he was mustered out, he was admitted to the practice of medicine in 1867. Early in 1876, the Reverend Smith, with his second wife Annie, and their three children, moved to Louisville, Ky.

Here, he heard about the Black Hills Gold Rush and joined the last gold stampede of the Wild West. He felt that there would be plenty of the Lord's work for him to do in preaching to the horde of fortune-hunters, and he hoped to be able to establish himself and then send for his family. Certainly, the mining camps would provide challenges for a servant of the Lord looking for sinners to save. Eventually, he boarded the Union Pacific, arrived in Cheyenne, Wyo., and joined a caravan, walking beside the wagons to Custer City, the first settlement in the Black Hills.

At Custer City, Preacher Smith met Capt. C.V. Gardner and asked to join his wagon train going north to Deadwood where everyone was headed. For when news of a big strike in Deadwood Gulch had reached Custer, where the gold-findings had proved disappointing, the latter soon became a deserted city with all these early birds flocking to Deadwood in May, 1876.

Capt. Gardner, a pioneer who became an outstanding leader in Deadwood, became an editor of the **Black Hills Pioneer,** the first newspaper in Deadwood. For years he wrote "Reminiscences" about his experiences and frequently included his recollections of Preacher Smith.

Both Gardner and Preacher Smith walked beside the mule-powered wagon train carrying supplies from Cheyenne; and at night Gardner, a Methodist himself, was surprised to find the tall, bearded Smith reading the Bible beside a campfire. When Gardner learned that Smith was a Methodist minister, he remarked that preaching might be a "hard proposition." Quietly, Preacher Smith replied, "Possibly so, but I will do the best I can."

Another prominent pioneer who knew Preacher Smith, first in Custer City, then later in Deadwood, was George V. Ayres, the witty hardware merchant. Ayres was also a talented diarist and reported that the "Reverend Smith held the first services in these hills. Congregation composed of 30 men and five women. I attended. He took his text from Psalms 34:7 [The angel of the Lord encampeth round about them that fear Him and delivereth them.] and preached a very interesting sermon." Ayres added that the congregation "paid strict attention to the sermon except when there was a dog fight outside."

Preacher Smith walked into Deadwood with the Gardner wagon train in late May, 1876. He began preaching on the jam-packed main street to

---

The highest peaks in America east of the Rocky Mountains, these are the Black Hills, the land of the golden fleece to whose shores the argonauts of the seventies sailed over the vast oceans of the prairies, many to perish on the voyage and others to die in the cruel clutch of the Monster, Avarice, that lay waiting them at the goal. **Black Hills Trails,** Brown and Willard

anyone who would listen—cut-throats, gamblers, prostitutes, speculators—
and undoubtedly a few respectable people.

Edward Kidd, also a pioneer with the Gardner wagon train, later recalled for his newspaper reminiscences that the minister went into the
saloons and gambling dives on Sundays and would say, "Boys, let us have a
little prayer," and everything would stop like magic. Then someone would
pass the hat and take up a collection for him. Kidd concluded: "It appears
like all the gambling houses and saloons took an interest in Smith's prayers
and liked to hear them."

A pioneer druggist of Deadwood, E. C. Bent, later recalled in a newspaper letter Smith's preaching on the street every Sunday, the busiest day in
the gulch, when the miners came in for supplies and excitement. Preacher
Smith would stand on a box above the crowd with his open Bible. Tough
grizzled miners, wearing six-shooters, would sit on the wooden planks or
stand in the dirty street to hear his sermons. He reminded his listeners that
the ever-loving Father was present here in a strange, gold-mad country and
"not to forget the greater riches of God and of home ties."

Doubtless the attitude and rough appearance of this open-air congregation were far different from the church-going Methodists in Connecticut
and Kentucky. However, there is no record of any disturbance interrupting
his sermon even though "the shout of the gamblers and the sports calling
for trade could be heard above his exhortations."

At least three pioneers of 1876 said that Preacher Smith often preached
in saloons; 48 years later Captain Gardner insisted that these stories were

---

Sodom and Gomorrah were both dull, stupid towns compared with Deadwood, for in a
square contest for the honors of moral depravity the Black Hills' capital could give the people
of the Dead Sea cities three points in the game and then skunk them both. **Heroes of the Plains,**
Buel

He was highly respected and while his ministrations were not very effective, exhorting the
miners to abstain from vice and sin, it was the fault of the material he had to work with and not
due to any lack of zeal or piety on his part. **Deadwood Pioneer-Times,** Aug. 21, 1914

It was certainly refreshing to have one among us who had wisdom enough to realize that
the pursuit of gold was not the only occupation to engage in by those who wanted to enjoy life.
Bullock article, **Deadwood Pioneer-Times,** Aug 21, 1914

We the jury chosen for the purpose of holding an inquest on the body of William Cowan,
lying dead before us, find that the deceased came to his death by the excessive use of intoxicating liquors and exposure. After the return of the findings of the jury, the funeral rites were immediately proceeded with Rev. H. W. Smith officiating. "Report on events of August 2, 1876,
the day of Wild Bill Hickok's Murder," **Black Hills Pioneer,** August 5, 1876

Within a year (1876) Deadwood was to have more than 200 stores (clothing sales for one
year topped $75,000); two large sawmills; three banks (one of them doing a $25,000 to $75,000
business daily); a public bath-house; 30 hotels and eating houses (the IXL Hotel fed 1,000 people one day); and at least 70 saloons and gambling houses. "History Catches Up," Case, **The
Black Hills,** Peattie, ed.

"pure fiction" and that the popular minister always did his preaching in the street.

Several historians claim that for street services, Calamity Jane often passed the hat for Preacher Smith; others scoff at what they term a "romantic lie." Whether she did or did not perform this service, it sounds like a good idea and typical of Calamity Jane when she was on her good behavior.

Even when his listeners did take up collections for him, Preacher Smith found it impossible to make enough money preaching to support himself and to send home to his family. Druggist Bent recalled how the street audience was generous in pouring a few grains of gold dust into the collection hat. Bent weighed the dust on his gold scales, and often the amount was $30 or $40. Bent recalled that Smith accepted the money with "considerable emotion and appreciation." He sent half of the first collection to his little church in Kentucky because he had promised to do so with the first gold he received for preaching.

Both Captain Gardner and George Ayres report Preacher Smith's doing manual labor; he did carpentry, chopped wood, and worked in a saw mill. The minister also performed the first marriage ceremony in the gulch. He attended the first murder trial in the gulch, that outdoor circus in Gayville, the miner's trial of Carty for the murder of Jack Hinch. Richard Hughes, reporter for **The Pioneer,** wrote that he loaned the preacher paper and pencil because he, too, wanted to take notes on the bizarre trial.

Although Preacher Smith was a licensed doctor, there is no record of his practicing medicine in the Black Hills. He might have found it easier to heal the broken bodies from the effects of gun-shot wounds, knifings, alcohol, and poison than to heal the souls of the lawless riff-raff who dominated Deadwood Gulch that murderous summer of 1876.

On Sunday, August 20, 1876, Preacher Smith delivered his usual Sunday-morning sermon to an audience gathered on the main street of Deadwood. Then he announced he was going to Crook City (no longer in existence), about 10 miles away, to preach a sermon there as he had done on previous Sundays.

Several friends warned him not to go because the Indians would often ambush lone travelers; but that if he were determined, he should at least arm himself with a gun.

Unafraid and trusting in the Lord, Preacher Smith refused the gun, saying, "The Bible is my protection. It has never failed me yet." So the man who placed duty above all else put his Bible in one pocket and his notes for the afternoon sermon in the other.

Thus armed, he set out on the wooded mountain trail to preach to his scattered flock in the tradition of the circuit riders, except he was not on horseback; he was walking alone on a perilous mission with only his Bible for protection.

Later that Sunday, a neighbor of Smith's, H. M. Chapman, found a

The painting by Charles Hargens depicting Preacher Smith choosing his Bible for protection instead of the gun. The insert in the corner is an old picture of the exact spot where he was killed on his way to Crook City to preach.

note on the cabin door: "Gone to Crook City to preach, and if God is willing, will be back at 3 o'clock."

He never returned alive.

A rancher came upon the body of Preacher Smith about three miles from Deadwood. He had been shot through the heart but he was not scalped or mutilated.

The rancher spread the alarm in the Crook City area, and a group of angry, sorrowful men loaded the body of their spiritual leader and sky pilot onto a hay wagon and brought it to Deadwood.

In the posse was Edward Kidd, now a carpenter, who had heard Smith preach on the streets of Deadwood. He later said, "It was the most pitiful sight I ever saw. We found him on his side with his little Bible in his hands as if reading it after he was shot."

"Killed by Indians" was the unofficial decision and so history has recorded.

None other than historian and pioneer of '76 John McClintock contradicted that verdict. He believed that the murder was done by a white man for some unknown motive. McClintock insisted that there were no signs of

The Sioux Chief who a short time before his accidental death on the Northwestern Railroad confessed to Capt. Seth Bullock that he led the war party of Indians who murdered Rev. Henry Weston Smith near Deadwood on August 20, 1876. Picture caption for photograph of Turning Bear by Archie Roosevelt, **Black Hills Daily Times,** June 1, 1878

Indians being in the vicinity that day; and that if the Indians had shot Preacher Smith, they would have followed their invariable practice of scalping the victim.

H. M. Chapman, Smith's neighbor who found the note, was responsible for the oft-circulated and oft-denied assertion that Calamity Jane and Kitty Arnold, two "soiled doves" or "female sports" laid out the preacher's body for burial in the Smith cabin. Chapman claimed he was there and witnessed the scene.

Chapman, quoted in later newspaper accounts about the Smith tragedy, is also the original source for providing another memorable Calamity Jane side-light: "With tears streaming down her cheeks, she said, 'Isn't it too bad that the only man who came here to tell us how to live had to be killed by Indians.' "

Estelline Bennett, the Deadwood authoress who knew Calamity, also repeated this quotation, except she had Calamity sounding more natural by saying "ain't" instead if "isn't". She also added a final line attributed to Calamity: "And we sure need the telling."

Calamity's lament sounds plausible and history should occasionally be believable as fiction. However, there are many historians who doubt that Calamity Jane had anything to do with Preacher Smith's burial or with making significant comments for posterity.

So runs the course of history, certainly not smoothly, and often careening from one side of the ledger to the other.

After Preacher Smith's murder, the gold camp was confronted with a new dilemma: how to conduct a proper Christian burial for a man of God.

The Board of Health, the only government in the gulch, drew lots to see which person would be in charge of the funeral. Seth Bullock, then a youthful newcomer to the camp, drew that awesome duty. Bullock, who years later wrote a long account about the murder and burial of Preacher Smith which was reprinted in the **Deadwood Pioneer-Times,** August 21, 1914, became the first sheriff. The fearless lawman recalled, "Went up against the most desperate emergency of my life." Doc Carter found a prayer book in a trunk. Then the committee sat down on beer kegs in Carter's saloon and looked through it for something appropriate and finally

Scarcely a day passes that questions of fact do not come up with regard to incidents that occurred during the years of 1875-1876-1877 in the Black Hills. In attempting to ascertain the exact date the trouble begins, as no two persons can be found to agree upon the date. The day on which Wild Bill was killed by Jack McCall was under discussion yesterday . . . The day of the murder of Rev. Smith was equally uncertain. **Black Hills Daily Times,** April 5, 1889

The night before Preacher Smith's murder there was an immense herd of horses, belonging to the miners in Deadwood gulch, numbering 500 or more, and this band was stampeded from their range on Centennial Prairie by the Indians. About 150 of the herd bolted, and were running over the hills in every direction. It was to secure these horses that brought the Indians so close to the city and it was one of these that met Rev. Smith. **Deadwood Pioneer-Times,** Aug., 1914.

settled on a prayer suitable for a minister killed by Indians.

Carpenter Edward Kidd made wooden coffins for Preacher Smith and for Charles Mason, a miner who had also been killed by Indians on the same day as had Preacher Smith. The funeral bier carrying two coffins was a wagon drawn by a pair of mules. Business on main street was entirely closed down, and the funeral procession was reportedly composed of every soul in town—except possibly John McClintock who on that day failed to observe what happened at the burial grounds.

As the funeral procession headed up the gulch, it met another wagon just arrived from Centennial Prairie carrying the bodies of two more casualties of Indian raids. The crowd went wild with the fearful excitement of four white men being killed by Indians in one day. One group of men left immediately to chase Indians, having been equipped with 50 of John Gaston's needle guns which he passed around with no questions asked.

The graveyard was in the Whitewood gulch in the area later known as Ingleside. Eleven people, including murder victims Wild Bill Hickok and Jack Hinch, were already buried there. Bullock, in his long report, wrote "all of the graves occupied by men who had died with their boots on except one which was occupied by a woman who had died of smallpox."

The two coffins were lowered into the same grave, Smith's coffin having been painted black to distinguish it from Mason's. Bullock said he was "immeasurably relieved" when Dean C. E. Hawley, an experienced churchman took charge of the funeral ceremonies.

Bullock reported that everybody sang "Nearer My God to Thee," whether they knew the words or not, "for it was the most serious business that ever happened in the Hills, a lot of wicked, illiterate miners burying a minister, a man of God. It was a scene worthy of the brush of a great artist."

Smith's entire worldly possessions consisted of his Bible, which Seth Bullock sent to his family in the south, together with a letter conveying "the sad intelligence" to his wife.

John McClintock, whom several of his contemporaries accused of being perverse, wrote in his book that although he was not present at the first burial of Preacher Smith, he did not think Preacher and Mason were buried in the same grave, and that he gave the story little credence.

The double burial was recorded by the **Black Hills Pioneer,** by Seth Bullock, and by Brown and Willard who later collaborated on a history. Further developments about locating and moving Preacher Smith's body

---

An Easterner visiting Fort Pierre asked, 'Does the stage run on Sunday?' A man from Deadwood going on the same stage replied, 'Stranger, there ain't no Sunday west of the Missouri River and no God west of the Cheyenne. If a man dies west of the Missouri, they don't bury him; and if he dies west of the Cheyenne, the coyotes won't eat him.' **A South Dakota Guide.**

seven years later proved the veracity of these accounts—in spite of McClintock's lack of credence.

On that August afternoon, a jubilant rider galloped into Deadwood, already in a frenzy over the multiple killings, and displayed a severed Indian head, dripping with blood. The gory trophy displayed to a delighted throng was but a repetition of the scene that had occurred on the day Jack McCall had shot Wild Bill.

On the day Preacher Smith was slain, three other white men were killed by Indians in the northern Hills, and the severed Indian head was symbolic of the hatred between whites and Indians. The **Black Hills Pioneer** concluded its account with these words: "May such a day never come again."

Six years after Preacher Smith's death, Capt. C. V. Gardner, who had been impressed with the humble man reading the Bible by a campfire, wrote an appeal in the **Black Hills Daily Times,** Sept. 8, 1882, requesting that everyone, regardless of denomination, donate money to help the destitute Smith family who by then had moved back to Connecticut.

Seven years after Preacher Smith's death, in Sept. 1883, the Rev. M. Cummings, new pastor of the Methodist church, decided that the body of the first sky pilot should be moved from the old Ingleside cemetery to Mount Moriah.

But no one knew which grave was Smith's because it had not been permanently marked. That problem didn't stop Rev. Cummings. He enlisted the aid of undertaker Henry Robinson, and **The Times** reported that "By a continued search and perseverance that overcomes all obstacles," the two men located Preacher Smith's body.

"The grave was the eleventh opened and there is but little doubt that the right one has been found at last. It is a double grave, with two boxes side by side, the Rev. Smith and Charles Mason who was killed at the same time." (Why didn't John McClintock take note?)

The reinterment of both Preacher Smith and Mason took place on Sept. 25, 1883, and was an elaborate outdoor ceremony with the Methodist choir singing "The Crown of Life Beyond This Vale of Tears." A large

---

The Reverend Smith Memorial statue fund is increasing quite satisfactorily, and work will soon commence on the statue. Mr. Alexander, owner of the Buffalo Gap stone quarry, has donated a block of stone worth at least $25 from which the statue will be cut. Harry Damon donated Black Hills marble for the wall around the grave and delivered the same to the cemetery. **Black Hills Daily Times,** Sept. 28, 1891

Reverend Weston Smith and Charles Mason were reinterred at Mount Moriah Cemetery. At the time of the killing of Rev. Smith, Mason had shot an Indian and had gone with a posse to show the body. Mason, in turn, was shot by another Indian, who was then shot by the posse. Texas Bill cut off the head of the Indian, and in the company of Calamity Jane and Dirty Em paraded through the saloons displaying the gruesome trophy. Seth Bullock took the head and buried it behind the Gem Theater. **Black Hills Daily Times,** Sept. 28, 1883

crowd met at the old cemetery to accompany the cortege to Mount Moriah. "Male pioneers led the way" with the ladies, who apparently did not qualify for the pioneer title "bringing up the rear."

The two coffins, decorated with flowers in the form of a cross, were buried just inside the boundaries of Mount Moriah. Four Methodist ministers took turns reading from the Bible, offering prayers to the Almighty, and delivering eulogies.

Amen! Nobody could say that Rev. Henry Weston Smith had not received a proper burial this time—and Charles Mason, too—even if this first move was never recorded in the Record Book of the Deadwood Cemetery Association.

In that same year, 1883, when Preacher Smith's body was moved for the first time, the editor of **The Times** began to correspond with Rev. Smith's daughter, Edna Tyler. Through the years several editors and officials of the Methodist church gathered additional information about the Smith family from corresponding with Edna and with other members of the family.

Mrs. Smith and her two daughters supported themselves by teaching and by public stenography. Mrs. Smith, a professional author, published an historic novel with an Indian background, entitled **Lords of the Soil,** a sympathetic portrayal of Indian life. She also published other novels and stories in magazines.

Edna wrote that her father was the youngest of three brothers, all of whom had met violent deaths. The family had never received money their father had sent home because, according to postal officials, the pony express rider had been robbed and murdered.

Often, Deadwood sponsored fund-raising drives for the benefit of Preacher Smith's family and invited them to move to Deadwood. The president of the Chicago and Northwestern offered free passes for the family to ride to Pierre on the train, with free tickets by stage to Deadwood. But because of the poor health of Mrs. Smith and of daughter Edna, the Smith

---

A story of Indian life among the Early English Settlers. Since the days of Fenimore Cooper there has been no Indian book so true to life, as brilliantly written or as interesting. Mrs. Jocelyn (pen-name) has championed the Indian cause in her novel, showing in vivid colors the gross injustice and rapacity of the early white settlers in their treatment of the magnanimous and unsuspecting "Lords of the Soil." Ad for Mrs. Smith's novel in the back of another of her novels, **The Black Mask** or **Bonnie Orielle's Lovers,** Copyright, 1898.

Mrs. Tracy donated a beautiful zephyr worsted scarf that Mrs. Kingsley told Mother was worth $50, and it was raffled off down at the Headquarters saloon at $.50 a chance for the benefit of the Preacher Smith family. It was on exhibition in the window, and we all made the most of the opportunity to go and look in a saloon window but we didn't see anything but that scarf. **Old Deadwood Days,** Bennett

family was never able to make the trip. Mrs. Smith died in 1912 at age 73.

In 1891, the body of Preacher Smith which had been re-buried eight years earlier near the boundary of the cemetery, was moved for the second time and re-buried in the middle section of Mount Moriah.

Then, on Nov. 1, 1891, the life-size statue of Preacher Smith, sculpted by Riordan and paid for by a subscription campaign, was dedicated. Dean C. E. Hawley delivered the main address; he was the man who had taken over the graveside services from a relieved young Seth Bullock at the first burial in 1876.

Read at the dedication of the statue in Mount Moriah was a poem written by Preacher Smith which he had sent to his family in the last letter they received from him. Entitled ''The Gold Hunter's Reverie,'' it was written on June 1, 1876, and since this first reading has been widely published.

The crowd at Mount Moriah to attend the unveiling of the statue of Preacher Smith in November, 1891. Read at the ceremonies was Preacher Smith's poem, "The Gold Hunter's Reverie."

Thirty-eight years after Smith's death, on August 20, 1914, another monument to his memory was dedicated at the highest point on Highway 85, the Deadwood-Spearfish road. The white stone shaft, overlooking mountain and plain, is not on the exact spot where his body was found, but it is in an accessible location for motorists who want to read the historical marker and contemplate the life of Preacher Smith whose church was God's outdoors.

The Society of Black Hills Pioneers erected this monument, and the people of Deadwood and the entire Black Hills contributed generously to

October, 1891—Rev. Henry Weston Smith, Preacher—first preacher in Deadwood. Killed in 1876, grave moved to Mount Moriah on this date. Record Book of the Deadwood Cemetery Association.

The sculptor Riordan beside the statue he chiseled of Preacher Smith. It was said to have been a perfect likeness. 1891

building it; contributors' names and the amount donated were published in the special issue of **The Deadwood Pioneer-Times,** August 21, 1914, dedicated to reviewing the history of the honored sky pilot.

Photo courtesy of Al Gunther.

Only the foundation for the statue remains at Mount Moriah. The statue of Preacher Smith was destroyed by vandals.

Presiding over the dedication ceremonies for the monument was the President of the Society of Black Hills Pioneers, George V. Ayres, the diarist and witty hardware merchant who had attended Preacher Smith's first religious service in the Hills. Ayres introduced all the important guests, Governor of South Dakota Frank Byrne, Congressman E. W. Martin, and other dignitaries.

Highlight of the program for the audience was hearing the sermon read aloud that Preacher Smith had expected to deliver at Crook City. However,

I again met Reverend Smith in June, 1876, when we were both working for a saw mill in Split Tail gulch, east of what is now the old Golden Reward smelter site, he firing the boiler weekdays and preaching Sundays, and I cutting the logs. Address of George V. Ayres, published in **Deadwood Pioneer-Times,** Aug. 21, 1914

102 Monument to the memory of Henry Weston Smith, the Pioneer Preacher who was killed by Indians, Aug. 20th, 1876. Erected by Society of Black Hill Pioneers, Aug. 20th, 1914.

THE UNVEILING, AUG. 20th 1914.

Photo courtesy of South Dakota Historical Society.

Monument to the memory of Preacher Smith on Highway 85, the Deadwood-Spearfish road. Not far from the spot where he was killed. Erected by the Society of Black Hills Pioneers and dedicated August 20, 1914.

according to historical sleuth Edward Senn, Preacher Smith did not leave a complete sermon, "only a blood-stained sheet of paper, containing notes or headings for the sermon. This was preserved and in later years the notes were elaborated into a sermon by some preacher, following the outline."

As the years passed, posthumous honors and memorials to Preacher Smith increased. In 1935, in a ceremony at Pierre, the state capital, a painting was dedicated to him.

In 1961, a new painting of Preacher Smith by Charles Hargens, commissioned by editor-historian Leland D. Case, was dedicated at the Layne Library at Dakota Wesleyan University in Mitchell, SD. The painting depicts the pioneering minister as a friend sought to press a revolver belt upon him shortly before he set off on the long journey from which he never returned. The preacher is holding up the Bible, his only protection.

In the summer of 1961, Preacher Smith's grand-daughter visited South

Some of the ways in which we can engage in the great work of preaching . . . **First,** without money. Christ sent His disciples forth without purse or script, but he did not intend that they should live without food. **Second,** by sustaining the social needs of Grace. All can do something here, and are required to do something, every man, according to his ability. **Third,** The Sabbath School. **Fourth,** by personal efforts to lead men to the Savior. **Fifth,** by holding up the life of a consistent God as a guide to our own lives. (Ending developed from notes for Preacher Smith's last and undelivered sermon.) As quoted by Edward Senn in **Preacher Smith—Martyr of the Cross.**

Photo courtesy of Deadwood Chamber of Commerce.

Daughter and granddaughter of Preacher Smith paying their first visit to the monument in memory of their famous relative. Both ladies, Mrs. A. G. Meriwether, and her daughter Mrs. Geraldine Holden were from North Troy, New York. August. 1933.

Dakota. She was Mrs. Geraldine Holden of Shrewsbury, Mass., and during the annual ceremony at the monument on Highway 85, she placed a wreath on the 85th anniversary of her grandfather's death. Mrs. Holden also played an organ prelude in the First Methodist Church, and the chimes of the Adams Museum played Preacher Smith's favorite hymns all day long to mark the day.

Henry Weston Smith has been eulogized by many speakers and writers. Although he did not live long enough in the Black Hills to actually make his mark, his contemporaries in the Gold Rush recognized that this humble man was a true disciple of the Master, a man they desperately needed. To Preacher Smith, like Wild Bill Hickok, violent death brought instant immortality. But to the unknown sky pilot, the drama of his tragic murder brought the glory reserved for a religious martyr.

A memorial ceremony on the anniversary of the death of Preacher Smith has become an annual event. At one time I was appointed a committee of one to secure a speaker . . . For the first time in the history of this annual event, I asked John T. Heffron, a devout Catholic, to give the dedicatory address . . . Before the ceremony there was some criticism because of the fact that I had selected a Catholic to give the address in memory of this Methodist preacher, but after hearing this address all were in accord that it was the finest address which had ever been given on this occasion. **Deadwood Doctor,** F. S. Howe, M.D.

THE GOLD HUNTER'S REVERIE
By Henry Weston Smith

I am sitting by the campfire now
  On wild Dakota's hills,
And memories of long ago
  Steal o'er me like the rills
Adown yon canyon deep and dark
  Steal through the leafy glades;
A glimpse, a murmur here and there,
  Then vanish in the shades.

This evening is the first of June,
  And the snow is falling fast,
The tall pines sigh, howl and moan
  Responsive to the blast;
The shades of night are gathering round
  The fire is burning low;
I sit and watch the dying coals
  And think of long ago.

I see a black-eyed, dark-haired boy,
  (That was forty years ago)
He draws a hand sled to the woods
  Amid the falling snow.
I see him slip and toil and tug,
  With steps that often tire,
He brings a load of wood to feed
  A widowed mother's fire.

They tell him at the village school
  That he has talents rare,
And, if he does not play the fool,
  He may fill a statesman's chair.
I am a toil worn laborer now,
  My hands are hard and dry;
And looking at that bright faced boy,
  I wonder—was it I?

I see a throng of worshippers
  Within a shady grove;
They listen to the oft told tale
  Of Jesus and His love.
And he who spoke the word that day
  Had surely felt the power,
And many a suppliant knelt to pray
  And blessed that gracious hour.

Says one, "He seems to have the power,"
  Another says, "No doubt
He'd make his mark upon the world
  But for one gracious fault."
I tread the forest paths alone;
  Alone I raise my cry
To Him who notes the sparrow's fall
  And wonder—was it I?

I see a lovely cottage home
  With humble comfort blessed,
I see at eve the workman come
  In loving arms to rest.
I am a lonely wanderer now,
  No friends or kindred nigh,
And gazing on yon love-lit home,
  I wonder—was it I?

And when I sit on Zion's hill,
  No more in need of gold,
And sing with those who love me still
  The songs that ne'er grow old
Perhaps I'll look on this sad eve,
  Beneath this stormy sky,
And think that this was long ago,
  And wonder—was it I?

(Deadwood City, D.T., June 1, 1876) As published in **Deadwood Pioneer-Times,** August 21, 1914

The 'one gracious fault' mentioned in the sixth verse, daughter Edna Smith Tyler explained thusly: 'The fault mentioned above was the giving away of every cent above his barest expenses to the needy, thus leaving nothing for future support.' **Preacher Smith—Martyr of the Cross,** Senn

The Deadwood Public Library received a very valuable gift in the form of two volumes written by the wife of Rev. Henry Weston "Preacher" Smith . . . The books were donated by the daughter and granddaughter of Rev. Smith who are in Deadwood on a visit at this time. **Deadwood Pioneer-Times,** Aug. 4, 1933

Potato Creek Johnny
Lucky Prospector

Potato Creek Johnny was the tiny bearded prospector who found one of the biggest gold nuggets in the Black Hills. His real name was John Perrett; and when he was 17 years old, in 1883, he emigrated from Wales to the Black Hills with his sister and father. Johnny was a young man looking for gold and excitement. Although the gold rush days were past and only the big mines were producing quantities of gold, many prospectors still worked the streams with their sluice boxes and rusty pans.

Johnny tried farming, cowpunching, working for WPA road projects, and carrying the mail before he settled down at 25 years of age to serious prospecting. He staked his claim on Potato Creek, a tributary of Spearfish creek near Tinton, now a ghost town, the whole area being one of the most beautiful in the Black Hills.

Only four feet, three inches tall was Johnny's height—no larger than a child. Perhaps his small size was one reason he always got along so well with children. As he grew older, he let his hair grow long and his whiskers grow every which way; and he looked just the way a prospector is supposed to look.

Early in his prospecting career he became an apprentice for a time to a barber in Central City, a gold camp located halfway between Deadwood and Lead, and panned gold in a gulch behind the barber shop. Other prospectors joined him and reportedly they all made a good living.

For over 30 years he lived in the log cabin he built himself by rollicking Potato Creek under the tall ponderosas, but he was not a hermit; he enjoyed being with people, playing his guitar and fiddle for country dances. How he loved to feed the birds and squirrels and chipmunks that shared their woods with him; often he coaxed wild creatures to eat out of his hand and to sit on his shoulders.

For many years Potato Creek Johnny panned gold, using a rocker and sluice box in the creek from which he got his name. Then one memorable day in May, 1929, he found the biggest gold nugget he had ever seen.

Johnny was so thrilled that he had to share his discovery; he ran to find his friend Goldbug Nelson who was working a nearby claim, according to the **Rapid City Journal** 21 years later in 1950. Goldbug recalled how Johnny had found him working his claim, pointed the gun-shaped nugget at him and commanded, ''Throw up your hands!''

Johnny's nugget which really looked more like the lower part of a dancer's leg than a gun, created a sensation whatever its form suggested. At first gold-miners and mineral authorities claimed it was the biggest gold

Placer gold and concentrates can be found by doing nothing more than just using water and a gold pan because placer gold is gold that has already been broken apart from rock by weathering, and is found, just mixed, among the mud, stones, gravel, and sand. **Gold Panning with Prospector John.** Prospector John, World Champion Gold Panner, 1973

Photo courtesy of Deadwood Chamber of Commerce.

Potato Creek Johnny panning for gold in Potato Creek that gave him his name. For many years he lived beside the creek in a rustic log cabin among the pines with only the squirrels and birds for company.

Photo courtesy of Centennial Archives, Deadwood Public Library.

**Potato Creek Johnny holding his nugget, one of the largest ever found in the Black Hills.
Some people suspected its authenticity. His watch chain is linked with nuggets that he found.**

nugget ever found in the Black Hills. But it turned out to be just one of the
biggest. Some people doubt its authenticity and wonder if Johnny pulled off
a hoax.

W. E. Adams, pioneer merchant of Deadwood and founder of the
Adams Museum, bought the nugget from Johnny for $250 and put it on
display in his museum. Today, an exact replica of the nugget is displayed on
the first floor of the museum. The weight of the original was 73/4 troy
ounces. On the fluctuating 1979 gold market the nugget would be valued at
$3,000 or so.

Goldbug Nelson was an intimate of the late Potato Creek Johnny Perrett of Deadwood
fame when the two were prospecting near Tinton shortly after the turn of the century. "It ain't
true that Johnny taught me how to find gold,' Nelson exclaimed. 'Why, I'd been prospecting
long before I met Johnny.' Bob Lee, **Rapid City Journal,** March 5, 1950

Potato Creek Johnny's genuine gold nugget was stolen once from its case in the Adams
Museum and was returned just as mysteriously as it had disappeared. Recollection of Mary
Adams Balmat, second wife of W. E. Adams, Black Hills Pioneer of 1877

With the discovery of his nugget, fame discovered Johnny. He soon became the greatest single live tourist attraction in the Black Hills. Tourists felt they had not seen the sights of historic Deadwood if they had not seen Johnny. Everyone wanted to talk with the little man who had realized every prospector's dream even if he hadn't really struck it rich.

Tourists wanted his autograph; they wanted to buy him drinks at the saloons; they wanted to hear one of his fantastic tales about how he and his burro were attacked by a vicious hummingbird; but most of all they wanted to hear Johnny with his unaffected Welsh charm tell about the leg-shaped nugget. "And I've been looking for the rest of that leg ever since," he used to say.

When Johnny became a celebrity, tourists and reporters often visited his homemade log cabin with the corrugated iron roof out in Potato Creek gulch. He used to offer visitors a cool drink of water from the spring he called "The Last Chance Saloon," and he didn't mind if they used his rusty tin cup hanging on a bush. He liked having visitors and invited them inside his two-room house with two brick hearths, one on top of the other, where he would often demonstrate how to make baking powder biscuits "so easy that you don't even have to wash your hands." The living area was stacked with magazines and old newspapers which Johnny claimed were just as good reading as the new ones.

A typical story about Johnny is the time he breakfasted at the home of some friends in Belle Fourche and was fascinated at seeing the toast pop up in an electric toaster. He said he was going to buy himself a toaster. "But what about the wiring?" his host asked. "Wiring? Shucks—I got plenty of barbed wire around my place," he said.

At one time Johnny was married, but his wife reportedly divorced him and moved to Belle Fourche.

Deadwood business people persuaded Johnny to appear in the "Days of '76" parade pushing a small wheelbarrow just right for his diminutive size. No one who saw him will ever forget the jolly little elf, wearing fringed buckskins, a big cowboy hat over his rimless glasses, his long scraggly grey beard floating in the breeze. Straight out of a story book, he looked like one of Snow White's lovable dwarfs or one of Santa's brownies. Johnny smiled and waved at the crowd, sometimes lighting a campfire in the middle of the street. He walked on his hands and often tossed pennies at the delighted children. No wonder Johnny was always the hit of every parade.

He was a member of the Deadwood Whisker Club which sponsored "The Trial of Jack McCall For the Murder of Wild Bill Hickok," a farce presented to summer tourists several times a week. Johnny played the part of a prospector in the jury; he was a natural and never needed any makeup.

Deadwood finally realized that it had a lively celebrity with commercial possibilities. During the summers in the late 30's and early 40's, he stayed in town and showed the Deadwood tourists how to pan gold, all the while talk-

Potato Creek Johnny showing how to pan gold. A sluice box is behind him. Tourists loved the tiny, talkative prospector but they bought him too many drinks in the saloons.

ing and explaining, "Placer mining isn't what it used to be. Too many folks in the Black Hills. They have riled the streams, dried them up, and so many amachoors have tried panning gold that all the good claims are staked by folks who don't know how to get the gold out."

Photo courtesy of Centennial Archives, Deadwood Public Library.

Potato Creek Johnny often danced a jig for the crowd watching the "Days of '76" parade. Sometimes he pushed a wheelbarrow; but when he got old and tottery, he rode a big horse and waved at the crowd. Whatever he did, the elfin showman was the hit of the parade.

Even without his beard Potato Creek Johnny is easy to recognize because of his small size.

The two ladies are portraying two notorious characters—Poker Alice and Calamity Jane. Potato Creek Johnny is the original—he's just being himself.

When Johnny grew too old and wobbly to push the wheelbarrow in the "Days of '76" parade, he rode on a big saddle horse with the stirrups set as high as possible to accommodate his short legs. The crowd loved having Johnny on horseback so they could see him better and exchange waves.

The Deadwood Chamber of Commerce persuaded a 73-year-old Johnny to go to the Chicago Travel Show, and by just being himself he ad-

Potato Creek Johnny Perrett has deserted his mining claims on Iron Creek, a tributary of Spearfish Canyon, at least until spring. He got pretty cold out there so he is spending the winter in town at a hotel, and last night celebrated his 75th birthday there. Anyway, placer mining isn't so hot anymore. Yuill, **The Sioux City Journal Magazine,** March 10, 1941

vertised Deadwood and the Black Hills. He was often interviewed on the radio, and he appeared on a "We, the People" broadcast.

When Johnny was 77 years old, he became ill and even Dr. F. S. Howe couldn't make him well. After an illness of two weeks, Potato Creek Johnny died in St. Joseph's Hospital, Deadwood, mourned by many, even by those who suspected him of being a phony.

"Potato Creek Johnny Crosses the Great Divide," was the headline in the **Deadwood Pioneer-Times,** Feb. 21, 1943. In the Episcopal rector's eulogy, he said, "His legacy to us is not gold for men to spend but a friendly smile and a word of cheer which will linger in our memory."

The Deadwood Chamber of Commerce requested that all business places be closed for the funeral which was held in the Masonic Temple with prominent businessmen acting as pall-bearers. As the cortege passed the

Photo courtesy of Black Hills Studios and Deadwood Chamber of Commerce.

Seven Deadwood businessmen who acted as pall-bearers and the Episcopal rector at the open grave of Potato Creek Johnny in Mount Moriah. 1943

Johnny went with the Chamber of Commerce people and looked at Chicago while Chicago looked at him. Chicago hadn't seen anything like Johnny since the last prospector brought the last covered wagon into town and set out for the west. Johnny panned gold in the Stevens Hotel and talked to the Chicago dudes. Mildred Fielder, **Potato Creek Johnny,** Bonanza Trails Publications, 1973, p. 14

Another well-known character that I attended in his last illness was Potato Creek Johnny . . . During his later years he spent his summers in Deadwood. He was constantly followed around by crowds of children. He was always kind to them and was a never-ending source of delight to the children as well as some of the elders. **Deadwood Doctor,** F. S. Howe, M.D.

Adams Museum, the carillion chimes which toll for the Black Hills Pioneers, both the official members and the unofficial like Johnny, tolled 77 times to signify his age and to honor the little goodwill ambassador.

Johnny Perrett is buried in Mount Moriah beside the graves of Wild Bill Hickok and Calamity Jane, all three having simple and indestructible markers embedded in the rock wall. Johnny could not have known Wild Bill who had died 67 years earlier. Undoubtedly he had known Calamity Jane. Who didn't? Johnny was an agreeable little man and probably rests comfortably beside his two flamboyant grave-mates who preceded him to Mount Moriah.

Today, this cluster of three graves is the most popular tourist attraction in Deadwood. The trio brought notoriety and fame to Deadwood, but Johnny was the one who brought mainly favorable publicity, the most beloved character the Black Hills ever claimed for its own. For many years after his death, people said wistfully that the "Days of '76" parade was never the same without him.

Potato Creek Johnny Perrett was laid to rest with this tribute: "God be with you and help you find in heaven the counterparts of your beloved Black Hills."

In honor of Potato Creek Johnny's memory, and through him to all Pioneers, we pause a moment in our program today. In respect to them, may we all stand.

Johnny, old pard, we hope you have found that claim
And that long-lost gold mine in the sky;
We hope you've said hello to all the friends to whom you said good-bye.
We hope you sit up there with them today,
Away from the worry, the sorrow, the pain and care of this life.
And watch the world go by.
"Days of '76" Tribute to Potato Creek Johnny by R. L. Ewing, August 8, 1943

Potato Creek Johnny was a stinker. I have prospected with him and he worked at the Tinton mill when I did. He was a sneak thief and could not be trusted. I myself—and there are many who agree with me—think that his famous nugget was a fake and that it was melted-down gold molded into a perfect shape. After the Chamber of Commerce got hold of him, they capitalized on his quaint appearance and talked him into performing for the tourists. He died an alcoholic. Recollection of Clyde Mitchell, son of W. A. Mitchell, Black Hills Pioneer of 1875; 1979-1980 President of the Society of Black Hills Pioneers.

III

VIGNETTES OF PIONEERS AND NOTABLES

J. J. WILLIAMS
PIONEER OF 1874

J. J. Williams was a Black Hills Pioneer of 1874, probably the only white person buried in Mount Moriah who came to the Hills that early. Williams came with the illegal Russell-Collins party, named after the organizers; it is also called the Gordon party, named for the guide of the expedition.

One of the organizers, Capt. Thomas Russell, eventually settled in Deadwood and became the first president of the Society of Black Hills Pioneers of 1876. Only five of these 1874 pioneers actually became permanent residents of the Hills, but these early trespassers who invaded the Black Hills, including Capt. Russell, J. J. Williams, Annie Tallent and her husband, became the most revered of all gold-seekers.

Annie Tallent, the only woman member of the party, later wrote the first history of the region, **The Black Hills** or **Last Hunting Grounds of the Dakotahs;** and Russell later wrote a short but interesting account of the trek.

Photo courtesy of South Dakota Historical Society.

Illingworth photo of Custer's permanent camp at French Creek (Golden Valley) in the southern Black Hills, August, 1874. Five months later in heavy December snows J. J. Williams and twenty-six other members (including Annie Tallent) of the illegal Russell-Collins party camped in this same area where the Custer Expedition had found the first gold in the Black Hills.

Little was known about the Black Hills until the summer of 1874 when the United States government ordered the Custer Expedition to explore them. Custer and his soldiers found gold at French Creek in the southern Hills. After Custer, in his official report, wrote a glowing account of the attractions of the Black Hills with gold found in the roots of the grass, the sacred Paha Sapa of the Sioux Indians were doomed.

That fall, even before the Custer gold discoveries were publicized in newspapers from coast to coast, the Russell-Collins party, in direct violation of the Laramie Treaty of 1868, and against the orders of the U.S. government to stay out of the Black Hills, made secret preparations to invade the forbidden territory. On October 6, 1874, the party of six covered wagons left Sioux City, Iowa. The expedition included 26 men and the valiant Annie Tallent who trudged beside the heavily-loaded wagon train.

Constantly tormented by visions of the scalping knife, Annie Tallent, who was accompanied by her husband and an 11-year-old son, described a hazardous journey across the barren plains and Bad Lands. When the caravan reached the valley of the Bad River, a sick man named Moses Aarons died an agonizing death.

Then J. J. Williams, whom Tallent described as a "skilled artisan and a genius in many ways," took charge of the preparations for the burial of a white man in Indian country on the desolate plains.

Williams made a coffin of small hewn timbers with wooden pins, and the men cribbed up the grave like a mine shaft. The gloomy mourners gathered in a snowstorm to hear Williams recite the burial ritual of the Order of Odd Fellows. Over the grave the men erected a wooden cross with an inscription for Aarons, realizing that this burial service and cross were inappropriate for a Jew, but hoping the rumor was true that Indians would not disturb a grave marked by a cross.

In another blizzard, the party found Custer's wagon trail leading out of the Black Hills about four miles south of where Sturgis is now. By backtracking Custer's route, the party arrived on French Creek near the present site of Custer City, on December 23rd in heavy snow. The group spent a miserable Christmas but soon began constructing the famous Gordon Stockade while hoping for spring and for reinforcements and praying not to be discovered by the military contingents they knew were searching for trespassers.

In February, 1875, the guide, Gordon, and another man decided to carry the best gold samples back to Sioux City to spread word of the gold discoveries and thus to encourage more illegal expeditions. Then in April,

Mr. J. J. Williams' claim immediately under this city is being worked day and night with about two shafts and a full force at each shaft and on tailings and paying well. **Black Hills Pioneer,** May, 1877

J. J. Williams is happy only when sinking a shaft somewhere. He attempted to sink one in Gold Street yesterday for which he was arrested and fined. He has appealed the case to the supreme court. **Black Hills Times,** Oct. 4, 1878

Photo courtesy of South Dakota Historical Society.

General Crook's soldiers in 1875 at the Gordon Stockade on French Creek. Built in two weeks during snowstorms, the stockade surrounded seven log cabins where the 27 members of the Russell-Collins party, including J. J. Williams, lived during the winter of 1874-1875.

six men, including J. J. Williams set off for civilization at Fort Laramie, Wyoming. Even though their reasons for leaving may have been valid, these desertions were of course extremely demoralizing for the 18 people who remained at the stockade.

Almost a month later, Williams and another man, presumably under duress, returned to the stockade with two military officers who bore orders to declare the entire party prisoners. Within 24 hours, the officers escorted the entire party, including Williams, and Annie Tallent riding a government mule, to Fort Laramie where they were all released without parole.

According to both Russell and Tallent who use exactly the same words: "Here the members of the Russell-Collins expedition to the Black Hills separated. Thus ended the memorable journey in and out of the Black Hills, with its dangers and hardships, the members of which gained nothing save a very dearly bought experience."

Whether J. J. Williams was considered an absolute traitor for deserting the group and returning with the military is not made clear by either Russell or Tallent. Certainly, he could not have been very popular at that time.

The United States government and the relieved army patrols soon gave up trying to stop the Black Hills Gold Rush, and thousands of fortune-hunters began pouring into the Indian reservation from all directions.

J. J. Williams returned to the Black Hills some time in 1875. By January 1, 1876, Williams was in Deadwood Gulch where the first gold-hunters had to lower the wagons down the cliffs with ropes and wind-lasses. He located No. 22 below Discovery, "from which he realized $27,000 in gold dust," according to Tallent. After he sold this claim, he located No. 14 above Discovery on Whitewood Creek "from which he realized $35,000 of the precious metal, the reward of his indomitable perseverance."

Be it resolved that no member of the expedition shall be permitted to return to civilization which we all voluntarily left; and, be it further resolved, that any attempt to return shall be deemed treasonable to the expedition, and that the offender shall be punished, by being disarmed and placed under guard, until the dangerous inclination subsides. (Resolution Adopted by Russell-Collins party) **The Black Hills,** Tallent

Photo courtesy of W. H. Over Museum.

Deadwood Gulch as it probably looked when J. J. Williams first saw it early in 1876. The first gold-hunters had to clear away much dead wood—hence the name. J. J. Williams helped lay out the town-site of Deadwood in April, 1876.

J. J. Williams helped lay out the townsite of Deadwood in April, 1876, and Williams Street is named after him. In addition to his mining interests, he also erected substantial buildings which were completely wiped out in the great Deadwood fire of 1879. Later, he became a contractor and carpenter.

In 1907, Williams spent several months in the Deadwood hospital, and his niece from New York state came to take him to her home, planning to have a stretcher bear "the feeble old gentleman" to the train. But before his niece could carry out her plan, J. J. Williams died at age 67.

According to the **Deadwood Pioneer-Times,** his funeral was conducted by the Deadwood Pioneer Hook and Ladder Company of which he was a charter member of 1877. His obituary credits him and his persuasive powers with saving the organization from breaking up because the members were fighting among themselves, wanting to disband and divide up the money. J. J. refused to take his share and convinced the others not to disband. "In this way," the eulogy concluded, "he has left behind him a lasting monument to his memory."

The Pioneer-Times reported that he had many friends, was a lover of Deadwood, thinking it the best place on earth to live. "He was always happy and contented even when physical sufferings overtook him and did not complain."

J. J. Williams is buried in the cemented-over firemen section of Mount Moriah, beside Jerusalem Street. The initials DPH & L Co. on top of his tombstone stand for Deadwood Pioneer Hook and Ladder Company of which J. J. was a proud charter member. Its equipment consisted of 100 canvas buckets and the running gear of an old wagon outfitted as a hook and ladder truck.

Fate was kind: J. J. Williams, who was old and sick and helpless, died before he could be carried out of the Black Hills, the new El Dorado which 34 years before he had entered so boldly with the immortal Russell-Collins expedition.

━━

While they were in the Black Hills that winter of 1874 and 1875, John Brennan, journalist in Sioux City, published a poem with the verse:

'Who'er may fail, or fortune get
Out in the golden land,
All generous souls will honor yet
Tom Russell's little band.'

The Russell-Collins 1874 Gold Expedition to the Black Hills of Dakota, Clowser, Ed.

SETH BULLOCK
FIRST SHERIFF

"Do you know why I sent for him to come to London?" asked Theodore Roosevelt, former president of the United States, of Estelline Bennett from Deadwood, when the two were chatting at a fancy tea in Chicago.

TR answered his own question. "Because I wanted those Britishers to see my typical ideal American." The man he was talking about was Seth Bullock, the first sheriff of Deadwood, who traveled to England with his wife Martha at Roosevelt's request.

"His friendships could run the gamut from Roosevelt to Calamity Jane and back again without stumbling. That was the West and Seth Bullock," reported Miss Bennett in **Old Deadwood Days.**

She should know. Her father, Judge Granville Bennett and Seth Bullock had pioneered together during the gold rush days, and these two men were chiefly responsible for enforcing law and order on tumultous Deadwood.

Seth Bullock was born in Ontario, Canada, in 1849; and early in life joined the gold stampede to Helena, Montana Territory. A precocious politician, he was elected to the Montana Territorial Senate when he was only 21 years old, where he introduced the resolution which eventually resulted

Photo courtesy of South Dakota Historical Society.

Seth Bullock, whom his friend Theodore Roosevelt described as "a splendid-looking fellow with his size and supple strength, his strongly marked aquiline face with its big mustache, and the broad brim of his soft hat drawn down over his hawk eyes . . . "

in Congress' establishing Yellowstone as the first national park. Bullock was elected sheriff of Lewis and Clark County in Montana Territory when he was 24 years old. His business partner and life-long friend Sol Star, also active in Montana politics, became the mayor of Deadwood and served 12 years in that office.

The two adventurous young men, no tenderfeet either in politics or gold rushes, soon became seasoned veterans of the frontier. During the spring of 1876 Seth Bullock and Sol Star heard about the exciting gold discoveries in the Black Hills; they decided to join this last frenzied gold rush in the Wild West, Bullock first sending his wife and infant by Missouri riverboat and then by train back to Michigan for safe-keeping.

Bullock and Star joined a party of 25 men, known as the second Montana Party, who wanted to try their luck in the Hills. At Fort Benton, Montana, they loaded all their supplies on a steamer going down the Missouri River to Bismarck. Here, they transferred their merchandise to an ox-drawn freight train and set off across the prairie wilderness to the Black Hills on what would soon become the Bismarck-Deadwood trail.

Seth Bullock and Sol Star arrived in Deadwood on August first, 1876. Instead of joining the mad search for gold, the two enterprising young men immediately went to work constructing a log building on the corner of Main and Wall streets. Soon they were busy selling picks and shovels, other mining equipment, even chamber pots which Bullock auctioned off on his first day in Deadwood. The firm of Star and Bullock eventually became one of the most prosperous in the Hills, and its owners two of the most respected citizens.

The day after their arrival in the gulch, on that memorable August 2nd, Jack McCall gunned down Wild Bill Hickok; a jubilant horseman displayed the severed head of an Indian to a blood-thirsty populace; the Indians were reported to be surrounding Crook City; Carty, who had been acquitted for the murder of John Hinch in Gayville, was escorted hurriedly through the gulch by an armed guard; and another drunk was found dead. All this violence and excitement was unlikely to perturb Bullock or Star who had survived gold rush initiation ceremonies in Helena.

It didn't take long for these two newcomers to be concerned that Deadwood had no government, no regulations, no organization. It was a lawless, haphazard settlement where all the floating population of the west had converged and succumbed to the contagious gold fever.

There were other responsible men who knew something had to be done if the camp were to survive and achieve a degree of stability. When several people came down with the dreaded smallpox, a group of citizens organized a "Board of Health and Street Commissioners" to take charge of the town. With Seth Bullock as treasurer, the Board proved to be the first public organization in Deadwood. The Board established a pest house for the quarantine of smallpox victims; the pony express galloped in with vaccine from Sidney, Nebraska, and an epidemic was averted.

Bullock, writing 40 years later, said that the Board took on many responsibilities including adopting ordinances to organize and protect the mushrooming city. These included organizing a police force and a fire department, levying taxes for licenses, regulating the lay-out and use of

Sol Star and Seth Bullock of Helena, Montana, arrived yesterday with a train loaded with merchandise. **Black Hills Pioneer,** August 5, 1876

Anyone who has been here for the space of a week and has witnessed the shooting, robbings, and brawls that enliven our nights and interrupt our days must realize that it is high time that some form of recognized law be established in Deadwood City. **Black Hills Pioneer,** July 10, 1876

Photo courtesy of South Dakota Historical Society.

A prospector guarding his claim in Deadwood where tents and brush shelters crowded up and down the gulch. When Seth Bullock arrived in August, 1876, and took over as unofficial sheriff, many of the disputes and gunfights were over claim-jumping.

streets, and establishing a cemetery, this first in Whitewood Gulch, later called Ingleside.

The Board of Health had a variety of problems confronting them: everything from settling disputes and shootings over claim jumping to drawing lots to decide who would read the prayers at Preacher Smith's burial. And Seth Bullock drew that duty which he called "the most desperate emergency of my life."

Bullock, with his experience as a sheriff in Montana, was a natural for

It can be said without fear of successful contradiction that those souls who have been sent to their Maker in our shooting affrays did, in most all cases, deserve their departure from the land of the living. On the other hand, it cannot be assumed that because a man possesses a pistol that he is qualified as judge, jury, and executioner. It is too good to be true that our good citizens can always be faster on the draw than the rascals and robbers of the Black Hills camps. **Black Hills Pioneer,** July 10, 1876

It was remarkable that with the number of outlaws of both sexes in the gulches, there were so few crimes of the graver character committed. This may be accounted for by the fact that preparedness was supreme; everyone went armed, and each carrier of a gun was supposed to be able and willing to use it. "An Account of Deadwood and the Northern Black Hills in 1876," Bullock, **South Dakota Historical Collections.**

the lawman role; in that hectic fall of 1876 he unofficially took on the duties of a sheriff. Not until the spring of 1877 when Lawrence County was organized did he actually become the official sheriff when Governor John Pennington appointed him to that position.

Bullock was determined to enforce law and order in Deadwood, to convince renegades that they should not kill, nor steal, nor rob stage-coaches, nor jump claims—and if they committed these crimes, they were in serious trouble with him. Tall and sinewy with a drooping black mustache, he had piercing gray eyes that made even the innocent feel guilty. Unlike Marshal Wild Bill Hickok who had relied on his lightning-fast guns to keep the peace in Kansas, Bullock relied on his wits and commanding personality to subdue criminals in the Black Hills. Although an expert marksman, there is no record of his killing a man while performing his duties.

That first year Sheriff Bullock cleaned up Deadwood without gunning down offenders. It was no easy job, especially when there was no jail except an abandoned mining tunnel or a dirt basement.

An oft-repeated story illustrating Bullock's resourcefulness involved breaking up a sit-down strike at the Keets mine in Hidden Treasure Gulch where about 30 miners, fortified with weapons and provisions, and holed up in the mine tunnel until their demands should be met for what they claimed were back wages. The miners were violating property rights, and it was up to the sheriff to rout them. But they refused to come out.

Then Bullock had an idea. He went shopping in Chinatown, then climbed up the mountain side and dropped burning sulphur down the air shaft. Soon, the rebellious miners, coughing and sputtering, scrambled out of the tunnel and surrendered to the waiting sheriff and his deputies. The episode may have been one of the first uses of tear gas.

This incident of a bloody confrontation being avoided received wide publicity throughout the country. Judge Bennett's daughter Estelline commented: "Father chuckled delightedly over that bloodless victory all the rest of his life. It verified and strengthened his high regard for Seth Bullock, who set a standard then to which all other sheriffs, as far as Father was concerned, had to measure."

It is generally acknowledged that great credit is due Sheriff Bullock for the efficient manner in which he conducts the business of his office. In the capturing of eight prisoners, he has shown a detective skill that is truly wonderful and proves fitness for the position he holds. It is unanimously asserted by the prisoners that his kindness toward them lessens the severe penalty of their close confinement. **Black Hills Times,** May 6, 1877

It was the universal verdict of the early settlers that to Sheriff Bullock was largely due the comparative peace and security prevailing in the county during the term of his appointment. **The Black Hills,** Tallent

The new hotel being built by Seth Bullock of this city stands upon the corner of Main and Wall streets and will stand as a monument to his pluck and enterprise for many years. It will be three stories in height: the front is solid white and pink sandstone, and an ornamental steel balcony will be placed around the entire building. **Black Hills Times,** Aug. 3, 1895

Unaccountably, Seth Bullock, a Republican, was defeated for sheriff in the first official election held in the Black Hills in November, 1877. Reasons given were that there were more Democrats than Republicans and that many frustrated lawbreakers didn't want such an efficient sheriff. In any event, the election was a wild one with accusations flying on both sides about stolen ballots and illegal voters.

Seth Bullock, although no longer sheriff, was still a deputy United States marshal and continued tracking down stage-coach robbers and outwitting criminals.

In addition to running his and Star's hardware store, he also invested in mining ventures and founded a cattle and thoroughbred horse ranch under irrigation in the valley of the Belle Fourche River. Bullock is credited with introducing alfalfa into South Dakota and with calling national attention to the great value of alfalfa as a forage crop.

One day in 1884, when Deputy Marshal Bullock was riding the range on his Belle Fourche ranch, he encountered a suspicious-looking trio of tired, dirty cowboys. One of the shady-looking characters turned out to be Theodore Roosevelt, a deputy sheriff who was then a rancher in the Badlands of northern Dakota. Roosevelt and another deputy had in custody a horse thief named Crazy Steve whom Bullock was also trailing.

Roosevelt, in his **Autobiography,** described his first meeting with Bullock, who "became one of my staunchest and most valued friends." Roosevelt wrote that Seth was rather cool at first but explained his attitude by remarking, "You see, by your looks, I thought you were some kind of a tin-horn gambling outfit, and that I might have to keep an eye on you!" Roosevelt summed up the meeting by writing that Bullock "then inquired after the capture of Crazy Steve with a little of the air of one sportsman when another has shot a quail that either might have claimed."

In 1898, when the Spanish-American war broke out, Bullock was commissioned Captain of Grigsby's Cowboys, known as the Black Hills Rough Riders, who to their chagrin, never saw active duty. From that time on, Bullock was always called "Captain."

When Roosevelt was inaugurated in Washington in 1905, Bullock

One day when Seth was paying a visit to the President in Washington, Roosevelt in the well-known impulsive Rooseveltian manner said, 'Seth, I'd like to have you down here with me in Washington. How would the commissionership of the General Land Office or of Indian Affairs suit you?' Those who knew Theodore Roosevelt realize how well he relished Seth's answer: 'Mr. President, there is just one position in Washington that I would accept, and you are filling that in a perfectly satisfactory manner.' Reprinted by permission of the Publishers, The Arthur H. Clark Company, from **Pioneer Years in the Black Hills,** by Richard B. Hughes

SCRUTON PEAK CHANGED TO SETH BULLOCK LOOKOUT, Pennington County, altitude 5,950, three miles south of Pactola and forming part of the divide between Rapid and Prairie creeks, was named for the Scruton brothers who had a hidden mine at its base . . . at the instigation of President Theodore Roosevelt the name of this peak was changed to 'Seth Bullock Peak' to honor his long-time friend whom Roosevelt appointed as the first supervisor of the Black Hills National Forest. **South Dakota Place Names**

rounded up about 50 cowboys with horses to pay their own expenses to the national capital by train. Lassoing bystanders, they galloped their broncos down Pennsylvania Avenue on Inauguration Day. The crowd was delighted and so was TR. **The Deadwood Pioneer-Times** in a national press release, Jan. 10, 1905, reported: "The President acted as though he would have enjoyed leaving the stand to run out and give Captain Seth Bullock a hearty grasp of the hand. Every cowboy had a salute for the President, all different."

Roosevelt, in his first year of office, appointed Seth Bullock a United States Marshal, a post Bullock held under three presidents.

Throughout their life-long friendship, the two men for whom ranching was only a sideline, carried on much correspondence and the families often exchanged visits. TR didn't want his sons growing up to be tenderfeet; thus he sent them out to the Bullock ranch to learn how to become cowboys— and bully ones, too.

It was after Roosevelt was no longer president, and he had just returned from a hunting trip in Africa that he had cabled Mr. and Mrs. Seth Bullock to meet him in London where he could show off the "splendid-looking" first sheriff of Deadwood as his "typical ideal American"—as he had explained to Estelline Bennett at the Chicago tea.

Seth Bullock, who made history in the Black Hills and in the West, was also concerned with preserving history and conserving natural resources. He began writing a book about Black Hills history which he never finished, but he did complete "An Account of Deadwood and the Northern Hills of 1876," an invaluable record and interpretation of that turbulent year. He was elected president of the Society of Black Hills Pioneers for 1890-1892, and he served on the first executive committee of the South Dakota State Historical Society.

The death of Theodore Roosevelt in January, 1919, was a dreadful blow to Captain Seth, who in that same year was failing fast from cancer. But he was determined to honor Roosevelt before he died. Largely through Bullock's efforts, the Society of Black Hills Pioneers, of which TR was an honorary member, erected a tower monument to him on what was then called Sheep Mountain, about five miles from Deadwood. Sheep Mountain was then renamed Mount Roosevelt, the first monument in the United States

Honorable Theodore Roosevelt, one of New York City's civil service commissioners and aldermen from the tenderloin district unceremoniously dropped into Deadwood yesterday from his own ranch in the northern part of the state, having driven the entire distance in his buggy. **Black Hills Times,** August 29, 1892

Capt. Seth Bullock of Deadwood, superintendent of the United States Forest Reserve in western South Dakota and T. J. Grier, superintendent of the Homestake Mining Company at Lead, presented masterly papers this forenoon on the relation of the public interests to mining. Capt. Bullock declared that mining depends on forest reserves. He complimented President Roosevelt for his efforts on behalf of the forests of South Dakota. **Deadwood Pioneer-Times,** Jan. 7, 1905

dedicated to the memory of Theodore Roosevelt.

A few months later, on Sept. 23, 1919, Seth Bullock died at age 70, joining the Cowboy President in "The Great Adventure," as Roosevelt had called death. **The Pioneer-Times** in a long eulogy, commented: "There is but little doubt that the work and worry incident to the task of completing the monument and carrying out the July 4th exercises of dedication served to bring on his old trouble and hastened his death."

The Lead Daily Call described Bullock as "Soldier, Patriot, Pioneer, and Good Citizen," whose death will be mourned by hundreds of people, "for he belonged not only to the Black Hills and the West but to the nation."

At his own request, Bullock was buried on the high trail to White Rocks towering above Mount Moriah cemetery. In 1919, from the Bullock grave-site one could see across the gulch to the memorial tower atop Mount

Photo courtesy of Al Gunther.

The grave-site of Seth Bullock about half-way up the trail to White Rocks. Bullock selected this location because it is across the gulch from Mt. Theodore Roosevelt, named in honor of his friend, a Dakota deputy sheriff who became president.

Roosevelt. Today, tall ponderosas obscure the view of the tower.

Both sites, especially Mount Roosevelt, provide panoramic views of the green valleys and peaks and forests of the Black Hills; and beyond roll the boundless plains and wide-open spaces of the ranch country, the Dakota

Trojan Mining Company to Chambers Kellar, who deeded to city of Deadwood, with exception of a parcel of land 50' square and in the center of the 25' lot surrounded by an iron fence being the burial place of Captain Seth Bullock. This grant is upon the express condition that the conveyed premises shall be used exclusively for cemetery purposes, and upon further express condition that burial lots shall be furnished free of charge to all members of Black Hills Pioneer Society, Record Book of Deadwood Cemetery Association.

Photo courtesy of South Dakota Historical Society.

Many climbers have admired this view from White Rocks far above Seth Bullock's grave. Historian John McClintock said the body of a young man was found here, apparently murdered for his gold watch.

both men loved and did so much to develop and preserve.

Seth Bullock, Roosevelt's "typical ideal American," had requested that no epitaph be inscribed on his tombstone. He asked for only one word, "Pioneer."

And that says it all.

Gold watch and chain to Kenneth Kellar. Copy of Last Will and Testament of Seth Bullock, Scrapbook in Adams Museum. (Kenneth Kellar, Bullock's grandson, in 1972, published a book about his grandfather entitled **Seth Bullock—Frontier Marshal.**)

"Mrs. Seth Bullock Passes Away at her Home, Wife of First Sheriff Has Thrilling Life." Mrs. Bullock married in Salt Lake City, leaving shortly after the ceremony in a wagon with a new team for Helena, where the Bullocks lived until the gold rush started in the Black Hills. Mrs. Bullock returned to the home of her parents in Battle Creek, Michigan, while her husband followed the gold trail in the Black Hills. She went to her Michigan home just before the Custer Massacre, and at one place Indians boarded the boat but did no harm . . . She was a leader in literary and musical circles, a charter member of the Round Table Club. **Deadwood Pioneer-Times,** March 11, 1939

GEORGE V. AYRES
WITTY HARDWARE MERCHANT

"Mount Moriah is the closest some of those rascals ever got to heaven," commented George Ayres about the riff-raff and crooks in wick-

Photo courtesy of Centennial Archives, Deadwood Public Library.

George Ayres, Black Hills Pioneer of 1876 and oft-quoted diarist, slogged through deep spring snows on the Cheyenne-Black Hills trail to reach Custer City, the site of the first gold discoveries. Later he invariably described the rugged trek in humorous terms: "lovely weather" and "delicious menus of beans-beans-beans."

ed old Deadwood. Asked how the respectable settlers coped with the bad guys, the witty hardware merchant said, "We just let the ruffians alone and they would kill each other off." And many did so with what was called "the little gun."

George Ayres, one of Deadwood's most prominent pioneers of 1876, always had a lot to say on every subject—politics, activities of the sporting fraternity, plans for improving Deadwood; ideas poured from him as though he were a wisecracking Mark Twain on center stage. And that is actually where he was—a colorful actor on the main street of Deadwood where he could keep track of the world from his busy hardware store; the fist fights and political arguments and shoot-outs, the arrivals and exits of the stage-coach and wagon trains, and later the comings and goings of the trains and the tourists.

Pioneering came naturally to George Ayres. He was born on a farm in Pennsylvania; moved westward by ox team when he was young, first to Illinois, then Missouri and Kansas; finally his family settled down at Beatrice, Nebraska, where he went to public school and grew to young manhood.

In the spring of 1876, the magic year, when George was 23 years old, he joined a small group of adventurers taking off from Cheyenne, Wyoming, for the Black Hills Gold Rush. That wintry March, they hired a team and driver to haul their provisions on a heavily-loaded wagon while the men tramped along through the snow. Without a tent, the tenderfeet had to sleep out in the open, and it snowed 10 out of the 17 days the group was trying to find the road to riches. Their meals consisted of sowbelly pork, beans, and coffee. George frosted his ears and nose in the intense cold. "It was lovely weather," George always said solemnly when reminiscing about the expedition, "and I arrived in the Hills flat broke."

Like many literate people of the era who must have sensed that they were characters in historic drama, George kept a diary of his experiences in the Gold Rush days; excerpts from his diary are quoted in many books writ-

Weather continued very cold. Left Six-Mile ranch about eight o'clock. Arrived at Fort Laramie at 10:30 a.m. Left Fort Laramie about 12 o'clock and crossed the Platte River. Here we left all settlements and entered the Indians' country. Diary of George Ayres.

Along about the last days of May, 1876, a flaxen-haired young fellow came into my store carrying a well-worn carpet bag . . . He introduced himself as George V. Ayres and said he was ambitious to open a small store and tin shop. I asked him if he had a kit of tools and he opened that old carpet bag. Bless me! All I saw in the way of tools was a soldering iron, a bar of solder, and a pair of tinners shears . . . George has made good. No man in the Hills who is better known in the business world than George. He has been a potent factor in the general development of the resources and prosperity of the Black Hills. "Brief Sketches of Pioneers I Have Known," C. V. Gardner, **Hot Springs Weekly,** 1882

A woman in man's clothes—we could see now that the head bull-whacker really was a bull-whackeress—was comforting a baby not more than a year old . . . She looked around and smiled at George Ayres who had come out of his hardware store to see what the trouble was. **Old Deadwood Days,** Bennett

ten about the Black Hills. His vivid account of the arduous trek from Cheyenne to Custer City has enabled historians to pin-point the location of the early camps and stage-stops: Left Horse Creek, Bear Springs, Chugwater, Chimney Rocks—all on the Cheyenne-Black Hills trail.

George described in his diary how a party of Indians, yelling and firing guns, invaded the sleeping camp; the men jumped out of their sleeping sacks without their boots, grabbed their guns, and hid behind trees in the deep snow. But the Indians did not return. George wrote that when it was his turn to stand guard, "I was not scared but I was nervous and mighty glad when daylight came."

Finally on March 25, 1876, the Ayres party, having slogged 260 miles through the snow, arrived in Custer City during a terrible snowstorm. Ayres stayed in Custer and thawed out until May. This was the time when he recorded in his diary that he had heard Preacher Smith conduct the first religious services in the Hills and that the congregation "paid strict attention to the sermon except when there was a dog fight outside."

He hiked on to Deadwood in late May, but here became very ill with mountain fever; and as soon as he was able to travel, in July, 1876, he returned to Custer where he stayed until the fall of 1877. When he received a telegram from Deadwood offering him a job in a hardware store, he tramped through snow a foot deep on the 60-mile trail from Custer to Deadwood.

By this time, floundering through the snow in every season must have seemed routine to George Ayres. At any rate, the young pioneer had regained his health and zest. He reported the next morning for work at his new job in the Lake hardware store. George worked in the hardware business more than half a century; and by 1909, he had become sole owner of this store on Deadwood's main street. At one time the Ayres hardware took over the old Star and Bullock hotel building.

Ayres, a Mason from Nebraska, affiliated with the Deadwood lodge in 1882, where he began a dazzling ascent up the Masonic ladder. After he had held all the offices in the lodge, he was chosen deputy grand master in 1889. Annie Tallent in her history of the Black Hills summed up his Masonic career: "Ayres was annointed High Priest in the Grand Council of annointed High Priests of South Dakota."

George Ayres, who was off a month, says he is now perfectly satisfied that there is but one country in the world he would be satisfied to live in and that country is the Black Hills. **Black Hills Times,** May 29, 1884

During the great fire of 1879 in Deadwood, George and two other men lifted Mrs. Lake's large square piano with a heavy rosewood case, carried it outside and a considerable distance up the hill before depositing it in a basement. Afterwards it took five men to lift it out. **Rapid City Journal,** Dec. 8, 1968

George Ayres, our popular hardware merchant, returned last evening from a purchasing trip in the eastern cities. He was so occupied with laying in his stock of goods that he forgot to get married. **Black Hills Times,** March 28, 1898

No wonder then that in 1908, **The Deadwood Pioneer-Times** reported that George Ayres was presented with a sparkling jewel, "the beauty and richness of which is emblematic of the high regard in which he is held by his brother Masons." The unnamed jewel was exhibited in Sol Levison's show window on main street.

Ayres, a staunch Republican who told funny stories about the Democrats, was city, county and state leader. He was a member of the city council of Deadwood, chairman of the Lawrence County board of commissioners, and was a representative for two terms in the state legislature. Twice, George Ayres was elected president of the Society of Black Hills Pioneers.

As chairman of the board of county commissioners, he convinced the people of Lawrence County to construct a gravel road from Deadwood to Centennial Valley. Capt. C. V. Gardner reported that "the old road was a mere wagon trail and at some times of the year was well nigh impassable for man or beast."

Ayres was chairman of two statewide good roads conventions which started work west of the Missouri River on the Black Hills-Yellowstone Park highway and the Deadwood-Denver highway. Fittingly enough, this pioneer of 1876 who had struggled 260 miles through the trackless wilderness to reach the Black Hills became known as the "Father of Good Roads in the Black Hills.

George was already an old man when he became president of the First National Bank in Deadwood. Like many who survived the hardships of the Gold Rush, he lived to an active old age.

The firm of George V. Ayres & Co., Inc., still operates in Deadwood under the ownership of his son Albro Ayres. The DuPont Chemical Company said the Ayres hardware was its oldest account for explosives in the world managed by the same family.

George Ayres died in May, 1939, at age 86. Those who attended his funeral packed the Masonic Temple whose cornerstone of 1900 is engraved with his name. The funeral, reported to be one of the largest in Deadwood's history, was overflowing with mourners from throughout the Black Hills; with state Masonic dignitaries and politicians; with tributes, flowers, and tears.

George Ayres' grave in Mount Moriah is at the crossroads of two good cemetery roads and not far from the Stars and Stripes which flies night and

He has a beautiful home high up on the mountainside in Deadwood where he and his kindly wife are always glad to meet the boys and girls of '76 and recount the stories of the early days. "Brief Sketches of Pioneers I Have Known," Capt. C. V. Gardner, **Hot Springs Weekly,** 1882

George Ayres' first wife Kate Towle died in 1892. He married Myrtle Coon of Omaha in 1898 who was a very fine singer. Myrtle Ayres frequently sang solos for public occasions; and in later years she told her friends how much she hated to sing at funerals because she was afraid the next funeral would be for George. But Myrtle's premonition was wrong. She died in May, 1937, and George outlived her by two years. Recollection of Marie Lawler, daughter of James Lawler, Black Hills Pioneer of 1876

Photo courtesy of Al Gunther.

The grave of Masonic leader George Ayres who was called the "Father of Good Roads."
It is located near the overlook where two cemetery roads meet, Moriah and Mary. The names
of streets, derived from Masonic ritual, are identified on an 1895 map of Mount Moriah Cemetery.

day, and near the scenic overlook which provides a spectacular view of Deadwood and the historic main street where he was always on center stage.

Unlike those rascals for whom "Mount Moriah is the closest they'll ever get to heaven," George Ayres is up there, and the Lord probably appointed him High Chancellor of the golden streets of paradise and chairman of their everlasting upkeep. Everyone who knew the friendly hardware merchant might be willing to wager that he is also Chairman of the Welcoming Committee to greet every soul who makes it through the pearly gates, especially the Masons and the Black Hills pioneers.

The writer and a friend from South America called on Mr. Ayres at the First National Bank shortly before his death. The South American was returning to Peru for at least three years. Mr. Ayres said: 'Harold, I won't be here when you return, but good luck to you.' My friend replied, 'Uncle George, whether you are here or not, I want you to know that in my opinion you will never be forgotten. You have influenced more young men by your life and counsel than any man I have ever known.' **Seventy Years of Banking,** Driscoll

Nancy Ford, travel editor in the Chicago **Journal of Commerce,** told this story in her column 'Going Places.' It seems that George Ayres and a toll-gate keeper at the edge of town boasted the first two telephones to come to Deadwood in 1880. George tried out the new contraption by calling the toll-gate keeper.

'Hello, Bill'

'Hello, George'

'Can you hear me, Bill?'

'Yes, I can hear you.'

'Don't it beat hell,'' said George, and hung up.

Local Celebrities Scrapbook, Adams Museum

JOHN McCLINTOCK
PIONEER HISTORIAN

"When antiquarians shall come as they have in all past ages,

They will find in Black Hills histories many blank pages,

Which could easily have provided an abundance of room

For the countless good stories which are enshrouded in the tomb."

Last verse of "The Vanishing Pioneers," McClintock, **Queen City Mail,** April 18, 1933

John S. McClintock was one Deadwood pioneer of 1876 who did his best to insure that "countless good stories" were not "enshrouded in the tomb," a situation he deplored in his verse quoted above.

This venerable historian, when he was 92 years old, published his now famous **Pioneer Days in the Black Hills,** a history book without "many blank pages." Instead, it is packed with countless straightforward and fascinating stories which he began arranging in book form when he was in his 80's. Publishers didn't think an informal history of the Black Hills would sell; thus McClintock had to borrow money to have the book published himself. Today rare copies of the McClintock history are collector's items;

Photo courtesy of Centennial Archives, Deadwood Public Library.

Venerable historian John McClintock driving the stage for the "Days of '76" parade. He operated a stage-coach line in the early days. Before the railroads came, the stage was the fastest transportation available, averaging about 8½ miles per hour on long trips.

in 1979, an individual copy in mint condition sold for $120.

Many chapters are based on historical articles which McClintock began writing in 1909 for the **Deadwood Daily Telegram** under the editorship of the puritanical and crusading newspaper editor, Edward L. Senn, who many years later acted as editor for McClintock's book. Many people suspect Senn cleaned up McClintock's colorful language. Senn wrote in the preface: "McClintock's reputation for veracity is unimpeachable. Because of this, and his remarkable memory, the writer has reached the conclusion that his stories are accurate except possibly in some minor details; and that in case of conflict with other writers, his recollections are most likely to be correct."

No one challenges McClintock's basic honesty, but there are those who would argue with Editor Senn's conclusions that McClintock's recollections are "most likely to be correct." However, there is not one aspect, not even a gold speck of Deadwood's history which has been settled to everyone's satisfaction. And this contradiction in memories and interpretation is what keeps history alive and kicking.

Young McClintock, with the tape-recorder in his head turned on, was often one of the supporting characters in historical drama; if not right on stage, he always had a front-row seat—a lucky break for a future historian.

Some historians insist that Wild Bill Hickok and Calamity Jane arrived separately in Deadwood. Not so, contended both McClintock and Richard Hughes, the first newspaper reporter; these two agree that the two superstars of the Wild West arrived on horseback in June, 1876, with the Colo-

rado Charlie Utter wagon train; and many years later both men wrote about this historic event in their pioneer histories. If two historians can agree, an almost incontrovertible fact is usually born of that union. Wild Bill and Calamity Jane galloped into Deadwood history together—and that's a fact.

Although McClintock was not one of the multitude who claimed to be kibitzing the poker game in the No. 10 saloon when Wild Bill was shot, he did happen to be standing across the street when Jack McCall burst out with his smoking gun.

A debunker of many sacred Deadwood legends, McClintock, interestingly enough, was chiefly responsible for promoting the tale that Wild Bill's corpse, after three years in a wooden coffin, had turned to stone, had become petrified. And McClintock was a member of the supporting cast in that scene of moving the body.

"Show me! I'm from Missouri," must have been the motto of this native Missourian. Of course, it is prudent for an historian to be skeptical instead of gullible, but occasionally even John McClintock might have gone along with what a crowd of people witnessed instead of giving the story "little credence"—i.e. the burial of Preacher Smith and Charlie Mason in a double grave in the first boot hill. Despite evidence to the contrary, McClintock was the only historian who insisted that Preacher Smith was killed by whites instead of by Indians.

Before the 25-year-old McClintock, called Mac, joined the rush to the Black Hills, he prospected in the Helena, Montana gold camp. In the spring of 1876, he boarded a riverboat at St. Louis and steamed up the Missouri River to Fort Pierre, 200 miles east of the Black Hills. From there he joined a 20-wagon train for the overland trek across the plains to the new El Dorado, encountering a number of Indians who did not attack the invaders.

McClintock's account of his arrival in Deadwood parallels the descriptions of most newcomers to the gold camp. The main street was a triple-wagon dirt road in filthy condition, and the gulch was packed with thousands of men, a few females, and a jumble of wagons and animals, the vehicles often getting stuck up to their axles in the stinking mud.

Mac soon built himself a cozy log cabin on upper main street, a perfect

---

Dec. 1, 1876, was an eventful night in Deadwood, for it was upon that day that the telegraph line connected that city with the outside world. They celebrated with a bonfire and 38 anvil salutes. Later in the evening there was a grand ball at the Grand Central Hotel and the enterprising reporter gave a description of some of the toilettes displayed by ladies present. The elite of the city glided through intoxicating mazes of waltz, polka, schottische, and quadrille. "Tales of the Hills," Alice Gossage, Scrapbook, Rapid City Public Library

Yes, I knew McClintock personally. He always wrote in long hand on big, yellow tablets. Although he prided himself on being an honest reporter, he was actually very biased and invariably took the opposite point of view from what other reliable historians had agreed upon. Recollection of Camille Yuill, author and veteran columnist for the **Deadwood Pioneer-Times**

location for one who would later write history. He had a good vantage point from which to observe the motley collection of fortune-hunters shoving their way in and out of the saloons in the wild gold camp. The many underworld characters—gamblers, con men, gunslingers, cut-throats—kept the town in a frenzy. McClintock saw it all from his lookout cabin on main street and from jostling his way through the jam-packed streets and sideshows in carnival town.

Unlike many of the young men jamming the city, Mac was an experienced prospector and soon had a job working the placers while looking for a promising claim of his own. Mac sunk shafts, then timbered up the hole to get out gold that was not available on the surface. Some times he was successful; working with a partner for two and a half months, the two were able to clean up $20,000. Only a few lucky ones struck it rich; and many miners lost out, their money wasted, typical of the bad luck in mining camps.

Eventually, McClintock branched out from mining gold. He owned and operated the Deadwood-Central City toll road. He established a livery and express business; and for over 30 years operated a stage line between Deadwood and Spearfish. Later he owned considerable real estate, including the Deadwood opera house, and the surface title to the site of the present Franklin Hotel.

Not until his later years did this astute businessman turn writer; and with the encouragement of Editor Senn, he then decided to write a history of his experiences and recollections. In his 80's and 90's, the old-timer with his cane hobbled about the city interviewing old and new friends about the old days. With persistence and vigor, this aged man with little education and a long, long memory succeeded in completing his book when he was 92.

Enjoying his authorship, he lived three more years and died at age 95, on April 8, 1942.

At his death, he was the oldest Lawrence County resident and the oldest living member of the Society of Black Hills Pioneers. He dedicated his book to the pioneers of 1876 whom he extolled as the highest type of congenial and enterprising people, excluding the criminal element, who settled in the Black Hills in defiance of the hostile Indians and of the orders of the United States government.

In the flowery tribute to McClintock in **The Pioneer-Times,** the writer extolled his virtues: "He often gave food to the hungry and aided the distressed." Because of his active work in placer mining, he was given much credit for the prosperity of Central City.

J. S. McClintock has heard nothing of his horse as yet. He has also sent out an officer to Minnesota to learn if he had gone there, but has telegraphed a description of the horse, saddle, and rider to Miles City, Montana, and Buffalo, Wyoming. It is a two to one bet that Mac recovers his horse even if the costs exceed the value of his property. **Black Hills Daily Times,** April 16, 1877

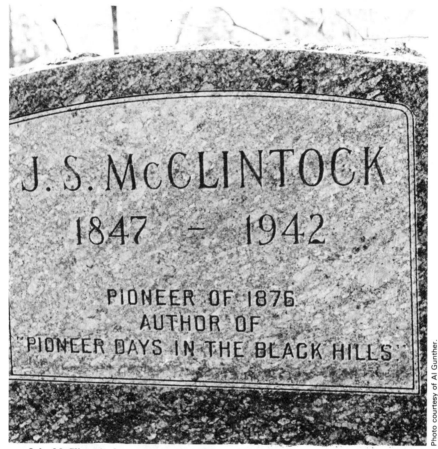

Photo courtesy of Al Gunther.

John McClintock also wrote verse, including a tribute to the stage-coach driver, "beset by road agents and many unseen dangers and Indian scares." Tombstone in Mount Moriah

As the cortege passed the Adams Museum on its way to Mount Moriah, the chimes tolled for the 95 memorable years of a remarkable pioneer of '76. The obituary concluded: "He has sailed on that ship which never returns homeward. John McClintock has left shafts to his memory more lasting than granite and more beautiful than the richest gold he ever mined."

"The Passing of the Overland Stage Coach and a Tribute to the Oldest Known Stage Driver" by J. S. McClintock

And for a decade or longer he cleared the trails
By buffeting the snowdrifts and breasting the gales.
He swung around craggy peaks in circuitous routes
And swept through gorges and canyons in his ins and outs.
(third verse) **Queen City Mail** clipping, Local Celebrities Scrapbook, Adams Museum

The Deadwood Opera House, under the management of J. S. McClintock, has been thoroughly renovated and decorated and now presents a very attractive appearance. Woolford-Sheridan Dramatic Company will make its first appearance before a Deadwood audience in a realistic drama, "The Smugglers," then "Shadow of a Great City" and "Mystic Mountain." **Black Hills Daily Times,** Sept. 1893

Deadwood, July 18, 1878. This is to certify that J. S. McClintock has furnished $150 to defray one half expense of W. Matkin on a prospecting tour to Bear Paw Mountains, and in consideration of said amount is to reap the benefits of one half of whatever may be obtained. Signed, J. W. Matkin. Deeds and Reports Scrapbook, Adams Museum

Mrs. George Murray, Jr. leads the "Days of '76" parade wearing a costume of black satin rhadame, made in the style of the early days of Deadwood. It has a basque waist and the skirt requires a hoop. Mrs. Murray is the daughter of J. S. McClintock . . . As a small girl, Mrs. Murray, who was born in Deadwood, begged to be allowed to ride with her father on the high seat of the rocking Concord stages, drawn by their prancing horses as they made their way from one city to another. Local Celebrities Scrapbook, Adams Museum

YUNG SET
UNKNOWN CHINESE

Yung Set was the name of a man from Deadwood's Chinatown, and most whites did not know or care that he was dead until the colorful Chinese funeral procession commanded attention on the clamorous streets of early Deadwood in 1878. According to **The Black Hills Daily Times,** Sept. 2, 1878, this funeral for Yung Set was the first public Chinese funeral in Deadwood, and thus a curious crowd of whites tramped after the parade up the steep hill to Mount Moriah, marveling at the bizarre and alien ceremonies. Thus began the Deadwood tradition of following Chinese funeral

Photo courtesy of South Dakota Historical Society.

This well-attended Chinese funeral in 1891 was for a man named High Lee. Note the tea pot, serving dishes, and joss sticks.

processions to the grand finale at the cemetery, the entire drama becoming a favorite form of free entertainment for the amazed audience.

For the funeral of Yung Set a horse-drawn wagon bearing the corpse in a cloth coffin led the funeral procession; then came the Celestials (as the newspapers often called the Chinese), dressed in white robes with white streamers floating from their hats; some carried lighted and scented tapers called joss sticks; others carried long staffs or gorgeous banners with Chinese inscriptions. Each Chinese wore a pink ribbon around his left arm.

At Yung Set's grave-site in the Chinese section of Mount Moriah, so many whites crowded around that there was scarcely room for the Chinese. Each Oriental threw his pink arm band into the grave, then piled up his white costume and "a lot of paper covered with heathen characters" beside the grave and set fire to the heap. Amid the firing of innumerable firecrackers, the Chinese lowered the coffin into the grave. Next, the funeral party passed around dainty sugar cakes to all those assembled. After shoveling dirt into the grave, they lighted four torches at its foot. Thus ended the burial rites for Yung Set, the first Chinese funeral witnessed by the whites.

Through the years the Chinese funerals with many variations and embellishments were often featured in the Deadwood newspapers. The clanging of a large gong from the Chinese church, a Joss House, usually signified a death in Chinatown, and the Chinese flag flew at half mast. Noisy and spectacular, their funerals were replete with mysterious incantations, dragon decorations, colored fire, the burning of incense, ear-shattering sounds from tom-toms and clashing cymbals—all of these rituals for the purpose of appeasing the gods during the flight of the soul of the departed to his future abode in paradise, the Flowery Kingdom. The progress of the soul to the other world was meant to be a gay procession, accompanied with every outward sound of joy, or the wrath of the gods would descend upon the living. The Chinese believed in celebrating death instead of grieving over it.

One of the rituals best-remembered by Deadwood was performed by a Chinese who sat beside the driver of the hearse. As the procession wound its upward way to the cemetery, he would scatter hundreds of small pieces of

---

The gayest thing about the Chinese was their funerals. **Old Deadwood Days,** Bennett

A Chinaman, 65 years of age, died yesterday and will be buried today. As the remains do not weigh over 40 pounds, it is highly probable that opium had much to do with the demise. Deceased was a Mason and will be buried in the order with the usual pomp and ceremony. **Black Hills Daily Times,** Aug. 1886

The recently defunct Chinaman left a number of bequests, including a magnificent poppy outfit to one of his old Anglo-Saxon customers. **Black Hills Daily Times,** Aug., 1886

Deadwood had a large Chinese population, and Rev. A. C. Dill of the first Hills church, the Congregational, instituted a school for them. He taught them to sing hymns and organized a night school, and with other workers taught them to read, write, and speak English. **Rapid City Journal,** Dec. 1929

colored paper with many tiny holes punched in them. These were to slow down the devil who must try to pass through each small hole before he could do any damage to the spirit of the departed. By providing this obstacle course, the Chinese gained enough time to bury their comrade and thus save him from the devil.

Often the Deadwood band in uniform led the procession. Most Chinese dignitaries, instead of wearing white costumes as in Yung Set's funeral, wore brilliant robes containing every color of the rainbow.

According to a report in **The Times,** May, 1896, a funeral for a member of the Chinese Masons was especially lavish, led by Dr. Von Wedelstaedt, the 'White Brother' and the coffin was lowered into the ground "amid chattering and hideous noises and contortions painful to behold." Often the mourners poured whiskey and rice on the ground, and near the grave set about quantities of roast pig, cooked chicken and geese, apples and oranges, cakes and candy. Some of this food was eaten by members of the funeral party, but much of it was left around and on top of the grave.

Usually two Chinese carried the pig on their shoulders to Mount Moriah where it was roasted in a ceremonial oven. The Chinese received permission to erect it in 1908, according to the minutes of the Deadwood Cemetery Association, preserved in the Record Book.

Many older Deadwood-ites recall how they, as children, tagged along after the exciting parade to hide behind boulders and tombstones until the coast was clear so they could sample the delicious picnic spread.

The reason given for the Chinese leaving a feast near the grave is that the soul which returned to the body before leaving on the dragon trip to the Flowery Kingdom might have provisions for its journey. **The Times,** April, 1889, said that Mount Moriah was crowded on Sunday so people "could observe the Chinese feeding their dead. An immense quantity of provisions were spread over the numerous graves."

An oft-told tale from Deadwood lore is that a white man asked a Chinese when the dead would arise from their graves to eat all the bountiful feast set out for them. The Chinese man replied: "Our dead will come up to eat our food when your dead come up to smell your flowers."

According to the **Deadwood Pioneer-Times,** June, 1914, Chinese funerals had ceased being elaborate. A Chinese official explained that "the younger generation of Chinese were becoming more Occidental in their beliefs and customs."

As the colorful style of Chinese funerals diminished, so did the Chinese population of Deadwood. About 250 Chinese were estimated to have once lived in the Northern Hills, working at placer claims, managing laundries and restaurants and shops. Gradually with the decline of the gold rush agitation and opportunities for livelihood, the Chinese began to leave Deadwood, either to return to China, or to settle in large American cities.

Photo courtesy of Centennial Archives, Deadwood Public Library.

The Wing Tsue Wong family. A successful merchant, Wing Tsue was the most prominent Chinese in Deadwood. The family eventually returned to China in 1902. A child of Wing Tsue's was buried in the Chinese section in 1895. According to the Record Book of the Deadwood Cemetery Association, Wing Tsue paid for many burial lots for the Chinese people.

Even many of the Chinese who had been safely planted in Mount Moriah before the devil could get to them did not stay put. Many male Chinese had a guarantee in their labor contracts that their bones were to be shipped back to their homeland no more than 10 years after their deaths. The relatives of the deceased often supervised the removal and paid for the costs.

Sometimes this removal of the bodies for shipment was recorded in the Record Book and sometimes not. Many entries are difficult to read, but probably about 60 Chinese were once buried in the Chinese section. About 20 removal notations are recorded. The name of Yung Set is not in the Rec-

Wing Tsue, our well-known and popular Chinese merchant and his wife are mourning the demise of their youngest child who died yesterday forenoon of bronchitis. It will be buried in the Chinese portion of Mount Moriah cemetery tomorrow. **Black Hills Daily Times**, Jan., 1895

The motto of some of the Caucasion League in the Black Hills is "Down with Chinamen, wholesale, retail, and pigtail." "Gulch Hash," **The Black Hills Daily Times**, May, 1878

An anti-Chinese meeting was held at Elizabethtown last evening. Speeches were made by Dr. Myers and others, giving our triangle-eyed brethren particular fits. **The Black Hills Daily Times**, March, 1878

An intelligent Chinaman interrogated concerning the custom of removing to the Flowery Kingdom the remains of deceased countrymen after resting while underground in this country, replied: "It is our custom to have all our relatives near to each other, to record them in their own family record and go to visit the relatives' graves yearly with the children. That is why we know all about our early fathers." **Black Hills Daily Times**, Aug. 25, 1886

ord Book even though his funeral in 1878 was the first one witnessed by whites.

Just how many Chinese—if any—are still buried in Mount Moriah is one of Deadwood's greatest historical controversies. Some historians believe that the bones of all the Chinese dead were shipped back in zinc-lined boxes; others insist that many Chinese still remain simply because they had no families or friends or employers to pay for the expenses.

Today, the Chinese section is mainly a steep slope of tangled under-brush and tall pines. The wooden markers with Chinese inscriptions have long ago disappeared. In this area are a number of paths and well-marked graves of white people, including a John Brown and a Joe Silver.

Although Chinatown has vanished, its inhabitants cast a lasting spell over Deadwood, becoming a legendary part of its mystique. Many beautiful Chinese artifacts are displayed in the Adams Museum. And if you follow a narrow trail down into the old Chinese section, you may imagine the aura of incense and the aroma of roasting pork still lingering over Mount Moriah.

Undertakers Henry and Charles Robinson recently dis-interred bodies of six Chinamen buried seven or eight years ago in Mount Moriah cemetery. The coffins were found to contain nothing but bones, each one of which was carefully wrapped in paper and replaced in metallic caskets for shipment to China, via San Francisco. This is done so that the spirit of the deceased may be at rest, the Chinese having a superstition that if their remains are not deposited in the sacred soil of China, the departed spirit will be forever a wanderer. **Black Hills Weekly,** October 12, 1895

Contrary to popular belief, the bodies of most Chinese buried in Mount Moriah Cemetery were not 'dug up and returned to China.' Many of the Chinese brotherhood remain on the rocky slopes of one of our nation's most historical and interesting burial grounds. **Deadwood Gulch—The Last Chinatown,** Sulentic

One day when I was in charge of the visitor's booth at Mount Moriah and it was closing time, I heard the sounds of an axe coming from the Chinese section. I found a college boy chopping up a wooden headboard with Chinese writing on it just as though he had every right to do so. I made a citizen's arrest of the vandal who then began crying. I took him to the police magistrate who gave him a good scare, but no charges were preferred. Recollection of A. H. Shostrom, Deadwood historian

KITTY LEROY
"SOILED DOVE" MURDER VICTIM

The most famous "soiled dove" of Deadwood's dens of iniquity was the beauteous bigamist, Kitty LeRoy, who came to a violent end. Reported to have had five husbands with several at the same time, she was always armed to her pearly teeth, stashing away at least two pistols and a couple of bowie knives in the voluminous gypsy costume she wore, and with a dagger tucked into her long brown curls and huge diamonds in her ears. A self-sufficient gold-digger, she needed protection from the love-starved miners, rejected suitors, and the gamblers she had swindled. Some say men had kill-

ed each other over her magnetic beauty and that Kitty herself was a murderess.

A professional dancer whom all the men cheered, Kitty also loved to gamble and conned many a bedazzled admirer out of his gold dust, one prospector losing eight thousand dollars to her tricks in The Mint, her home base in Deadwood Gulch. Legend had it that she married her first husband because he was her only lover reckless enough to let her shoot an apple off his head while she galloped by at full speed, a lady William Tell, Wild West style.

She married her fifth husband, faro-dealer Sam Curley, in the Gem Theater, the most notorious of all Deadwood's combination brothels, gambling dens, and saloons. Sam was terribly jealous of his gorgeous and unfaithful wife; they quarreled; he left town in a rage. Later he returned incognito to Deadwood and sneaked up to the Lone Star saloon where Kitty lived with his rival.

The Black Hills Daily Times, Dec. 7, 1877, reported what happened under the headline, "All For Love": "A thrill of horror ran through the community last night as the intelligence passed from mouth to mouth that Kitty LeRoy had been shot and instantly killed by her husband Sam Curley, who in turn killed himself." The reporter described every gory detail: pools of blood, brain-spattered walls, oozing wounds, glazed eyes, protruding bones—with provocatively-dressed Kitty lying there dead with a bullet hole in her pretty bosom. Right beside her lay Curley with his brains blown out. Somehow Kitty's paramour escaped the vengeance of the cuckolded husband. Kitty was 28 years old, had a legal husband in Michigan and a child in California.

After the funeral for Kitty and Sam, held in the Lone Star saloon, they were buried in a double grave, each in a separate pine casket. Probably in this first cemetery at Ingleside no permanent markers were placed on their graves.

Their names are not listed in the Record Book. Like many other people whose bodies were eventually moved from Ingleside to Mount Moriah, the bodies of Kitty and Sam were unidentified when they were reburied in the mountaintop cemetery, and there is no record of when or where or if.

A month after the tragedy, **The Times** reported that the Lone Star had become a haunted house with disembodied spirits floating about which observers could identify as the shadow of a comely woman followed by the tread and ghostly form of a man. "The double phantoms are seen to recline in loving embrace and finally melt away in the shadows of the night."

The Times concluded its tale of the supernatural phenomena witnessed by the reporter and by many others with this paragraph: "Whatever may have been the vices and virtues of the ill-starred and ill-mated couple, we trust their spirits may have found a happier camping ground than the hills and gulches of the Black Hills, and though infelicity reigned with them here, happiness may blossom in fairer climes."

Kitty Curley drew an holographic will in ink on the day prior to her death. The estate amounted to $650, more than half of which was claimed by and allowed to Kitty Donally, and the expenses have doubtless consumed the balance. **Black Hills Daily Times,** Jan. 7, 1878

Many bodies have been removed to Mount Moriah cemetery, but still quite a number remain within the old enclosure. These removals only complicate the difficulties of identifying the remaining dead because in the majority of cases only a rude board with the name written in lead pencil was placed over the dead. A few months suffice to rot away the board and obliterate the writing. **Black Hills Daily Times,** Nov. 21, 1881

CHAMBERS DAVIS
GOLD ASSAYER

Chambers Davis, an assayer who came to Deadwood in 1877 from an assaying position with the Denver mint was an expert who tested the gold ore that the eager prospectors brought to him.

His office building at the head of main street contained a complete metallurgical business. "He had an assaying credit of $100,000 with which to purchase ore here for California companies," according to an article in the **Black Hills Daily Times,** May 27, 1877, about early Deadwood industries. In Davis' laboratory there were three furnaces, one used for melting gold dust, and the other two for crucible assays of ore. In the same building he also had a two-stamp mill run by steam engines.

The Times also reported that Davis fixed up a hot and cold water bath arrangement in his building, "the first private institution of its kind in the Hills." Another Davis innovation was the erection of several solid posts

outside his building for the bullwhackers to buck against because they had a "habit of driving their wagons into the gutterspout while turning the corner and blockading it with dirt."

Chambers Davis and his wife Adrienne were a popular young couple, mentioned frequently in the social columns of the newspapers. In June, 1878, Adrienne died at age 33. **The Times** reported "that there is no death that has occurred here that has excited such general regret and unfeigned sorrow . . . Her cultivated mind and noble qualities of heart made her a favorite."

Two days after her death, this **Times** item appeared: "The lonely grave of Mrs. C. C. Davis on the point at the head of Centennial Avenue was numerously visited by friends on Sunday afternoon who literally bedecked it with wild flowers." Why was Adrienne Davis buried first on Centennial Avenue?

In April, 1879, not yet a year after his wife's death, Chambers Davis died at age 38. **The Times** in a long obituary praised him highly as "brilliant, hard-working, well-known, and respected."

The Times also suggested a dark mystery by writing: "The painful and distressing circumstances that seemed to have encompassed his life during the past year are too well-known to need repetition at this time, but they excited the universal sympathy of this community." In the Record Book, the cause of death listed for Davis is "softening of the brain."

Photo courtesy of Al Gunther.

"Remember now thy creator in the days of thy youth" is inscribed around the Masonic pulpit with the stone replica of the Bible. According to the names listed, 18 people, including the Davises, are buried in the Masonic Circle.

Both Chambers Davis who was a Mason and his wife Adrienne are buried in the Masonic circle in Mount Moriah. Their names are on the Masonic lectern as well as inscribed on a weathered, pillar-shaped tombstone nearby. Masons buried Chambers Davis with the last rites of their order: "where in God's good time we will meet again. Until then, dear brother, until then, Farewell."

D. P. Webster of Helena, Montana, arrived in the city yesterday to look after the grave of his daughter, Mrs. Chambers C. Davis, whom our old timers remember well and who died early in the year 1878 and was buried in the old cemetery. The body was moved when Mount Moriah was laid out, and Mr. Davis who died subsequently was buried beside his wife. Mr. Webster visited the cemetery and had no trouble locating the graves of his children. He has arranged with Henry Robinson the undertaker to improve the ground and put up a temporary headboard and in the near future will erect a nice monument. **Black Hills Weekly,** Aug. 10, 1895

JOHN GASTON
FOUNDER OF SOCIETY OF
BLACK HILLS PIONEERS

A wagon-load of members belonging to the Society of Black Hills Pioneers at a picnic in the Lead city park. No date. Holding the reins is James W. Allen, a charter member of the society which John Gaston is given much credit for organizing.

John Gaston, a Black Hills Pioneer of 1876, is credited with originating the plan for the organization of the Society of Black Hills Pioneers, according to historian John McClintock. At the organizational meeting held Jan. 8, 1889, McClintock reported that arguments arose which caused Mr. Gaston to drop the leadership role and to destroy the membership papers

which had already been signed. However, Gaston recovered from his tantrum and was finally persuaded to sign the new membership papers. Although Gaston was not elected to office the first year, he did serve as treasurer for two terms, 1890-1892, and was always regarded as a public-spirited citizen.

The original requirement for membership in the exclusive and prestigious society was that a member must have arrived in the Hills by December 31, 1876. This ruling, which offended many pioneers who had come a year or two later, gave rise to a popular saying in the Hills that "if your family didn't come in '76, you don't amount to a damn."

As the years passed, the membership requirements were liberalized to include children of members, living or dead, eligible for membership; in 1921, this was amended to include wives and widows of pioneers. Finally, in 1932, an amendment provided that children and grandchildren of pioneers were eligible if the latter had arrived in the Hills before the date of the big Deadwood fire, Sept. 26, 1879. By the first meeting in October, 1889, 153 members were enrolled; 90 years later, in October, 1979, there are over 300 members.

According to the constitution of the society, the aims and objects are these: "To cultivate social intercourse and form a more perfect union among its members; to create a fund for charitable purposes in their behalf; to collect and preserve information connected with the early settlement and subsequent history of the country."

John Gaston, the temperamental founder of the society, was a prominent merchant, a mine and real estate broker. A widower, he married Marie, a charming English lady, in 1882. He died at age 58 on March 17, 1895. At the extremely large funeral held in the Gaston home, his many friends reminisced about his life. They recalled that wild August day, almost 20 years before, when Preacher Smith had been found murdered. It was John Gaston who had loaned 50 needle guns, with no questions asked, and had provided ammunition for a posse to go out after the suspected killers, the Indians.

Filing by the open casket, after they had taken a last look "at one who had endeared himself to all," many of the mourners shed tears for Gaston, affectionately called "Uncle John," whose countenance looked "calm and exceedingly life-like." His long and complimentary obituary in the **Black Hills Daily Times** called him "one of the sturdy trail-blazers who opened up the Black Hills for settlement in the face of all dangers."

A surviving group of trail-blazers, the Society of Black Hills Pioneers conducted the funeral for John Gaston, its members all wearing white gloves and badges of mourning. The burial rites at Mount Moriah concluded with these words: "Let us hope that as we each depart from this life on that unknown journey that we will find the trails to everlasting peace and comfort, so well-blazed by the Pioneers who have gone before that none will be lost on the way."

Welcome Pioneers
by Allan Penfield
Make way for the Pioneers!
Fall back—hats off—three cheers!
Three rousing ones for the Pioneers.
They came on foot, they came on mules.
They wallowed in gumbo with placer tools.
The spade and the pick and the trusty gun,
The many for wealth, the few for fun.
Some dug, some saved, some others stole.
The latter class were soon in the hole.

Their boots went with them, traditions say,
And hence their absence on pioneers' day.
But the brave and true, the fittest survive.
The Hills are their home, the house of their pride.
We welcome ye heroes at the gateway,
We welcome, thrice welcome on Pioneers' Day.

Poem recited at Society of Black Hills Pioneers' Picnic held at Canyon Lake, **Rapid City Journal,** July, 1892

M. O. Gaston, son of the late John Gaston, while enroute to the Gaston ranch on the Redwater from this city, was thrown from his horse and sustained injuries of a dangerous nature. **Black Hills Daily Times,** March 21, 1895

John and Mrs. Gaston returned from Hot Springs. John is thoroughly cured and reasonably enough, cannot speak too glowingly of Hot Springs, its beauties and virtues as a health resort. **Black Hills Daily Times,** July 16, 1886

MARIE GASTON
FIRST LIBRARIAN

Marie Gaston, Deadwood's first librarian, emigrated from England to Deadwood in 1879. The attractive Englishwoman married widower John Gaston, a mining and real estate broker, in 1882. For 11 years the marriage was a happy one until he died in 1895. She then took over his brokerage business.

That same year, 1895, when she became a widow, Mrs. Gaston was elected president of the Round Table Club, the first woman's club in Deadwood. This group of five women led the drive for establishing a library, an educational advantage sorely needed to help civilize the mining camp. The first library was set up in the Syndicate building on main street where Mrs. Gaston served as librarian without pay for seven years. The first catalogue of books lists 100 volumes of fiction, history, and reference. This lady who loved books and respected education also served for many years as treasurer of the school board.

The library in the Syndicate building was a good start, but Mrs. Gaston was determined that Deadwood should have a permanent library building, and with the support of the Round Table Club, the Thursday Club, and other women's clubs, she stimulated a great deal of interest in the project.

At last, with the help of Congressman E. W. Martin, Mrs. Gaston was successful in getting a Carnegie grant of $15,000 to build a library. The Deadwood Library Board also sponsored dances and flower shows to raise additional money to buy books. The city of Deadwood contributed $863 to the fund and also donated land for the site, which had formerly been a stone mason's yard on Williams Street.

Then on a cold, blustery November day in 1902, Mrs. Gaston attended the funeral of a friend and caught a bad cold which quickly turned into "ty-

Deadwood Carnegie Public Library, dedicated November, 1905, three years after the death of Marie Gaston who led the fund-raising drive for the library and was instrumental in Deadwood's receiving a Carnegie grant.

Photo courtesy of Centennial Archives, Deadwood Public Library.

phoid pneumonia.'' She died suddenly on November 28, 1902, at age 57. **The Deadwood Pioneer-Times** expressed the city's shock and sorrow at the death of this popular and effective community leader, writing: "She had lived a life of good deeds until the summons came for her to join her husband in the other world.'' One of the saddest aspects of her untimely death was that she had not lived to see the new library take shape, for it took three years to construct the library building which was not dedicated until November, 1905, three years after her death.

Marie Gaston is buried beside her husband John in Mount Moriah, and the two share the same tombstone with the inscription, "A Pioneer Family.''

The lady with the English accent who did so much to convince many of the uneducated miners that a library was worth its weight in gold has not been forgotten. Today, in the Deadwood Carnegie Library hangs a youthful picture of Marie Gaston, depicting a pretty, intelligent-looking blonde with a bouffant hair-do. And on Arbor Day in 1915, memorial trees were planted in her memory on the south side of the library.

> How vainly we struggled to save her,
> Around her how deeply we mourned,
> When back to the Maker who gave it
> Her beautiful spirit returned.

The Deadwood Pioneer-Times, Dec. 2, 1902

Anna Karenina, Adventures of Sherlock Holmes, A Mountain Woman, David Copperfield, Stories of a Western Town, The Luck of Roaring Camp, The Oregon Trail, A Summary of Greek Civilization. "Catalogue of the Public Library,'' Deadwood, SD, Incorporated 1895

The second annual ball of the Deadwood Public Library was given at the City Hall last night and over 150 of Deadwood's best people were in attendance. **Deadwood Pioneer-Times,** Nov. 23, 1897

PATRICK CASEY
SPECTACULAR SUICIDE

Patrick Casey was one of the many suicides in Deadwood's first quarter century. Venerable historian John McClintock, who totted up 97 murders and suicides in Deadwood's first three years, lists Casey's suicide in 1890; however, it did not occur until May, 1897, according to the **Black Hills Daily Times** and the date of death on Casey's tombstone. Such are the contradictions of Deadwood's history.

At any rate, Patrick Casey died by his own hand in the capricious gold camp where the wheels of fortune spun crazily, the dice were often loaded, and life itself was a gamble. Casey was an Irish immigrant who had been at every gold camp in the west and was reputed to have won and lost several fortunes. He came to Deadwood at the height of the gold rush in 1876, continued prospecting, and opened up a saloon.

"Ended his Woes" is the headline over the long front-page story in **The Times** about Casey's spectacular suicide in his saloon on the corner of Main and Lee streets. Casey invited Colorado Charley Steinmetz and another friend to have a drink with him, reached under the counter, pulled out a revolver, announcing, "Good-bye, boys, I am going to kill myself!" Then he fired a shot into his left breast, saying, "That didn't hurt a bit." By this time, the two friends had recovered from their astonishment and tried to grab the revolver from Casey, imploring him not to kill himself. In a flash, Casey pushed the gun muzzle into Colorado Charley's face, yelling, "Get out or I'll kill you!"

Casey fired the gun into his chest again, managed to throw the revolver

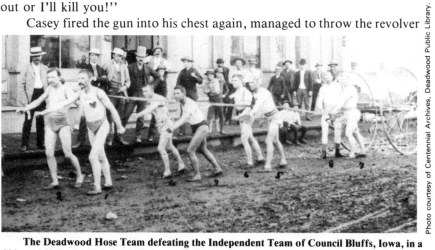

Photo courtesy of Centennial Archives, Deadwood Public Library.

The Deadwood Hose Team defeating the Independent Team of Council Bluffs, Iowa, in a 300-yard Hub and Hub Hose Race in Deadwood. Pat Casey often acted as judge for races between hose teams when not in his saloon where many brawls, as well as his own suicide, took place.

on the counter, staggered from behind the bar and fell to the floor, blood gushing from his body.

Attracted by the shots, a large crowd gathered including Dr. Morris Rogers, who summoned another doctor, but the two doctors could do

nothing to save Casey. Quickly, friends brought Casey's wife Lillian to her fallen husband. **The Times** reported: "The scene which followed was heart-rending and those who witnessed it will not care to behold it again. Agonized by grief, the unfortunate woman threw herself prostrate upon the body of her dead husband, and in the most endearing terms called him to come back to her again. With much difficulty Mrs. Casey was removed and subsequently taken in charge by friends who took her home." Crowds gathered to stare at the bloody corpse until the coroner came and removed it.

Why did Casey commit suicide? A dozen years before Casey had shot a man named Dorrity who had tried to burn his saloon. In the subsequent murder trial, Casey was acquitted on a technicality, but the murder weighed on his mind; and as the years passed, he became increasingly irritable and depressed. On the day of his death, he was rumored to have had a misunderstanding with his wife who had heard gossip concerning his interest in a "soiled dove" or "demi-monde," as the newspapers variously called the prostitutes.

Casey left a suicide note, found under the counter at the bar, saying he had no money, nor home, nor friends, nor religion, and that he was not afraid of heaven or hell. He requested no funeral and asked that his body be given to Dr. Rogers for scientific purposes.

His anguished wife did not respect his wishes because she had a funeral for him at their home conducted under the direction of the Society of Black Hills Pioneers of which Casey was a member. His body was not given to Dr. Rogers.

Like it or not, Patrick Casey is buried under a handsome granite marker in the top section of Mount Moriah nearest the overlook where many prominent people are resting in peace.

Lillian Casey lived 40 more years, eventually remarried. She died in 1937 and is buried beside her first husband, Patrick. A large lilac bush flourishes inside the Casey lot, enclosed by a wrought iron fence.

Contemplating Casey's grave and his life, one wonders if his spirit found heaven or hell, or had he already experienced the two extremes in his half century on earth?

The largest nugget yet unearthed from Whitewood No. 90, Cape Horn, was taken from Pat Casey's bar. It weighs 36½ pennyweights. **Black Hills Daily Times,** Oct. 8, 1877

Although quite well off at different times, Casey died a poor man, in which respect he did not differ from many others who have followed life in the mining camps. **Black Hills Daily Times,** May 6, 1897

Rather a serious fracas occurred in Pat Casey's saloon last evening. Four of the 'regulars' were at the bar when a stranger came in, quite intoxicated, 'rung in,' words ensued. Two of the men started slapping each other. At this Casey jumped over the bar in an attempt to separate them. Witnesses said Casey kicked Sparks, one of the pugilists. A bystander stepped up with an iron poker and dealt Sparks a hard blow on the head which dazed him. Sparks was taken to doctor by friends and had only a slight scalp wound. **Black Hills Daily Times,** April, 1893

GRANVILLE G. BENNETT
FIRST FEDERAL JUDGE

"Father was over six feet tall with black hair and mustache, dignified and a little stern of aspect, the handsomest man who ever lived," wrote Estelline Bennett about Granville G. Bennett, the first federally appointed judge of the Territorial District Court in the Black Hills.

Judge Bennett was undoubtedly a handsome and popular man, although probably not always as honorably just as his adoring daughter Estelline depicts him in **Old Deadwood Days,** a delightful book dedicated to his memory, which provides a vivid picture of the stage-coach era in Deadwood in the late 19th century.

Born in Ohio, Granville Bennett continued to move westward: to Illinois; to Iowa where he served in the territorial legislature; then to Vermillion, Dakota Territory, where he was appointed to a federal judgeship. He came to the Black Hills, reports his daughter, "with the love of new land in his heart and the authority of the United States Government in his hands," a Black Hills Pioneer of 1877.

Judge Bennett held his first term of federal court in Spring Valley at a cluster of cabins called Sheridan, about 40 miles south of Deadwood, now a drowned hamlet at the bottom of man-made Sheridan Lake.

This first courtroom in the Black Hills was a one-room log cabin with a dirt floor, mud roof, and crude cut-outs for doors and windows. There were no accommodations for the judge, lawyers, jury, marshal, the accused law-breakers, and spectators who had arrived by stage-coach or horseback over the rough mountain trails. Visitors to Sheridan had to camp out or sleep on the dirt floor of primitive cabins—even a judge.

The first cases tried involved robbers, horse thieves, road agents, violators of internal revenue laws. Estelline Bennett tells the story of her father's first day in court when a man convicted of robbery was placed in the custody of a United States marshal; that night both marshal and prisoner, unhandcuffed, lay down together and went to sleep on the dirt floor. In the morning the prisoner was gone, having dug a hole under the bottom log of the cabin wall and escaped.

Holding court at Sheridan must have been a trial, and Judge Bennett quickly moved his court to rowdy Deadwood which, by comparison,

An innocent-looking piece of paper recalls a famous trial in Deadwood. This warrant was issued for witness fees in a case celebrated in the annals of the Black Hills courts as being the first murder trial tried in the Hills. The case was tried at the June term, 1877, of the district court. Honorable Granville G. Bennett, Judge, and Seth Bullock was sheriff. **Black Hills Weekly Times,** Feb. 9, 1895

The school board held a meeting about erecting a school house in Deadwood in Judge Granville Bennett's office. There seems to be a lack of healthy sentiment among our people in school matters which augers bad for the education of the future eminent Black Hillers. **Black Hills Daily Times,** Sept. 21, 1877

seemed more civilized; and most cabins had wooden floors.

The first courtroom in Deadwood was held in the upstairs rooms of the Bonanza, a saloon on Lee Street. **The Black Hills Daily Times,** in October, 1877, commented on the advantages and suitability of the location, concluding: "The appearance of faro, nutshell, and vingtum tables was a little incongruous at first, but the novelty soon wore away and the court settled down to legitimate business by swearing in the bailiffs."

Judge Bennett had many challenges to meet besides trying to sit in authoritative comfort on the hard wooden bench and administer justice; although the government had legalized white settlements in the Black Hills in February, 1877, many renegades continued to fight the power of judicial government, of lawmen like Sheriff Seth Bullock, of law and order and other threats of the spread of civilization. In addition to the routine crimes of murder and robbery there were many lawsuits between claim jumpers and among the newly-formed mining companies, a tangle of conflicts over mineral and water rights with no guiding precedents.

How the Black Hillers loved the new judge when he ruled in the fall of 1877 that the Laramie Treaty of 1868 did not actually prohibit white men from prospecting and from acquiring property in the sacred Paha Sapa of the Sioux Indians. Although his amazing decision was unaninously over-ruled the next year by the supreme court, Judge Bennett was promptly enshrined forever in the hearts of the Black Hillers. Of course, everyone knew the whites had a right to wrest the Black Hills from the Sioux—treaty or no treaty.

Quickly, Judge Bennett had made many friends but he apparently had also made enemies, for according to the **Black Hills Daily Times** of October, 1877, he was accused of "arbitrariness, ignorance of mining laws, refusal to issue subpoenas in the interest of prisoners unless costs were previously paid, allowing parties interested in civil cases to approach him outside of the courtroom, and general corruptness." However, Judge Bennett was later exonerated of all charges which his loyal daughter never mentions in her book.

Judge Bennett presided for a year over the territorial court held in a Deadwood saloon. During this judgeship, his daughter reported that he was against capital punishment and would have quit being a judge if he had to send a man to the gallows; that he believed a child belonged with its mother, no matter how depraved she might be; and finally, that "the laws he was sworn by his profession to uphold were as sacred to him as the Ten Commandments."

After a year of being the honorable judge in the fiesty environment of the frontier, he decided to run for Congress as a representative from the Black Hills. There was nothing that he ever wanted more in his life than to be elected Congressman, confided Estelline. With strong support from the mining communities whose interests he shared, the judge was easily elected to Congress.

Estelline did not comment on the family's life with Congressman Bennett for one term in Washington except she concluded that the family acquired "a little smattering of knowledge about a world outside a gold camp." Back in Deadwood Bennett sported a high silk hat until several old-timers told him that his wearing a fancy hat threatened all the traditions of the West. He never wore it again.

Granville Bennett, always called "Judge," settled down in Deadwood to become the silver-tongued barrister of the Deadwood bar, which was

Photo courtesy of Centennial Archives, Deadwood Public Library.

A galaxy of Deadwood's early-day lawyers, Judge Granville Bennett is seated in front row with arms crossed. Next is W. H. Bonham, publisher of the *Deadwood Pioneer-Times* who wrote in 1914: "The Deadwood Bar was made up of the best legal talent from the mining states and territories of the west and were surpassed by none . . . I believed they were the truly great of the earth and I have never been disillusioned."

famous throughout the west for its sparkling legal ability and brilliant oratory. At one time, in the early 1900's, there were at least 80 lawyers practicing in Deadwood with apparently enough legal business to support all of them, mainly because of the endless conflicts over mining interests.

The Bennett family—Judge and Mrs. Bennett with two girls, Estelline and Halle, two sons, and Mrs. Bennett's brother, General A.R.Z. Dawson —lived a comfortable and satisfying life in an attractive house with a mansard roof which is still there on Williams Street.

Here, observant Estelline stored up images, impressions, and facts for the book she later wrote. She and her diarist friend Irene Cushman, along with other respectable young people, all dying of curiosity, promenaded on lofty Williams Street overlooking main street to wonder at the goings-on in

Judge Bennett called the grand jury before him this morning and gave a strong solid charge. He said society was becoming terribly demoralized and something must be done to check the lawlessness in the Hills. We coincide with the Judge that things are altogether too wild in the gulch. **Black Hills Daily Times,** April 29, 1878

A most enjoyable, successful social was given by the Congregational Society at the cheerful home of Judge and Mrs. G. G. Bennett on Williams Street, the commodious parlors were filled to the utmost with musical people. Piano duets, male quartettes, piano solos were performed. After the program was rendered a lunch was served that was faultless in quality and was enjoyed by all. The entertainment was a gratifying success. **Black Hills Daily Times,** March 23, 1895

Father and Seth Bullock went through a great deal together, and it was no idle compliment that a railroad official in laters years paid them when he said: "It was the Bennetts and the Bullocks that brought law and order to the Black Hills." **Old Deadwood Days,** Bennett

the forbidden "Bad Lands," especially when the band played from the balcony of the notorious Gem Theater, whose windows gleamed upward "like the eyes of hell."

The Bad Lands and Chinatown were fascinating, but off limits to the daughter of a judge. During the years Judge Bennett practiced law in Deadwood, he was the unofficial counsel for the Chinese and was determined to see to it that the Chinese received a fair trial when they were arrested for selling opium. The Bennett family received many lovely Oriental gifts at Christmas, including embroidered shawls, decorative teapots, scarlet chopsticks. Both Estelline and her friend Irene Cushman helped teach English to the Chinese who attended night school at the Congregational Church.

Conversation flourished at the Bennett dinner table where Judge Bennett and General Dawson dominated the discussions. "They probably didn't tell us everything," Estelline suspected, but the two men talked about the coming of the railroads, politics, gamblings, and the intense rivalry between East River and West River with the Missouri River dividing the state into warring camps.

With a passion for books, Judge Bennett had the largest library in Deadwood. He was particularly fond of history, biography, poetry, thinking fiction too frivolous. The Bennetts were a musical family, and the Judge played his guitar and sang Irish songs with Estelline accompanying him on the piano.

Judge Bennett supported women's suffrage; he led the drive to build the first school in Deadwood; he was the first president of the Society of Black Hills Pioneers of 1877; he was a leader for all worthy causes. But his greatest contribution to Deadwood was his daughter Estelline.

Estelline Bennett's book presents a colorful picture in **Old Deadwood Days,** when "Of all the mining camps of the frontier, Deadwood flared highest and brightest." This talented author takes the reader along for a stage-coach ride and for a ringside seat in December, 1890, when the first railroad "strained and thundered triumphantly up the grade into a shouting tumult that frightened a grizzly bear in his winter quarters at Ragged Top, reverberated up and down the gulch and around the head of Terry's Peak." But the arrival of the train ended the stage-coach era that had made Deadwood famous, and everybody sensed it and felt sad because the last stage-coach had left Deadwood the day before, never to return.

Judge Granville Bennett, who died in 1910 at age 77, Mrs. Bennett,

Granville G. Bennett, judge of the county court, and the Deadwood Board of Education yesterday deeded to the Deadwood Cemetery Association a strip of ground 60 feet wide along the east side of the cemetery. This is to be utilized as the county burial ground for the burial of paupers. **Black Hills Daily Times,** April 13, 1895

Honorable Granville Bennett accepted an invitation to deliver his entertaining and instructive lecture, "Books and Reading," for the benefit of the Congregational church on Thursday evening. **Black Hills Times,** Nov. 7, 1877

their son Robert, who drowned as a boy, are all buried under imposing tombstones near the Masonic Circle in Mount Moriah.

Estelline, who never married, is buried in Chicago, where she had been employed as society editor for newspapers. When she died in January, 1948, the **Rapid City Journal** and the Deadwood press wrote proudly about "the hometown girl who had made good" and whose book was hailed as a classic of western literature.

Yes, Judge Bennett undoubtedly helped balance the scales of justice and fostered both culture and education in Deadwood Gulch, but it was his daughter Estelline who explained Deadwood to the world.

Yes, we have enjoyed living in the historic Bennett house for 35 years. It's been remodeled several times. We removed the old cat-walk which ran from Estelline's bedroom to the hillside. That's where she used to sit outside and read. A surprising number of strangers who have read **Old Deadwood Days** have appeared at the door, asking permission to tour the house. Recollection of Mr. and Mrs. Don Fletcher, long-time residents of Deadwood.

In the early days of the Black Hills there were many true and good women who came with their husbands and families, some hoping to have a share in the carving of a new country and all with the true pioneer spirit . . . Mrs. Granville Bennett was another whose life had its influence for good upon those with whom she came in contact. The writer knew her from childhood and respected and loved her. Too many articles have been written about such women as Calamity Jane and Poker Alice. "Tales of the Hills," Alice Gossage, **Rapid City Journal,** April 24, 1928

Bennett was affable, an interesting conversationalist, an excellent speaker, his charming but unpretentious home was full of books, magazines, pictures, and musical instruments. It was a home of refinement and culture. **The Memorial Biographical Record for the Black Hills.**

Down that road and past the schoolhouse, I remember, there used to come funeral processions on their way to Mount Moriah, the cemetery on the hill, when a miner had been killed in the up-gulch mines, and with a dramatic fitness that impressed us as we stood on the schoolhouse steps and watched and listened, the brass band always played, "Flee as a Bird to the Mountain." The lilt of the melody and the high waiting mountain with its crooning pines seemed to take away all the sting of death. **Old Deadwood Days,** Bennett

COLONEL JOHN LAWRENCE
FIRST COUNTY TREASURER

Photo courtesy of Centennial Archives, Deadwood Public Library.

Col. John Lawrence, the man for whom Lawrence County was named, died in 1890. His grave was moved in 1897. In 1913 it was decorated for Memorial Day. In 1979 the grave of John Lawrence cannot be located. If anyone should find it, please notify the cemetery sexton.

Col. John Lawrence, the man for whom Lawrence County was named by Governor John Pennington, was the first county treasurer. A former member of both houses of the Dakota Territorial legislature and a Deputy U.S. Marshal of Dakota Territory for 12 years, he was a well-known political figure, having lived at both Yankton and Sioux Falls, the civilized cities of eastern Dakota. Lawrence had survived a fire on the steamer "Corral" which had burned on the Missouri River.

Col. Lawrence arrived in the Black Hills on April 26, 1877, to take over his appointment as County Treasurer. According to the **Black Hills Daily Times,** he came by stage-coach via Fort Pierre; he stopped first at Crook City (now disappeared), believing that city had won the heated contest for the county seat, unaware that Deadwood, the wildest and largest settlement in the Hills, had captured the honor despite its reputation for lawlessness.

A handsome bachelor, known as a ladies' man, he was often mentioned in the frank early newspapers—sometimes in a complimentary way, sometimes not. In 1877, the **Times** wrote that "the position Lawrence held was a credit to himself and the county that bears his name; later in 1880, the **Times** complained that "it is anything but complimentary to the citizens of several Hills towns to have it said that the Colonel (?) is manipulating caucuses and engineering their politics." After serving as an appointed treasurer for one year, he failed to win the election when he ran for the treasurer's office.

An affluent leader in government contracts and in mining deals, Lawrence often suffered from poor health, including rheumatism and an ailment called dropsy. His ailments and activities were frequently mentioned in the newspapers whose content was often highly personal and picturesque. In 1880, the **Times** wrote: "Col. John Lawrence was seen by a Deadwoodite in Lead City, and the Colonel looked as though his chimney smoked or he had been in a battle and had no time to recuperate."

Finally, in the old Wentworth Hotel, at age 52, Lawrence died an agonizing death from "liver and heart disease," on April 26, 1890, 12 years to the day from the time he had arrived to become the first county treasurer. His obituary, like most obituaries was kind: "The colonel was a generous and whole-souled man, and was always prominent in charitable deeds, of a generous and liberal character."

His death is recorded in the Record Book with a section and a lot number; there is also a notation that his grave was moved in March, 1897, to a new location and lot number, but where it is, no one knows. In 1913, the location of Lawrence's grave was known because a news item states that his grave was decorated for Memorial Day, along with those of Wild Bill Hickok and Preacher Smith.

A large map of Mount Moriah, drawn in 1895, identifies many sections and innumerable numbered lots—but few names—and the map does not accurately represent the cemetery as it is today. However, by combining the information in the Record Book with the map drawings, this researcher

Photo courtesy of Al Gunther.

An old marker still standing and legible even though Judge Henry Hill died 22 years before Col. Lawrence. Hill's death is recorded on pp. 144-145 of the Record Book. Listed as the cause of death was "softening of the brain," certified by a physician.

assumes that Col. Lawrence's grave should be in the section across the road to the north of where George Ayres is buried and west of the rest rooms.

In this section, surrounded by roads, there is a large lot enclosed in a wrought-iron fence with no identifying marker; could this grave be that of John Lawrence? Perhaps no permanent marker was ever placed on his grave. Or is it possible that a stone marker may have been carried off by vandals?

The Times, in the obituary, reported that Lawrence's nephew from Omaha was completely worn out from the constant vigil at his uncle's bedside. The nephew said that Lawrence "repeatedly made the request that in the event of his death, he be buried wrapped in the American flag and in the

Photo courtesy of Al Gunther.

One of the partially buried stone markers beside the main thoroughfare in Mount Moriah. As the "City of the Dead" grew in population, wider streets and more cross-roads became necessary. Many lost graves are rumored to be covered by the gravel and debris of road construction. Could this misfortune have befallen the grave of John Lawrence?

county which was named after him, which request will be complied with."

Undoubtedly, Colonel John Lawrence, peaceful and unaware, and wrapped in the Stars and Stripes is lying somewhere in Mount Moriah, Lawrence County, in the Black Hills of South Dakota.

Treasurer Lawrence is appealing to the taxpayers to step up to the Colonel's office from the post office and settle up—or else. **Black Hills Daily Times,** Nov. 12, 1877

Rumors were put in circulation some time since by either designing persons or busy bodies, to the effect that the accounts of our former County Treasurer, John Lawrence, were in bad shape, and that he was defaulted to a considerable extent was also whispered. Recently the gentleman has been confined to his bed, suffering from bronchitis, which deterred him from carrying on an examination of his accounts by the proper persons . . . A certificate published yesterday from the County Board of Commissioners and over their signature, puts this matter to rest and fully exonerates the gentleman. **Black Hills Daily Times,** Jan. 16, 1878

Lawrence County was organized in April 1877, but the destruction of the records by fire in 1879, makes it impossible to give the exact date as the recollection of the earliest settlers do not always agree. **Andreas Historical Atlas** of Dakota, 1884

GENERAL A. R. Z. DAWSON
FIRST COLLECTOR OF
INTERNAL REVENUE

Andrew R. Z. Dawson has the distinction of having two tombstones in Mount Moriah, and nobody knows which one he is buried under. Another of his many distinctions is that he was the adored uncle of Estelline Bennett, author of **Old Deadwood Days,** whose book provides many insights into his character and charismatic personality.

A Black Hills Pioneer of 1876, General Dawson, as he was known,

GEN A.R.Z. DAWSON

BORN MAY 10, 1835
DIED JULY 19, 1896

ANDREW R. Z. DAWSON

COLONEL
187ᵗ REGT
OHIO INF.

MAY 10 1835
JULY 19 1896

came to Deadwood Gulch in its first wild year as—of all things—a Deputy Revenue Collector for the United States government in the Black Hills, which until February, 1877, was the legal domain of the Sioux Indians. During all of 1876, the white settlers were trespassers, but they soon learned that no matter where they lived, death and taxes were inevitable.

Despite holding a traditionally unpopular appointment, the General, an educated and cultured man, was an extremely popular person, making friends easily with the miners and exerting leadership in helping to civilize the gold camp.

The long-bearded General was a brother of Mrs. Granville Bennett, and after the arrival of Judge G. G. Bennett in 1877, he lived with the Bennett family until he eventually married. In his niece Estelline's book, he is listed in the cast of characters as "my avuncular guide." He is also mentioned affectionately in Irene Cushman's diary; the two girls were best friends and shared many of the same experiences and companions.

Through the various stages of her growing-up, Estelline was fortunate to have such an understanding and knowledgeable guide as the General. He took her by the hand and walked her up and down the hills and the wooden stairways connecting the terraced streets to check out the town: to see the stage-coach come dashing down the hill or to watch the colorful Indian parade led by Chief Red Cloud.

Her uncle also explained to her in baffling Victorian terms why "nice people" should never go inside the fascinating Gem Theater where the gaudy girls beckoned to male passers-by. A big event was the day the General introduced her to his friend Calamity Jane and her stepdaughter; at dinner that night he and Judge Bennett held one of their revealing discussions, this time about the merits and demerits of the controversial Calamity.

In the General's room at the Bennetts, his Civil War sword hung on the wall. He had served in the Ohio Infantry during the Civil War, receiving many commendations for his bravery and leadership. Although his permanent rank was that of colonel, he was breveted a Brigadier General, and as was customary, was always addressed by the higher rank.

His miltary service in the Civil War and his experiences in the days of '76 were the highlights of his life, and how he loved to reminisce about those exciting years.

The General played a key role in the first Fourth of July celebration in Deadwood, 1876, that Centennial year when the disorderly inhabitants called a truce on lawlessness for one entire day to honor the nation's 100th birthday. First, they cut down the tallest pine tree for a liberty pole to fly Old Glory, which was created from unmentionables contributed by patriotic ladies. The crew, by pulling on the attached ropes, erected the flag pole

We cannot but regret the defeat of General Dawson which was not owing to his unpopularity but to combinations and trades on the day of election. His personal and political popularity today is as great as it was on the day he was "downed" by the tricks of local politicians and liars. "Fifty Years Ago," **Deadwood Pioneer-Times**, Nov. 4, 1930

Photo courtesy of Centennial Archives, Deadwood Public Library.

Fourth of July celebration in Deadwood before 1887 with what could be a Chinese banner in front. Stars and Stripes visible. At the first Glorious Fourth in 1876, General A. R. Z. Dawson, a powerful orator, read his "Memorial to Congress" requesting the United States government "to extend a protecting arm and take us under its care." All the trespassers signed the petition and spent the day anvil-firing, shooting 300 guns, building bonfires, singing patriotic songs, and listening to speeches.

on main street in front of the speaker's platform, decorated with evergreen boughs. The public-spirited throng, although expatriates from the United States, sang patriotic songs, fired 300 guns in salute, and listened to orations.

Reputed to be an eloquent speaker with an inimitable style, Dawson read the entire Declaration of Independence to the outdoor audience of many nationalities, his powerful voice ringing out grandly on the balmy mountain air: "When in the course of human events—"

Another highlight of the celebration also starred General Dawson. To the packed crowd on main street, estimated to be in the thousands, he read the document he had drafted, entitled "A Memorial to the Congress of the

On the Centennial Fourth with the rising of the sun there was mingled with the heavy reports a continuous cracking of musketry through the town and the gulch, almost every cabin wreathed in rifle smoke. **The Black Hills Pioneer,** July 8, 1876

United States" which "respectfully petitions for speedy and prompt action in extinguishing Indian title to, and the opening for settlement of, the country we are now occupying and improving." Further, the petition entreated "that the government for which we have offered our lives at once extend a protecting arm and take us under its care."

There was no trouble getting signers for that petition.

During his 20 years in Deadwood, the General, who became the first Clerk of Courts in the Black Hills and the third president of the Society of Black Hills Pioneers, was most sympathetic to the problems of the diverse group of people congregated in Deadwood. He had a reputation for being helpful and wise in matters large and small.

The beloved General Dawson died of tuberculosis in June, 1896, at age 60. According to three Deadwood newspapers, his funeral was the largest ever held up to that time: 150 Black Hills Pioneers of '76 marched at the head of the long funeral procession, followed by area members of the Grand Army of the Republic, then came 75 buggies, and additional mourners on foot. At Mount Moriah, a male quartet sang, "Rest, Soldier, Rest"; and while taps were played, hundreds of people wept at this farewell for a not-so-old soldier and an unforgettable pioneer of '76.

Dawson was buried a few feet south of the graves of other Civil War

Photo courtesy of Al Gunther.

The wooden cross marking the area where nine Civil War veterans are buried. The simple stone of Col. A. R. Z. Dawson is down the slope to the left and set apart from the graves of the other soldiers.

veterans, an area which now includes nine graves and is marked by a large wooden cross. His small white marker, similar to the other Civil War markers, identifies him as a colonel in the 187th Ohio Infantry.

Some time after his death, as several of Deadwood's oldest residents recall, his wife Elizabeth and the Bennett family decided he deserved a more imposing marker and erected a large granite tombstone near the Masonic Circle. This engraving labels him as "General." Whether or not his body was moved to the new site is unknown. As the years passed, his wife Elizabeth, his brother-in-law Judge Bennett, his nephew Robert, and his sister Mary were, one by one, buried in this lot.

Perhaps it doesn't matter which gravesite he is buried in or which military rank identifies him, for his life on earth is what counted. Summing up his influence, Annie Tallent, in her history of the Black Hills, wrote: "General A.R.Z. Dawson, the memory of whose name causes the heart of every old pioneer to thrill with intense pride . . . and his taking away was a sad blow to the people whose staunch friend he ever proved."

General Dawson, on Williams Street, has about completed one of the coziest-looking cottages in the city. Several others on Williams are nearly completed and will soon make a better appearance than before the fire. **Black Hills Daily Times,** April 23, 1880

General Dawson returned from Hot Springs where he had gone for rheumatism. He left it all at the springs except for a slight memory in his right hand. **Black Hills Daily Times,** May, 1890

SUSAN CLARKE-WELLING
WALKER ON THE CHEYENNE—
DEADWOOD TRAIL

Susan Clarke-Welling walked 260 miles from Cheyenne and Fort Laramie to Custer City on the Cheyenne-Deadwood trail, "and I used to start out with the wagon but I never fell back more than half the length of

the wagon train in the 16 days it took us to reach the Black Hills," she recalled in an interview for the June 17, 1938 **Black Hills Weekly.** The interview took place 62 years after this pioneer of 1876 had made it to Custer City, the first settlement in the Black Hills, walking beside the long, heavily-loaded wagon train which was protected from Indian attacks by an armed escort of 500 men on horseback.

Her first husband, George Clarke, brought in a load of groceries and supplies to use in the locksmith business. He had also packed his two favorite books, Mark Twain's **Innocents Abroad** and Cervantes' **Don Quixote.** Susan brought some heavy sad irons for which the freight charge was $.15 a pound. The irons were a scarce item which most pilgrims didn't bring. When Susan lived in Custer City, she recalled that the irons never had a chance to cool off because she continually rented them out for specks of gold dust.

Susan and her husband lived in a log cabin at Custer City that had been General Custer's quartermaster house during the Custer Expedition of 1874. When the first stage-coach came in a few months later bringing mail and passengers, Susan and another young woman tossed their handkerchiefs in the air "with mad excitement" during the hullabaloo when the isolated pioneers greeted the first stage.

In Custer City in December, 1876, there were only about five respectable women. To celebrate Christmas these five and their husbands attended a dinner at the nicest hotel. When some of the couples began waltzing, Mrs. Clarke took her baby and left because "I wasn't going to stay where there was dancing."

After her first husband, George Clarke, died, Susan married John Welling. He also died, leaving her a widow for the second time. During her declining years she lived with her daughter's family in Deadwood.

Then on January 30, 1940, "a final summons came to Susan Clarke-Welling" at the home of her daughter in Deadwood, wrote the **Deadwood Pioneer-Times.** Susan was 84 years old when she died, a typical pioneer woman who had braved many dangers to walk to the Hills of Gold. She was

---

Fort Laramie, estimated about 92 miles north of Cheyenne, was perhaps the most important station on the Cheyenne and Deadwood route, because at the time the through stage line was inaugurated it was the base of military operations against the Sioux in their last stand against the white man's invasion of the Indian country . . . When the gold rush began in the mid-seventies, Fort Laramie was the 'jumping off' place for the vast, unsettled country to the north of the Platte. It became a focal point for prospectors. **The Cheyenne and Black Hills Stage and Express Routes,** Spring

O you daughters of the West!
O you young and elder daughters! O you mothers and you wives!
Never must you be divided, in our ranks you move united,
Pioneers! O Pioneers!
"Pioneers! O Pioneers!", Whitman

a loyal member of the Society of Black Hills Pioneers, having served as a director of that society for Lawrence County.

"She had thousands of friends throughout the west," her obituary concluded, "and if there be another world in which charity is a virtue, in which fidelity is loved and justice honored, then all is well today with Susan Clarke-Welling."

Today, many people walk beside the roadside grave of this legendary walker who now rests in Mount Moriah near the main entrance road.

JOHN GRAY
MANAGER OF WASP NO. 2 MINE

John (Jack) Gray was one pioneer of '76 who actually struck it rich in the Hills of Gold. Handsome Jack with the walrus mustache was also a big-time gambler, and the story goes that one morning after a poker party he was surprised to find the deed to a saloon among his prize-winnings. However, at one point in capricious Jack's career the banks had a rule not to cash any of his checks for more than $100.

A Cornish Englishman with a heritage of mining, Jack prospected for gold in South America, Idaho, and Wyoming before he romped into Deadwood Gulch with the Wild Bill Hickok-Colorado Charlie Utter wagon train from Cheyenne. Unlike Wild Bill, Jack didn't gamble day and night, but immediately set to work prospecting and was one of the first to profitably work a placer claim in Deadwood Gulch.

Photo courtesy of Centennial Archives, Deadwood Public Library.

Placer mining in Black Tail Gulch with an entire family involved in the work. 1908. Jack Gray (not shown) was one of the first to successfully work a placer mine in Deadwood Gulch.

Jack and his wife Mary Ellen settled in Terraville, then as now, an incredible hamlet perched precariously on a mountaintop between Central City and Lead. Here, the Grays managed the Caledonia boarding house for a time. Jack was the fifth president of the Society of Black Hills Pioneers, and his wife designed and sewed an elegant and treasured banner used for many years by the Society.

Despite Jack Gray's being a bon vivant and a gambler—or maybe because of it—he became one of the most successful gold mine operators in the entire west. His partner, banker Robert H. Driscoll, called him a "McKinley sound-money Republican." Against the advice of mining experts, Gray decided to process low-grade gold ore; and with the new cyanide process which enabled him to handle the quartzite cheaply, he created what was known as a miracle mine, the Wasp No. 2. It continued for years to turn out a profit of from $5,000 to $15,000 a month to the small coterie of stockholders; and for a $15,000 investment, Driscoll from 1901-1920, collected $350,000 in dividends.

Showman Jack, whose life was one of constant action, liked to hitch up a matched team of bays to his yellow-wheeled buggy and prance down the dirt road carrying the bullion from the Wasp No. 2 to the Deadwood bank. One time when the horses ran away, to save his neck Jack had to jump out; and by the time he caught the runaways and the buggy, two bars of bullion were missing, worth $40,000 apiece. Jack rounded up a search party which soon found the bars glittering under a wild strawberry patch.

This man with the Midas touch died in 1915 from a combination of injuries caused from being kicked by a horse and a fall into the open cut of Wasp No. 2. Today, all that remains of this lucrative mine near Yellow

Photo courtesy of Centennial Archives, Deadwood Public Library.

The Open Cut of Wasp No. 2, a money-making mine. Manager Jack Gray fell into the Open Cut. He sustained injuries which contributed to his untimely death. For many years the huge piles of sandy tailings from Wasp No. 2 have been used for grading county roads and railroad beds.

Creek road a few miles from Lead is a tailings pile and some crumbling foundations.

No flowers blooming in the winter on the Gray tomb. John Gray left $1,000 for perpetual care of his grave beside Jerusalem Road in Mount Moriah.

In Mount Moriah there is an attractive lot, adorned with large urns and enclosed by a wrought-iron fence. Bordering on the left of Jerusalem road, the cemented-over tomb looks as though it should have affluent occupants —and it does. Here lie Mr. and Mrs. Jack Gray. Two things are sure: Jack enjoyed being the last of the big spenders, and never in this world did he want to be the richest man in the cemetery.

Only those who have lost dear ones by death know the heartaches and sorrow left by the merciless reaper . . . By the death of Mrs. John Gray, this community was robbed of a woman of noble character . . . Her heart-broken husband refuses to be comforted . . . Mr. Gray wishes to extend his heart-felt gratitude to those many kind friends who attended his beloved wife during her fatal illness and administered so tenderly to her comfort. "Where is Thy Victory?" **Deadwood Pioneer-Times,** March 17, 1898

The program has been arranged for Carnival Day. John Gray of Terraville has been chosen as king of the carnival and already the committee has the promise of 20 floats for the parade. **Deadwood Pioneer-Times,** June 29, 1901

Jack Gray, a member of the Black Hills Pioneers, paid Calamity's expenses in Terry and perhaps paid for her funeral—and it could be that other of the Society's members chipped in, too. **Here Comes Calamity Jane,** Klock

RESOLUTION: Be it resolved by the Trustees of the Deadwood Cemetery Association that we accept the trust of the fund of one thousand dollars ($1,000) left by the late John Gray, and that we agree as trustees, and the same shall be binding on our successors to see that the graves of Mr. and Mrs. John Gray have perpetual care in the way of seeing that flowers are planted on the graves each year. Signed, W. E. Adams, President; L. W. Stilwell, Secy. Record Book of the Deadwood Cemetery Association, June 21, 1921

JOHN BAGGALEY
"SOONER" AND MINE BROKER

Photo courtesy of Centennial Archives, Deadwood Public Library.

John Baggaley, a Black Hills Pioneer in 1877, learned about prospecting in Two-Bit Gulch where every pan of gold was not always worth two bits. This early prospector became a successful mine broker.

John Baggaley, accompanied by his wife Jennie and small daughter May, was a pioneer who set out in 1875 for the Black Hills, before they were officially opened to settlement. These early gold-seekers were often called "Sooners"; some like Annie Tallent and the unauthorized Russell-Collins party reached the New Eldorado before they were banished; others, like John Baggaley and his family who got as far as Fort Pierre, were turned back by government troops. The military had a busy time enforcing the Laramie Treaty after the Custer Expedition's gold discoveries of 1874 had been widely publicized.

Disheartened, the Baggaleys, who had started out from Galesberg, Ill., back-tracked as far as Iowa to wait for the inevitable opening of the golden gates. By the latter part of 1876, the horde of prospectors pouring in on the trails from Fort Pierre; Cheyenne, Wyo.; Sidney, Neb.; and Bismarck, D.T. were too many for the army to handle and for the vacillating United States government to legislate against. Thus, in February, 1877, the sacred Paha Sapa of the Sioux were officially opened to settlement. And everyone rejoiced—except the Indians.

Early in 1877, on their second try, John Baggaley and his family made it all the way to the Black Hills by wagon train. They built a cabin in scenic Two-Bit Gulch near Deadwood where they could often hear the uproar

from the wildest gold camp in the Hills. Here in this lovely valley, John Baggaley, whose background was farming, began learning how to mine and to prospect for gold.

One story about how Two-Bit acquired its name was that a miner panned two bits worth of gold every time he worked the creek. Another version was that the panner lost two bits every time he tried to coax some yellow flakes to stick to the bottom of his pan.

At any rate, John Baggaley was not able to accumulate as many quarters and dollars as he would have liked. His son George was born while the Baggaleys lived at Two-Bit. Eventually, John decided to give up haphazard prospecting, move to Deadwood, and go into a more stable business.

John started a curio shop where he sold Indian artifacts and unusual mineral specimens. Later he sold insurance and real estate, then became a mine broker. He continued to invest in mining properties, particularly the Golden Crest at Two-Bit and the Iron Hill Mining Company, a silver mine at Carbonate Camp near the rim of Spearfish Canyon.

John Baggaley II, a third-generation Baggaley, now a retired banker in Deadwood recalled that his bearded grandfather was a formal and reserved man who always wore a stiff collar, coat, tie, and spats—even when on a picnic or while working in the yard. A charter member of the First Baptist Church, he was deeply religious and did not believe in playing cards or dancing; of course he hated the gambling and prostitution in Deadwood.

A traumatic experience for seven-year-old John II was losing his mother during the flu epidemic of 1918. On the stormy day of his mother's funeral, John and the other children were quarantined with measles and could not attend the sad rites. The road up Lincoln avenue was so icy and slippery that no horse or vehicle could make it up the steep hill to Mount Moriah. Thus, on this blizzardy day, about 30 volunteers took turns carrying the casket of Alice Baggaley up the treacherous hill. Her grave had been dug with much difficulty by grave-diggers using picks and shovels in the

---

John Baggaley has added another rare specimen to his fine mineral cabinet at his office. It is a queer freak of nature or monstrosity in the shape of a fish, about a foot long that has the head and face of a monkey and arms and hands of a frog. He bought it from a Chinaman . . . It is a very curious thing and is well worth inspecting. **Black Hills Weekly,** March 16, 1895

About 75 of the many friends of Mr. and Mrs. John Baggaley gave the estimable couple a surprise party last night, upon the occasion of the 25th anniversary of their wedding. The affair was a complete surprise. The pretty lawn surrounding the house was lighted with Chinese lanterns and was very picturesque. The evening was passed in an enjoyable manner with music and games. **Black Hills Daily Times,** August 10, 1895

John Baggaley dealt in mining stock for years, selling and buying stocks at various mines through the Black Hills. He purchased stock in 1892 in the Good Enough Mining Company . . . In 1893 he purchased Victory stock . . . In 1894 it was Yankee Boy stock . . . serves to prove the point that Baggaley was a financier in the mining game. Mildred Fielder, **Silver is the Fortune,** North Plains Press, 1978, p. 59

frozen ground. It was a terrible day for the Baggaley family.

After his mother died, young John lived with his grandparents for a while. His grandfather said grace before every meal and required his children and grandchildren to attend prayer meetings, Sunday school, and church services. Young John respected and liked his grandfather, although the older John was too preoccupied with business and church work to have much time to get acquainted with his grandchildren.

John II recalled how good-natured Grandmother Jennie was. She was a fabulous cook who served delicious meat, potatoes, and chocolate cake, believing that setting a good table was an important duty for a housewife.

About his handsome father George Baggaley, John II has vivid memories. Like his father, George was also extremely religious. He eventually became a partner with his father in various business enterprises. George had many interests. He owned one of the first automobiles in Deadwood, becoming an expert racer on the gravel roads. In the 1920's he drove a Chandler roadster from Deadwood to Sioux Falls in eight hours; he liked cars so much that he eventually became an automobile dealer himself. A fine athlete, George was a champion bicyclist and tennis player; and according to his son John, "went bananas over golf," often telling hilarious stories about his golf game.

Being a good Baptist was a tradition with the Baggaleys. George played the organ at the Baptist church, donated an electronic organ to the church, and once taught a Chinese Sunday school class. Active in community affairs, he was president of the Chamber of Commerce, of the "Days of '76," and of the Custer Battlefield Highway Commission.

Eventually, George married again. His second wife was the popular kindergarten teacher, Imogene Stevens, who became a wonderful mother to his three children. George and Imogene also had a son. George died in 1950 at age 68.

The log cabin where George Baggaley was born in Two-Bit was eventually brought into Pine Crest park and became a tourist attraction. Ironically, it was not displayed as a cabin of genuine pioneers; instead, it was advertised as the cabin of the fourth man posing as the fictitious Deadwood Dick.

When the patriarch and "sooner" John Baggaley died in 1922 at age 73, he owned a batch of worthless mining certificates. Although he had made a comfortable living, he had never accumulated the fortune he dreamed of from his long-term mining investments.

One of his favorite mines, the Golden Crest, established in 1876, on a divide between Two Bit Creek and Strawberry Gulch, is now a wreck with crumbling timbers, rusty machinery relics, sagging floors, collapsed roofs, and an empty safe. The forlorn ruin is now silent as the tombs at Mount Moriah, where the Baggaley lot is on the left side of Jerusalem road.

No, John Baggaley never got rich, but perhaps what he earned was better than gold. In his obituary, full of praises for his honest business deal-

Photo courtesy of Centennial Archives, Deadwood Public Library.

The Golden Crest or Commonwealth Mine was idle in 1920. Originally known as the Weber mine, it produced gold off and on into the early 1900's. Golden Crest was one of the best preserved of the old mines in the Black Hills until a fire in 1972 destroyed most of the buildings.

ings, **The Deadwood Pioneer-Times** paid him a remarkable tribute: "If the citizens of any town would only live the upright life of our brother John Baggaley, such a place would be an ideal community."

John Baggaley and wife, after a two-month visit east and at the Worlds Fair have returned to the Hills and are now at Hot Springs in attendance at the Baptist Conference. **Black Hills Daily Times,** August 24, 1893

JOHN BAGGALEY AND SON, BROKERS—ESTABLISHED 1886. Some of the leading Black Hills stocks to buy are Spearfish, Potsdam, Oro Hondo, Hidden Fortune, Grantz, Deadwood Standard, Phoenix, Jupiter, University, Pluma, Columbus. Advertisement in **Deadwood Pioneer-Times,** June 5, 1903

Horace Clark, the Mr. Real Estate of Deadwood-Lead, once said to me: 'Your grandfather sold me many mining stocks but the only one that turned out to be any good was the Homestake.' Recollections of John Baggaley, grandson of John Baggaley, Black Hills Pioneer of 1877.

DR. VON WEDELSTAEDT
"WHITE BROTHER" OF
THE CHINESE

"White Brother" was the name the Deadwood Chinese conferred upon Dr. Von Wedelstaedt who helped them organize a Chinese Masonic lodge. The grateful Orientals always asked their White Brother to lead the colorful funeral procession when a Chinese Mason was buried in Mount Moriah. In **Old Deadwood Days,** Estelline Bennett described Dr. Von Wedelstaedt leading the parade: "He had jet black hair and whiskers, and he wore his high silk hat, swung his gold-headed cane, and threw his head and shoulders back, proud of being the only man of his race among the Chinese masons."

In 1877, the Prussian-born physician whose complete name was Henrich Alexander Leopold Von Wedelstaedt came to the Hills to practice medicine and was "family physician to half of Deadwood, and carrying a personal interest in our health, for which he felt entirely responsible, but in our general welfare no less," wrote Judge Bennett's daughter, Estelline.

This German-born doctor who became a naturalized citizen was an example of the cosmopolitan mixture of ethnic backgrounds in early Deadwood. There were Germans, Scandinavians, Finnish, Italians, English, Scots, Irish; some came directly from their homelands; others came from "back East."

Four races were represented in the gold camps: white, yellow, black, and red. Their relationships were often more antagonistic than harmonious. The Chinese people of Deadwood had their own Chinatown in lower Deadwood; and seldom did they welcome white people into their lives and secret societies. Dr. Von Wedelstaedt was an exception.

In addition to being an honorary member of the Chinese Masons and permitted to share the secrets of the Orientals, the doctor was also a member of the Deadwood Masonic order, the Knights Templar.

The gregarious doctor was definitely a joiner; he was a member of the Odd Fellows, Knights of Pythias, and 23 other secret societies. A Jacksonian Democrat, he was a member of the Episcopal church and a firm believer in Sweedborgrandism and was said to have derived much comfort from its mystical teachings.

At the time of his death in March, 1900, the first year of the new century, the **Deadwood Pioneer-Times** called him "a unique physician; he was kind, gentle, and hope inspiring in the sick chamber, but never gave illusive promises. In desperate cases, he would say, 'God only knows—we can only do the best we can.' "

The Pioneer-Times eulogized him both as a doctor and as a liberal, creative thinker, "as true an American as anyone who was born on this soil."

In describing the circumstances of his death, the newspaper reported: "He fell asleep and never woke on the scenes of this world. He went down like a shock of corn, fully ripe, with his work done and well done. Who can mourn such a death? Hail and Farewell!"

The large funeral was in charge of the Deadwood Masons, the Knights Templar, who were present in a body as were the Odd Fellows and the

We had a pleasant call today from Dr. H. Von Wedelstaedt of St. Paul who arrived last evening by Bismarck coach. Dr. has practiced his profession in St. Paul the last 20 years with much success, and wishing a change, proposed locating in this country, whether here or in Central City, he is undecided. **Black Hills Daily Times,** Aug. 17, 1877

Dr. Von Wedelstaedt celebrated again last night one of his numerous birthdays in his cozy little shack on City Creek, in the circle of a few of his numerous lady and gentlemen friends. "Twenty Years Ago Today" **Deadwood Pioneer-Times,** Oct. 17, 1920

Chinese Masons. The crowded Episcopal church was decorated with potted plants while a beautiful display of flowers covered the casket, including carnations, the doctor's favorite. The Chinese Masons brought dozens of roses for their floral offering.

At the request of the family, there was no sermon, only the text from Timothy: "I have fought a good fight, I have finished my course, I have kept the faith."

The doctor's widow was reported to be so prostrated with grief that she was unable to attend the funeral. Only two daughters represented the family. The rest of the eight children, including five sons, were said either to be too ill to attend or too far away to arrive in time for their father's funeral.

The Redman's band, furnished by the Chinese Masons, preceded the hearse and led the procession to Mount Moriah. Masonic leader George V. Ayres conducted the Masonic burial rites at the grave which is located just outside the Masonic circle and lectern.

As the funeral procession moved down the hill from the cemetery, the mourners could look back and see the flag of Chinese Masonry flying over the grave of the only American belonging to its order, and one who had been a member of the American Masonic order for 56 years, the oldest Mason in South Dakota, "one who had gone into the land to which their fathers have gone before them."

Just a few minutes before the Chinese Masons had planted their flag,

Photo courtesy of Al Gunther.

When the "White Brother" was buried, his Chinese friends planted a Chinese Masonic flag beside his grave. Tombstone in Mount Moriah

the swords of the Knights Templars had made the emblem of Christianity over the grave and the Christian ministers had offered prayers. **The Pioneer-Times** concluded that the combined rites of several religions "was symbolic of the broad liberality of Dr. Von Wedelstaedt."

There will be consigned to its home a form and figure which has been familiar on the streets of Deadwood for almost a quarter of a century. He will not only be missed in our public thoroughfares and places of social gatherings but in numerous homes where his professional visits came like ministrations of mercy and helpfulness to those who had almost lost heart and hope. **Deadwood Pioneer-Times,** March 22, 1900

DRAMATIS PERSONAE
When Cold-Deck Johnny
And Jimmy-Behind-the-Deuce
Were dealing Old Man Wadsworth
And Alden Eaton
At Morton's New Club House
For Gents only,
Eyed by W. P. Taylor, U.S. Marshal,
And O'Hara from Spearfish
And Boone May of the Bully Reserve;
While Alabama Jane and Cayuse Laura
Poured and sang to Judge Kukyendall,
Who liked singing and Jane and Laura;

While Swill-Barrel Jimmy
And Coal-Oil Johnny Spencer got underfoot
And died,
And Madame Hayes of the Badlands Boarding House
Bought a lot of Cashmere and Gingham
For eighteen cents a yard;
While Crow Dog was killing Spotted Dog,
Doctor Von Wedelstaedt
Became the only white member
Of the Chinese Masonic Lodge.
The Hills Aren't Black. A Collection of Black Hills Poetry, Larry C. Nelson

JOHN HUNTER
FIRST SAW MILL FOUNDER

Instead of bringing a gold pan, pick and shovel to the Gold Rush of 1876-1877, John Hunter of Minneapolis, Minn., brought a portable saw mill to the Black Hills to seek his fortune. Like a number of merchants and suppliers, he did better financially than some of the inexperienced gold-seekers who expected to find nuggets sparkling on the Deadwood streets.

Enterprising John Hunter, in 1877, shipped the saw mill by train to Bismarck, then brought it by ox team to Polo Creek near Deadwood, and finally moved it to Crook City, an early settlement which has long since disappeared.

His business started off with a bang—and the noise of saws and hammers—for most of the settlers were eager to buy lumber to build homes and businesses for permanent settlement on the challenging frontier. The sounds of Hunter's sawmill were the sounds of civilization.

John Hunter had left a wife and three children in Minneapolis for safekeeping until he could provide a home and be assured of a reasonably safe environment in country only recently wrested from the Sioux Indians. Whenever he could, he went back to Minneapolis to visit, but that arrange-

John nd Elizabeth Hunter with son George, 7, who celebrated his 93rd birthday in 1979. He has a remarkable memory for Deadwood history.

Photo courtesy of Centennial Archives, Deadwood Public Library.

ment was unsatisfactory for both him and his wife.

Elizabeth Hunter had lived through the 1862 Sioux Uprising in Minnesota. She was willing to face the dangers and uncertainties of the wilderness rather than stay alone in Minneapolis with three small children. Determined and unafraid, she decided to join her husband but did not inform him of her decision until she had leased her house in Minneapolis for a year, and thus had enough money to make the journey.

Mrs. Hunter, with two little girls and a baby, came on the Northern Pacific to the end of the line at Bismarck in northern Dakota Territory. Then all three children became ill. Fortunately, she met two Deadwood men who were friends of her husband; they helped her care for the sick children on the bumpy stage-coach ride when accommodations were primitive or non-existent on the Bismarck-Deadwood trail. At one point when the driver thought Indians were approaching, he handed Elizabeth Hunter a loaded gun. But to her great relief, the Indians did not appear.

When at last the stage reached Crook City, Mr. Hunter was there to welcome his family. It was a joyful reunion. Proudly, he took them by horse and buggy to his busy sawmill in Speagle Gap where he had built a brand-new cabin of carefully-cut logs.

Upon arriving in her frontier home, Mrs. Hunter, exhausted from the difficult trip over the alkali plains, lay down with the baby to take a nap. The two little girls, Lillian and Daisy, recovered from their illness, were excited by their new environment and ran into the woods to explore. When their mother awakened, she looked and looked, called and called, but she could not find her children.

Mr. Hunter gave the alarm to his sawmill workers, and soon every prospector and resident in the Speagle Gap-Crook City area began searching for the missing children. Carrying lanterns, the men searched throughout the night in the deep woods thinking of wild animals, falls over cliffs, drownings in rushing creeks.

At daylight, the distraught parents heard three shots, fired in quick succession, the signal that the children were found. When the searchers appeared carrying the two little girls, unharmed, their parents rejoiced and thanked the Lord. The men reported that they had found them sitting on the edge of a cliff, Daisy, the younger of the two, sleeping with her head in Lillian's lap.

John Hunter visited on Sunday last with his family at Mystic and in company with his little seven-year-old son Georgie went out fishing. The little fellow strayed a short distance from his parents, but soon his cries alarmed them, and coming quickly to where Georgie was, found him struggling with a two-pound trout which he landed safely without their assistance. Mr. Hunter thinks he has a smart son and probably he has. John caught not even a bite. **Black Hills Daily Times,** August 3, 1897

Let no one forget the sociable tomorrow night at Mr. John Hunters on Forest Hill. Mr. Hunter's house is one of the most spacious in the city and its hospitality is as spacious as its hall. "FORTY YEARS AGO" **Deadwood Pioneer-Times,** Jan. 20, 1932

Mrs. Hunter, who must surely have been tired but happy, gathered up her strength and prepared breakfast in her new home for the hungry men of the search party. Such was Elizabeth Hunter's introduction to the life of a pioneer in the Black Hills.

The sawmill business flourished. John Hunter efficiently provided a product sorely needed by the gold-seekers pouring into the northern Hills.

On Sept. 27, 1879, a rider galloped breathlessly up to the sawmill to confront John Hunter. "I'll buy all the lumber you have right now," he said, offering a good price.

John began to bargain with him and was about to close the deal when another rider galloped up yelling, "Don't sell any lumber, John. Don't sell for God's sake! Deadwood burned to the ground last night!" and pointed to the smoky haze hanging over the mountains.

After the big fire of 1879, which burned forever more in the pages of Deadwood's history, John Hunter's lumber literally rebuilt Deadwood. He had a reserve supply of lumber on hand and cut more as fast as he could. Hunter ran his mill 24 hours a day and put on four-horse teams to haul the wood to the ruined city, flattened and lying in smoking ashes. The indomitable pioneers rebuilt much of Main Street and Sherman Street with both lumber and bricks before snow fell that winter.

In 1883, John Hunter joined forces with J. M. Fish who operated a saw mill in Two-Bit Gulch. The two men became partners and established the Fish and Hunter business. Although this enterprise started out in a tumbledown shack in Chinatown, it soon prospered. Through consolidation and purchase, they added other lumber men and additional mills. The Company branched out with lumber yards in several Black Hills cities; they also added a large merchandising establishment on Sherman Street, selling hardware, groceries, meats, and staples of all kinds. The Fish and Hunter Company is still in existence in Deadwood.

John Hunter died February 10, 1920. **The Deadwood Pioneer-Times** published a lengthy, complimentary obituary: "He always enlisted his services in every movement for the betterment of the community. His business was his first thought and his success in this line was due to his untiring efforts and his straight-forward policies. He was a home-lover and a good provider; when not in his office, he was at home with his family."

Mrs. Hunter outlived her husband and died in 1928. **The Deadwood Plain Dealer** described her as "always cheerful, kind and gentle." She was more than that. In addition to raising a large family, this strong woman was

Mr. and Mrs. John Hunter left on the Northwestern last evening for an extended visit at Jacksonville, Fla., and other places in that vicinity. They will probably visit Cuba before returning to Deadwood. **Deadwood Pioneer-Times,** Feb. 4, 1914

Dear Harvey: The Fish and Hunter Company are dealers in building materials at Deadwood, SD, all of which proves that out in that country where ducks fly low and fish swim high, men have mastered the business of pleasure as well as the pleasure of business. Lloyd Maxwell, **Deadwood Pioneer-Times,** Dec. 13, 1953

also a highly respected business adviser to her husband throughout his successful career.

At the time of Mrs. Hunter's death, only two of her eight children were living: Lillian (one of the girls who became lost and grew up to marry Dr. F.S. Howe) and George, who organized the Black Hills Mercantile Company.

Tragic misfortunes befell the Hunter children: one by one, the six died: from falling off a porch, from drinking lye by mistake, from diphtheria, from dread maladies with no names and no known cures.

The twins, Thadeus, who died after one month of life, and Theodore, who died three months later, are buried in the old Crook City cemetery; however, their brother George had markers placed for them in the Hunter family plot with nine markers in Mount Moriah, near the overlook.

The Pioneer-Times summed up John Hunter's life thusly: "He left a record behind that was seldom surpassed in that day when it took courage and character to make a place for oneself in pioneer country."

Surely, Elizabeth Hunter, like so many women who settled the Black Hills, also demonstrated "courage and character" and all the other qualities associated with the heart-stirring word, "pioneer."

"Conquering, holding, daring, venturing as we go the unknown ways." "Pioneers! O Pioneers!", Whitman

George Hunter, preparing for open house to mark the Golden Anniversary of the black Hills Mercantile Company, found original ledger sheets dating back to its formation. Thirteen businessmen pledged $10,500 to organize a cooperative fruit-dispensing firm. **Lead Daily Call,** Feb. 20, 1964

Be it resolved . . . and recognizing the long and faithful service of John Hunter with this corporation . . . I, George Hunter, nominate John Hunter as the first Honorary President of the Fish and Hunter Company. Resolution unanimously passed by directors, Jan. 16, 1918. **Deadwood Pioneer-Times,** Feb. 14. 1920

DR. MORRIS ROGERS
BELOVED PHYSICIAN

Dr. Morris Rogers, one of the most popular and respected doctors in Deadwood's early years, died an alcoholic at age 67. A Kentuckian, Dr. Rogers graduated from an Iowa medical school and became a pioneer physician in Deadwood in 1877. Because of his ability and personality, he soon built up a large practice, often making his rounds by horse and buggy over the rough trails to visit his patients. Known for his gentleness, courtly polish, and generosity, Dr. Rogers' name became a household word in almost every home in the northern Hills.

As the years passed, he became a "victim of his own weakness"—presumably excessive drinking. At last his relatives and friends convinced the doctor to commit himself to a sanitarium for treatment.

The Deadwood Pioneer-Times reported: "So successful was he up to this time, despite his shattered health, there are many who prefer him to any other doctor in the world . . . He is regarded by hundreds with the deepest gratitude because it is known that there are thousands of dollars of services which Dr. Rogers rendered that have never been entered in his books."

After several months of treatment for alcoholism, Dr. Rogers was pronounced cured of his sickness and returned to Deadwood.

But the cure didn't last. The police chief was shocked to find Dr. Rogers lying unconscious in an alley. Despite all efforts to revive him, he died in the local hospital, August 18, 1905, leaving a wife and four grown children.

The Pioneer-Times published a sympathetic eulogy: "There is the deepest regret that Dr. Rogers' life should have gone out in such a manner. Over his own weakness all are willing to draw the mantle of forgetfulness and remember the man only as he once was—cultured, brilliant, devoted to his profession, overflowing with kindness of heart and love of humanity, a charming conversationalist, and a sincere friend."

A large and sorrowing congregation, with Deadwood doctors as pall-bearers, attended the funeral in the Methodist Church where the casket was completely covered with floral offerings. The Deadwood Fire Department led the way to Mount Moriah, followed by mourners on foot and in carriages.

For many years grieving patients and friends made pilgrimages to Dr. Rogers' grave; and on Memorial Day, they decorated it with garlands, wreaths, and bouquets of wild flowers and "fragrant gems from the garden" in memory of this beloved physician with the fatal flaw.

Vera Ella Fargo, daughter of Mr. and Mrs. J. W. Fargo. Miss Vera is a living tribute to the skill of the late Dr. M. Rogers, who cured her after her feet and legs had become paralyzed by a fall. (Caption for picture of a two-year-old girl, **Deadwood Pioneer-Times,** Aug. 31, 1905)

JOHN TREBER
WHOLESALE LIQUOR DEALER

John Treber, a Black Hills Pioneer of 1877, and his partner Herrmann, were the first wholesale liquor dealers in Deadwood, and their first street sign can be easily read in the famous picture of Deadwood's main street of

This photo is often incorrectly identified as "Deadwood in 1876." The year is 1877. The Herrman-Treber sign is clearly visible on the left. John Treber did not arrive in the gulch until April, 1877, according to records of the Treber family and of the Society of Black Hills Pioneers.

August, 1877.

Treber, born in Germany, immigrated to the United States when he was 21 years old and became a naturalized citizen. He worked in a brewery in St. Louis and was employed in Kansas before coming to Deadwood Gulch and going into the liquor business with Herrmann.

The Black Hills Daily Times, August 10, 1878, reported: "The Treber-Herrmann large fire-proof buiding is chock full of whiskies, wines, St. Louis beer and cigars; these goods are piled to the very ceiling, the front store room has been painted and arranged in style, and these enterprising wholesalers are now ready for a big rush of business." Another item states that the firm was expecting 94 barrels of St. Louis beer shipped from Fort Pierre and "that they had double that amount on other wagon trains enroute on the other trails to Deadwood." Thus, because of the Treber-Herrmann partnership which lasted for seven years, the saloons in Deadwood were able to set 'em up for the thirsty populace.

John Treber journeyed to Kansas to claim his bride in June, 1878 and brought her back to Deadwood. On the first day of their trip, the stage-

coach broke down, and Treber had to set his bride Hermina out on the open plains in the rain without a blanket or umbrella while repairs were made. **The Times,** June, 1878, reported that John said his bride after that experience looked as though she was sorry that she had married him, "but since their arrival Mrs. Treber is looking more cheerful."

Mrs. Treber lived the rest of her life in Deadwood. Eventually the Trebers and their three sons moved into a huge, rambling home with three parlors on Lincoln Avenue (now an apartment house). People still talk about Hermina's beautiful Bavarian china and her wonderful German cooking, especially applestrudel.

John Treber, his business and his activities, were often mentioned in the early newspapers. In May, 1878, Treber "was down the Sidney road yesterday and is delighted with the condition of the country in the foothills, bespangled with wild flowers, and the grass grows so rapidly that one can

Photo courtesy of Centennial Archives, Deadwood Public Library.

John Treber, a German immigrant who became a loyal and successful American citizen. After one visit to his home-land, he was thankful to spend the rest of his life in Deadwood and to sell kegs of his favorite beer, Anheuser-Busch.

hear it." In July, 1885, **The Times** reported the hard luck he had with his hired help suffering accidental injuries. In 1910 **The Times** announced that Treber had decided to erect a concrete ice-manufacturing plant this side of Pluma at a cost of $25,000.

After John Treber arrived in Deadwood during the gold rush, it didn't take him long to become a successful and wealthy businessman known for his generosity. In 1891, he decided to take his wife and three sons back to

Germany for a visit with his and his wife's relatives and friends. Shortly after his arrival, Treber was arrested and thrown into prison because he had left Germany without serving in the army as was required of all subjects of the Kaiser. His distraught wife Hermina, with the three boys, rented a small house near the prison while doing everything she could to obtain his release.

The State Department in Washington went to work untangling the red tape and informing the German government that it could not imprison a United States citizen.

Mrs. Treber wrote letters to Deadwood, and news about the Trebers' plight was published in the **Black Hills Daily Times** to keep their many friends informed of developments. In January, 1892, Mrs. Treber, in a letter to Mrs. Harris Franklin, wrote that she expected her husband to remain in prison for eight months and the boys were attending college nearby. At last, in March, 1892, much earlier than expected, John Treber was released from prison, according to a telegram from Busch, a partner in the famous brewing company of Anheuser-Busch.

In May, the Trebers were delighted to return to Deadwood unexpectedly and "surprise their many friends and avoid all ovations." **The Times** commented, "John is the same jovial and easy-going John, but he lost 25 pounds in prison."

According to John Treber's granddaughter, Dorothy Treber Hoherz of Deadwood, the story handed down in the family about Treber's incarceration is that despite the State Department doing its best, nothing seemed to happen. Not until a liquor salesman contacted Busch of the Anheuser-Busch brewers. Busch cabled Kaiser Wilhelm of Germany, who had often been his drinking partner, and requested the release of one John Treber of Deadwood, SD, USA. And that is how John Treber was sprung from a German prison long before anyone expected him to be.

John Treber and his family were happy to resume life in Deadwood, John declaring that he would never leave America again. Active in community affairs, he served on the Deadwood city council for 24 years and was also elected a member of the South Dakota State Legislature. After a long and useful life, at age 83, he died peacefully in his sleep in October, 1937. His son Albert, a Deadwood native, lived to be 96 years old and died in 1979.

There is an article sold in many saloons, imported by Hermann and Treber, that is called Benedictine and covered all over with labels and strange devices. It is not only alcoholic but also medicinal and said to be possessed of rare curative powers. Manufactured by Benedictine monks since 1410. Local News, **Black Hills Daily Times,** April 23, 1880

Your skin should be clear and bright if your liver is in normal condition. Dades' Little Liver Pills act on the liver and headaches. Constipation and biliousness disappear. Price $.25 SOLD BY JOHN TREBER. Advertisement in **Deadwood Pioneer-Times,** Oct. 16, 1907

John Treber suspended operation of his bottling works last Monday, for a week, to give all employees a vacation, and on that day they all started for the Belle Fourche river to hunt and fish. **Black Hills Daily Times,** May, 1893

John Treber sleeps in Mount Moriah, next to his Hermina and other family members. The Treber lot is not far from the Stars and Stripes that flies day and night on the mountain-top cemetery, the symbol of freedom that meant so much to John Treber, American.

The following telegram yesterday received at business house of John Treber: 'Upon request of State Department, Washington, our friend John Treber has now been released and returned to his family. Three cheers. Hope he will soon arrive at his home hale and hearty. Yours truly, Adolphus Busch.' **Black Hills Daily Times,** March 13, 1892

In 1932, John Treber reminisced for the interviewer about the aftermath of the big Deadwood fire in Sept. 1879, stating 'that the construction of new buildings began at once, lumber was ordered from John Hunter's sawmill, other supplies arrived, and a brick factory was started on upper main street. Because the weather was so mild that fall, building went ahead rapidly and structures on main street were ready for occupancy in 90 days.' **Rapid City Journal,** June 1, 1932

WILLIS H. BONHAM
MOST POPULAR
NEWSPAPER EDITOR

Willis H. Bonham, who became the most popular and least controversial of Deadwood's many newspaper editors, had a colorful early life, but in his mature years settled into an untroubled and comfortable career. A self-educated man, his only schooling was in a log school house in Illinois, the state where he was born in 1847. Young Bonham, like many other adventurers on the frontier, joined the crowd riding the Union Pacific railroad to Cheyenne, Wyo., the main headquarters for the prospectors, or pilgrims as they were often called, during the Black Hills Gold Rush.

In Cheyenne, Bonham managed the Black Hills Outfitters Store, then decided that instead of selling gold pans, picks and shovels, it would be more fun to take off for the Hills of Gold. He traded his Wyoming homestead for 130 Mexican burros, got a job as foreman of a wagon train hauling machinery for stamping gold. He led the burro train over the plains, mountains, and gorges without losing a pilgrim, a burro, or a pack.

After covering 300 miles on the Cheyenne-Deadwood trail, Bonham and his burro-train trotted into roaring Deadwood Gulch in July, 1877, the second year of its existence. Deadwood, jammed with prospectors and entrepreneurs, had a population estimated at between 15,000 and 25,000.

After selling his cargo and his burros, Bonham got a job running a hand press for the **Black Hills Pioneer,** the first newspaper in the Hills, then a year old. Later, he also worked for the first daily newspaper, **The Black Hills Times,** whose first issue had appeared two months earlier in May, 1877.

WILLIS H. BONHAM, 1883-4-5

W. H. Bonham, leader of a burro train over the Cheyenne-Deadwood trail. He never ran out of subjects to write about for his newspapers.

By 1885, the ambitious Bonham became sole owner of **The Pioneer;** and by 1897, he bought **The Black Hills Times** and consolidated the two leading papers into one, **The Deadwood Pioneer-Times.** He then installed the first linotype machine in western South Dakota. **The Pioneer-Times** became the most powerful newspaper of the Northern Hills and is still in existence today.

As the newspaper, born of a merger, grew in circulation and influence, it gradually became more conservative, perhaps reflecting the old gold camp's struggle to feel natural in the guise of a respectable twentieth-century city. As the years passed, the reporting and editorializing was neither as picturesque or as libelous as they had been in the first two rival and name-calling newspapers of the late nineteenth century.

The Pioneer-Times greatly affected people's thinking and attitudes toward the happenings and problems of the times. Bonham, as was often said, was always in favor of a progressive Deadwood. He did not question the business practices of the wealthy and powerful city leaders, as did

radical socialist Freeman Knowles, editor of **The Lantern;** nor did he agitate against gambling and prostitution as did prohibitionist Edward Senn, editor of **The Daily Telegram.**

Little is known about Bonham's personal life except that he was once married, and that a Bonham child is buried in Mount Moriah.

As the years passed, Bonham gradually turned over the management of **The Pioneer-Times** to his two nephews, the Morford brothers. On the morning of the day he died, on November 30, 1927, Bonham had waved a cheery "hello" to his physician, assuring the doctor that he felt fine. But later that day the 80-year-old pioneer who had published and edited the successful merger of Deadwood's first two newspapers for nearly half a century "passed peacefully to The Great Beyond."

Eulogies from editors throughout the state poured in for Bonham "who had more friends and fewer enemies than most newspaper editors." The accomplishments of the veteran newsman were reviewed: organizer of the Deadwood fire department, director and stockholder of the Franklin Hotel, part owner of several gold mines. He, along with Theodore Roosevelt, was an honorary member of the Society of Black Hills Pioneers, for he had guided the burro train on the Cheyenne-Deadwood trail in 1877 instead of 1876, which was the first required year of arrival for membership in that illustrious society. Bonham was described as "level-headed, warm-hearted, courteous, generous, fearless, accommodating" and many other nice adjectives. However, unfavorable obituaries of businessmen are hard to find in the files of Deadwood newspapers.

Interment was made in the south part of Mount Moriah, Bonham's nephews wrote, "on a slope overlooking a large part of the city where the deceased had lived so long and loved so dearly."

The new editors did not forego publication of the newspaper for even one day, in keeping with their uncle's wishes and with newspaper tradition. The special editorial, dedicated to his memory concluded: " 'Thirty' has arrived for Willis H. Bonham, but his spirit will continue to be a guiding

---

The Times and **The Pioneer** will cease as individual newspapers and the wedding will take place during the early hours of this day, the ceremony to be strictly private. The individuality of the two separate papers ends and what of good (if anything) they contain will be concentrated into THE DAILY PIONEER-TIMES which in consolidated form will make its bow tomorrow morning. **Black Hills Daily Times,** May 13, 1897

In the future the weather forecasts as telegraphed from the Weather Bureau will be communicated to the public of Deadwood by means of flag signals displayed from the Pioneer-Times building. **Deadwood Pioneer-Times,** October 5, 1897

Editor Bonham of the **Pioneer-Times** has written an interesting article on the early history of Deadwood which appeared in the Homecoming number of the **Sioux Falls Argus-Leader** which follows: 'The early days of Deadwood were one huge, concentrated life that never considered eight hours and $3.50 per day. Deadwood was strictly cosmopolitan, composed of every race and character, from every land and clime that made it so.' **The Lead Daily Call,** June 24, 1914

beacon to his successors who will ask nothing more than to be able to publish **The Pioneer-Times** as well as did he.''

Few men have been paid the compliment that was tendered W. H. Bonham at the Deadwood business club last evening, and few men so richly deserve the honors that were so heartily heaped upon the veteran editor of the **Pioneer-Times** . . . the club having styled it a ''homecoming celebration'' and extended invitations to all the newspaper men in the Black Hills. **Deadwood Pioneer-Times,** May 23, 1914

HARRIS FRANKLIN
THE RICHEST MAN

Harris Franklin, for whom the Franklin Hotel in Deadwood is named, was the personification of the American dream; he was a poor Jewish immigrant who came to this country as a boy and died a multi-millionaire, a highly respected leader of the gold camp he helped to develop. Three biographical sources list three different birth places: Poland, Russia; Hanover, Germany; Prussian Poland. In America, the young immigrant went first to Rochester, New York; then to Iowa; Nebraska; Cheyenne, Wyoming. Somewhere in his travels west, he changed his name from Finkelstein to Franklin.

Harris Franklin first tried his luck in the Black Hills Gold Rush in

Photo courtesy of Centennial Archives, Deadwood Public Library.

Harris Franklin, a poor Jewish immigrant, who became a multi-millionaire in Deadwood.

1876, but not until 1878, when he was 29 years old, did he decide to make Deadwood his home. Here he settled down to make his fortune, rumored to be five million by the time he died.

First, he established a wholesale liquor business which prospered quickly among the thirsty miners. Then during the severe winter of 1886-1887 when ranchers feared all the cattle on the open range would perish, he bought up the survivors of 23 brands. When spring came, Franklin had won his gamble, because more cattle survived than anyone predicted. He soon became one of the biggest cattlemen in the west, at one time reportedly owning 30,000 head of cattle on the range in South Dakota, Montana, and Nebraska.

Franklin's next profitable venture involved mining, and his associates quickly hailed him as a "genius in the business world." He organized the Golden Reward Mining Company and held controlling interest in the Ruby Basin Company. Sponsor for the erection of the original Deadwood chlorination works, purchaser of the Deadwood-Delaware smelter, prime mover in the establishment of the American National Bank in Deadwood, the sagacious financier was also the heaviest investor in building the Franklin Hotel, which bears his name.

Photo courtesy of Adams Memorial Hall Museum.

Harris Franklin built this mansion on Van Buren Street for $10,000. That was in 1892. The turret is partially hidden. This house, where Theodore Roosevelt was entertained, was the scene of many galas when the Franklins lived here and later the W. E. Adams family. It is now known as the Adams House.

Harris Franklin was a serious businessman and not overly friendly, but Deadwood awarded him and his family the universal adulation reserved for the very rich—especially for one who had earned a fortune from scratch. The Deadwood newspapers usually wrote about him as though groveling at the feet of a golden god.

Even when the Franklin mansion caught fire, more space was given to extravagant adjectives than to the facts, the bedazzled reporter writing how "the elegant mansion" escaped destruction when a servant discovered an oil burner ablaze in the "elegant men's smoking room" and subsequently smothered the fire with an "elegant Turkish rug."

Surely, one of the most memorable social events of Deadwood's golden age was the much-publicized celebration of the Franklin's 25th wedding anniversary. On the front page of the **Black Hills Times,** Jan. 3, 1895, banner headlines announced: "THEIR SILVER WEDDING—MR. AND MRS.

Photo courtesy of Centennial Archives, Deadwood Public Library.

Harris Franklin and his wife, Anna, riding in their buggy. A favorite Sunday drive was "Around the Belt": Deadwood to Central City and Lead; then down Gold Run Gulch to Pluma and Deadwood.

HARRIS FRANKLIN OBSERVE THE EVENT IN A BRILLIANT MANNER—RECIPIENTS OF A LARGE NUMBER OF BEAUTIFUL AND VALUABLE PRESENTS. The palatial home . . . was the scene of one of the most brilliant and successful social events that have been given in this city."

Harris Franklin will leave today for Fort Worth, Texas, where he will close the purchase of and ship nearly 3,000 head of young cattle to his range on the Belle Fourche. **Black Hills Times,** April 8, 1893

This week Seth Bullock sold between 500 and 600 head of cattle to Harris Franklin of Deadwood. Mr. Franklin purchased the hay and grain here on the home ranch east of Belle Fourche and will feed the stock this winter. A force of men was engaged in branding the stock Sunday. **The Belle Fourche Bee,** Nov. 10, 1895

One wonders if the awed newspaper reporter present was peeking from behind draperies which were undoubtedly elegant to describe in ecstatic terms the "100 large incandescent lights and numberless candelabra; the profusion of Chinese lanterns; the horseshoes woven from arbor vitae and draped with smilax, hyacinth and roses; the rich material and drapes decorating the doors, windows, mantles, furniture."

At this turreted castle, the showplace of the area (now known as the Adams house on Van Buren street), was served "the most delicious dinner ever given in Deadwood," which included oysters, grouse, goose, filled dates, turkey, French peas, chicken salad, plum pudding with brandy sauce, five kinds of cake—all served by "numberless servants." While the men retired to the smoking room to enjoy their Havanas, the ladies visited and entertained the Franklin grand-daughter, who must have been a precocious three-month-old baby to have "enjoyed the event hugely."

Right smack on the front page of **The Times** were listed the names of the invited guests with the "elegant present" each offered at the door like a ticket of admission also listed. Many gifts were of "solid silver," including an elegant chest full of a dozen each of sterling silverware. One guest brought just a pillow—undoubtedly elegant.

Despite the lavish anniversary celebration, time-honored Deadwood gossip preserves another view of the marriage, which may not have been made in heaven. Mrs. Anna Franklin, remembered for her kindness, died in January, 1902. The story goes that Harris ordered a crew of his employees to struggle with the lifting, loading, and unloading of the mammoth tombstone transported by a horse-drawn wagon up the steep ruts to Mount Moriah. When at last the workmen planted the heavy marker over Mrs. Franklin's grave, the usually non-commital Harris is supposed to have exclaimed, "There—now she can't get at me anymore!"

Eventually, Harris married a widow with two children and subsequently moved to New York City where he lived the rest of his life.

Nathan, the only son of Harris and his first wife, was a popular mischief-maker in school, married the town beauty, then worked closely with his father to manage the widespread Franklin holdings both in the Black Hills and in New York City. Nathan, also an influential man in Deadwood, several times ran for mayor in hotly-contested elections. He was victorious only once, and that was when he overwhelmed the opposing candidate, Edward Senn, the unpopular newspaper editor who was determined to

The Franklin Hotel management has installed a new towel device in the toilet room. Cloth towels of the ordinary size are used, but each is punctured with a brass-rimmed hole, through which a brass rod passes. The towels are stacked on top of a rack and are used while still attached to the rod. After being used, they slide down the rod onto the soiled towel basket. **Deadwood Pioneer-Times**, July, 1914

Miss Mildred Franklin, daughter of Mr. and Mrs. Nathan E. Franklin, opened The Carnival by touching a button and the doors of the Mineral Palace swung open and the ceremonies were over. **Deadwood Pioneer-Times**, July 4, 1901

rout gambling and prostitution from Sin City.

Another highlight in the saga of the Franklin dynasty was the inaugural ball of "THE FRANKLIN—SPLENDID NEW DEADWOOD HOTEL" which opened to the public with royal ceremonies in June, 1903. The newspaper accounts do not state whether Harris Franklin was present.

Five-hundred guests were ushered in for dancing in the ballroom or listening to a concert while "partaking of refreshments" on the balcony decorated with evergreens and festooned with Chinese lanterns.

The Pioneer-Times, June 6, 1903, described many "rich costumes" worn by over 150 women, including:

Mrs. Nathan Franklin—lace over silk; diamonds
Mrs. John Treber—black lace; diamonds
Mrs. George Ayres—black voile and jet
Miss Blanche Colman—white embroidered chiffon
Mrs. A.D. Wilson (diarist Irene Cushman)—pink dotted swiss and lace

The names of other ladies present were listed but their costumes were not described; one of these was Mrs. Freeman Knowles, wife of former Congressman Freeman Knowles, the socialist newspaper editor who often attacked Nathan Franklin in his columns.

When Harris Franklin, age 74, died of pneumonia in New York City in April, 1923, his old friend of 45 years, Henry Frawley, a prominent attorney and rancher of Deadwood, wrote a long obituary for **The Pioneer-Times:** "Again has the bell tolled for a pioneer . . . He was a far-seeing adroit operator . . . He was never known to foreclose a mortgage . . . He paid little attention to social affairs or to politics . . . E. J. Harriman, financier, paid him a business visit to Deadwood. So did John Jacob Astor and other well-known capitalists . . . Harris Franklin—your work is done. You lived to see consummated and prosper many of your designed enterprises . . . The Black Hills mourn your demise. You did much for their development . . . Peace to your ashes, eternal happiness to your soul."

Today, the Franklin tombstone looming over the graves of Harris Franklin and his first wife Anna is the largest marker in Mount Moriah and is located at the corner of the cemetery at the very top of the Jewish section.

Nathan ran for mayor once against Mac the Saddler McDonald. The election looked like a walkaway until Harris Franklin sent down $1,000 to bet on his son. Money was snapped up and everybody betting against Franklin got out and worked hard to defeat him. Mac the Saddler won, rather bewildered. **Black Hills Weekly** feature by Elizabeth Howe, March, 1940

WAR DECLARED: Beginning Monday and continuing until entirely exterminated, I hereby request all property owners and renters of Deadwood to wage war on the DANDELION. This is a call to arms which I trust will meet with success. Nathan Franklin, Mayor. **Deadwood Pioneer-Times,** May 23, 1914

NATHAN FRANKLIN ACCUSES ME OF TEACHING FREE LOVE, BUT HE PRACTICES IT. **The Lantern,** Freeman Knowles, editor, March 28, 1909

The author admiring the largest tombstone in Mount Moriah.

One can ascend the steps of the imposing tomb and gaze down over the silent city from the final resting place of Harris Franklin, king of the hill.

According to a telegram from Nathan Franklin, funeral services for Harris Franklin were held in New York City today. Several floral decorations from the Black Hills will appear on the casket, sent by former business associates, the Society of Black Hills Pioneers, and others who held the deceased in high estimation. Nathan wired: 'Later the ashes will be buried beside my mother, in accordance with my father's wishes, on Mount Moriah, overlooking the city that was his home so many years.' **Deadwood Pioneer-Times,** April 12, 1923

MAJOR ANDREW JACKSON SIMMONS
VERSATILE WESTERNER

A comparison of the accomplishments of Major Andrew Jackson Simmons and those of Wild Bill Hickok would put the Kansas marshal in his place—just a careless gunfighter. Yet, because of the inconsistencies of fame and the vagaries of immortality, thousands of people have made pilgrimages to visit Hickok's grave but have never even heard of Simmons. His tombstone, in the last row of graves nearest the overlook, is tops at Mount Moriah, just as it should be. Simmons, appropriately named for Jackson, the frontier U. S. President, was an adventurer, lawmaker, mining expert, philanthropist, politician, educator, and Special Indian Agent—all on the frontier.

A born pioneer and adventurer, Simmons, who grew up in Indiana, at age 19, joined a wagon train to California in 1853. During the six-month journey he survived hair-breadth escapes from hostile Indians, from equally hostile white outlaws, and from the floods of rampaging rivers—all authentic material for an exciting western tale, supporting the adage, "Truth is stranger than fiction."

After several years of prospecting for gold in California, he rode horseback over the Sierras into Nevada to learn whether the fantastic stories of Nevada mineral discoveries were true. Later, when the Comstock Lode was discovered in 1859, the prospectors were mad with both gold and silver fever, and Simmons, too, had a bout with the malady.

Young Simmons took an active part in developing Nevada, was elected to the Nevada Territorial Legislature three times; and when he was only 27 years old, became Speaker of the House in 1863-1864 during the tumultous time when Nevada became a state.

Simmons collaborated with United States Senator Stewart in framing the federal laws on mining which controlled for many years the location and acquisition of lode and placer claims in the United States.

While in Nevada, Simmons roomed with a young newspaper correspondent named Samuel Clemens who later became Mark Twain, that giant of American literature. The two became life-long friends.

The youthful legislator and mining expert was rumored to have made a fortune in the Comstock Lode; he then returned to California and reportedly lost money in investments because of the manipulation of dishonest

bonanza kings—another fascinating though depressing facet of Simmons' life.

Next, Simmons, always optimistic, decided to try his luck in Montana, where he accepted an appointment from President Ulysses Grant as Special Indian Agent with the title of Major. Simmons led a party to the Indian reservation to negotiate with Sitting Bull and finally persuaded the uncompromising Sioux leader to grant right of way to the Northern Pacific railroad, much to the later sorrow of the Indians. Simmons also accompanied a group of Indian leaders to Washington to meet the Great White Father in 1872.

Being an Indian Agent was not exciting enough for Simmons; he resigned to take up the mining game again, this time to placer mine in Montana.

Again, in 1878, the spirit of adventure overcame Simmons, and he responded to the magnetism of the Black Hills Gold Rush. With his wife Kate, he settled in Deadwood, invested in mining properties, and became active in developing the community.

Later, Simmons moved to Rapid City where his leadership qualities were quickly recognized; and in 1886 he was elected Mayor of Rapid City. Simmons visited the Dakota Territorial Legislature and is credited with securing the establishment of the School of Mines at Rapid City. He and another generous man donated a five-acre tract of land on which the School of Mines was built. Subsequently, he was elected president of the first board of trustees of the college.

In 1897, the Major returned to Deadwood to live, became involved in several mining properties; in his later years, he was manager of the Echo mine in Maitland, not far from Deadwood. His wife Kate died in 1906. Major Simmons died in 1920 at age 86 in the Denver home of his only child, son Jesse, also a mining expert.

After Simmons' death, many of his contemporaries commented on his enthusiasm for the Black Hills which he believed contained an inexhaustible supply of gold, silver, and other important minerals. **The Deadwood Pioneer-Times,** Dec. 30, 1920, described his life as a "Big One," declaring that he had "few if any enemies and numbered his friends by the number of acquaintances. His life was gentle and the elements so mixed in him, that

Jack Simmons' smile still illuminates our streets. **Black Hills Times,** Jan. 4, 1880

In approximating the value of a gold mine, it is well to bear in mind two fundamental principles: first, mining is not an exact science; second, the laws of nature, as applied underground, are not fixed and immutable. "Looking Backwards Fifty-Six Years," A. J. Simmons, **Black Hills Illustrated,** 1904

Major Simmons remembers Clemens as a young man who had the faculty for bringing out the lighter spots in the usually dull sessions of the Nevada legislative body; he lent to his correspondence a piquancy and spice that put it outside the class of tiresome reading. "Major A. J. Simmons' Personal Recollections of Samuel L. Clemens," **The Deadwood Pioneer-Times,** April 24, 1910

Photo courtesy of Centennial Archives, Deadwood Public Library.

The United States Assay Office in the Federal Building, Deadwood. 1909. Mining engineer Jesse Simmons, only son of Major A. J. Simmons is seated at the desk. U.S. Assayer Col. W. J. Thornby is standing. A Mason and Black Hills Pioneer of 1877, he helped lay out Mount Moriah.

Photo courtesy of South Dakota State Historical Society.

Henry Newton, like Major Simmons, has received little acclaim. Newton was geologist for the Jenney-Newton Expedition of 1875 which mapped the entire Black Hills and determined their geology and mineral resources. He died in Deadwood of typhoid in 1877 and his body was shipped back east. In *Black Hills Booktrails,* historian J. Leonard Jennewein concluded: "A monument and glory for Wild Bill Hickok who did nothing for the hills but to die there; nothing for Henry Newton."

nature might stand and say to all the world: 'this was a man.' "

Certainly, his complete history would parallel the history of the western experience in the United States. With his contributions to the development of Nevada, California, Montana, and South Dakota, he is surely more deserving of being raised to a hero's status in western history than is Wild Bill Hickok. Who knows? Maybe some day crowds will gather about the grave of Major Andrew Jackson Simmons, wondering if he found that gold mine in the sky.

Fortunate indeed was Rapid in having a chief executive of the Jack Simmons' order; and thankful indeed are the guests of this city that Jack was on deck. A more tireless and effective as well as unostentatious worker could not have been selected. (Feature on Rapid City Jubilee upon arrival of first through train.) **Black Hills Daily Times,** July 18, 1886

Any old-time veteran miner may recall from his stock of fading reminiscences the prospects he has abandoned or could have controlled for a trifling consideration, which have since been developed into great mines. "Looking Backward Fifty-Six Years," Simmons, **Black Hills Illustrated,** 1904

Mrs. A. J. Simmons of Thursday Club went as a delegate to the biennial meeting of the Federation of Women's Clubs in St. Louis, May, 1904. The Thursday Club of Deadwood contributed attractive pictures for school rooms and influenced the city council to bring about better sanitary conditions. "Women's Literary and Social Clubs of the Black Hills," **Black Hills Illustrated,** 1904

W. E. ADAMS
MERCHANT AND
PHILANTHROPIST

W. E. Adams is not buried in Mount Moriah, nor is any member of his family. However, on the left side of Jerusalem Street is a memorial marker which he had erected, dedicated to the memory of his family: his first wife Alice; two daughters, Lucille and Helen; and a newborn grand-daughter. His wife, his daughter Helen, and his grandchild all died within two days in June, 1925. The entire family, including Mr. Adams himself, are buried in the family mausoleum at the foot of Mount Wilson in California.

W. E. Adams had a big heart, and one could say that he left a good share of his heart—and his fortune—in Deadwood.

His magnificent gift to the city of Deadwood was the Adams Memorial Hall, more popularly known as the Adams Memorial Museum. He erected the building at a cost of $75,000 in 1930, four years before his death; and it was dedicated October 4, 1930.

This fascinating museum preserves and displays historical objects and materials related to the history and geology of the Black Hills. One of the outstanding exhibits is the Thoen Stone, the first record of a gold discovery in the Black Hills. Another is the first railroad engine in the Black Hills, brought in by ox team.

Photo courtesy of Centennial Archives, Deadwood Public Library.

W. E. Adams, Black Hills Pioneer of 1877, who presented the museum to the city of Deadwood. At the dedication ceremonies, his presentation address consisted of these few words: "To my friends—to my neighbors—and in memory of the dear ones who have graced my fireside I offer this as a token of my love for the Black Hills."

Special displays include a gun collection; gold-mining equipment, geologic formations; historic documents; replica of Potato Creek Johnny's nugget; various possessions of Wild Bill Hickok, Seth Bullock, Calamity Jane, Annie Tallent, Dr. F. S. Howe. Also displayed are a Chinese collection from Deadwood's Chinatown, a pioneer room, and Indian artifacts. This free museum, visited by over 100,000 people yearly, is on Sherman Street, next to the Post Office, and across from the Adams building.

Eventually, after Adams' triple bereavement, this dignified, austere man fell in love with Mary Mastrovich, a vivacious young woman from Lead, many years his junior. He wrote her innumerable letters proposing

Photo courtesy of South Dakota Historical Society.

Every year an average of over 100,000 people visit the free Adams Museum containing many documents, relics, and artifacts of pioneer days.

marriage and begging her to marry him, saying, "I lay everything I have at your feet." Because of the disparity in their ages, Mary was fearful that a marriage could not be successful. She also knew that he carried a great burden of grief, but finally Mary consented to marry W. E. Adams.

Their seven-year marriage turned out to be an exceedingly happy one, ended only by his death at age 80. Dreaming of by-gone days, Mary Adams Balmat said, "Yes, he was the most wonderful man in the world. They don't make men like W. E. anymore. The best word I can use to describe him is 'benign.' "

Adams kept diaries through the years, and sometimes Mary re-reads them. "He wrote so beautifully about his love for his two daughters, Lucille and Helen," she said wistfully. "I never knew them or his first wife, Alice Burnham Adams, who contributed so much to his success."

Mary lived with Adams in the same mansion where he had also lived with his first wife. "The house itself radiated a sense of harmony and I was very happy there," Mrs. Adams Balmat recalled.

This turreted old house on Van Buren Street, now known as the Adams House, was built by Harris Franklin, another Deadwood millionaire, then later purchased by W. E. Adams. Full of servants, fireplaces, gold bathroom fixtures, three staircases, inlaid wood, stained glass windows, this ele-

An Observation Party was held at the W. E. Adams home on Forest Hill. Thirty-five items were placed on a table surrounded by a curtain. The participants were permitted to observe items for a few minutes, then try to recall them all. Delightful refreshments were served and there were many prizes. Two of the top prizewinners were Estelline Bennett and Mrs. A. D. Wilson (Irene Cushman). **Black Hills Daily Times,** May, 1892

Since W. E. Adams announced the dedication of the museum to house the historical relics of the Black Hills in Deadwood, offers have been arriving from every quarter to place private collections in the building when completed. **Deadwood Pioneer-Times,** May 29, 1929

gant Victorian home was once a showplace of the town when first the Franklins and later the Adams lived there. During the late 19th and early 20th centuries, the hey-day of Deadwood's glittering social life, it was the scene of many gala parties and social affairs. Theodore Roosevelt was entertained in this historic mansion.

W. E. Adams first came to the Black Hills in 1877 on the Bismarck-Deadwood trail, driving a team of horses and a wagon. Old newspaper accounts state that the wagon train of 50 people was caught in a terrible April blizzard, and consequently four people died. However, Mary Adams Belmat said that she never heard her husband mention the blizzard; instead he often talked of the raging prairie fire the wagon train encountered. In April, in the Land of Infinite Variety, extremes of nature are certainly possible.

Adams established the Adams Grocery Company, both retail and wholesale, which turned out to be a highly successful business. Eventually, W. E. became president of the First National Bank of Deadwood. Much interested in civic affairs, he was president of the Deadwood Cemetery Association, served six terms as Mayor of Deadwood when he spearheaded the drive to brick-pave the business streets of the city and thus rescue Deadwood from its historic mud.

A public-spirited man, Adams personally provided American flags for both schools and churches (the flagpole from the Adams house is now in the rodeo grounds); he had watering troughs built throughout the city for the horses; and from his own pocket he paid the Boy Scouts, in addition to providing them with drinking water, while they worked on his favorite project, the construction of the road to Mount Roosevelt.

It was a sad day on June 16, 1934, when the **Deadwood Pioneer-Times** wrote: "At high noon, as the beautiful carillion chimes of the Adams Memorial Hall tolled the hour, William E. Adams, pioneer Deadwood businessman and philanthropist, passed away at his home on Van Buren Street, following a brief illness."

His funeral was held in the Adams Museum, and hundreds of mourners gathered across the street at the Burlington Depot to pay their last respects as his casket was borne to the train which carried the body of this outstanding pioneer to its final resting place in California.

When W. E. Adams died, his estate was said to have been the largest ever to pass through the Department of Internal Revenue for the Black Hills district.

As a young man, I worked as a bookkeeper for Mr. Adams, a man of few words. Adams was the first man to use paper money for his personal use instead of gold and silver dollars. One time he sent me to collect a $480 bill in Lead and instructed me not to come back without the money. The man with the unpaid bill unlocked a roll-top desk full of gold, counted out $480 in twenty-dollar gold pieces for full payment, and told me to go back and tell Mr. Adams what I had seen. Recollection of George Hunter, son of John Hunter, Black Hills Pioneer of 1877

In addition to providing an endowment fund for the Adams Museum, his will made large bequests to established charities such as the South Dakota Children's Home and the Shriner's Home for Crippled Children. He bequeathed legacies to many relatives and friends, including all employees who had worked for him for at least a year. His widow, Mary Adams Balmat, recalled that many people have told her how their inheritance from Mr. Adams helped them get started in life.

Photo courtesy of Deadwood Chamber of Commerce.

Commissioned by W. E. Adams, this etching by New York artist Mark Young was featured in the souvenir booklet prepared for the dedication of the Adams Museum in October, 1930. The purpose of the museum is to "preserve concretely for all time the history of the Black Hills, the last Frontier of Western America."

He left many kinds of legacies. The generous Mr. Adams had always been man of action—not words. Typical of his modesty was his Presentation Address at the dedication ceremonies of the Adams Memorial Hall: "To my friends, to my neighbors—and in memory of the dear ones who have graced my fireside—I offer this as a token of my love for the Black Hills."

Who could forget W. E. Adams?

We can all rejoice that in his last years he found comfort and companionship in the loving, faithful, and devoted service of his wife Mary Adams who gives this beautiful window we dedicate today. "Memorial Service at St. John's Episcopal Church," **Deadwood Pioneer-Times,** June 17, 1940

The chimes of St. John's Episcopal Church played several selections last Saturday in memory of William E. Adams, a pioneer member of St. John's church who died 45 years ago on June 16 . . . The Adams Memorial Hall stands as a loving tribute to all pioneers of the Black Hills and especially to those endeared to us by sacred human ties. Article contributed by Katherine Thornby and Marie Lawler, long-time residents of Deadwood. **Deadwood Pioneer-Times,** June 18, 1979

CHARITY ELIOT
CENTENARIAN AND DAUGHTER
OF A REVOLUTIONARY SOLDIER

Mrs. Charity Eliot of Deadwood celebrated her 100th birthday on April 9, 1895. She enjoyed a gala celebration at the home of her daughter, Mrs. Moody, wife of Judge G. C. Moody, who presented her mother with a beautifully decorated cake. The guest of honor also received many gifts including books, dainty china, and imported wines. Especially welcome were innumerable letters and telegrams of congratulations from children, grandchildren, and great grandchildren in addition to friends from all over the country.

The Black Hills Daily Times reported that "she seemed brighter than she had been for many days. Mrs. Eliot remarked, 'It is worth living 100 years if only to enjoy so many kindnesses.' "

The Times described her as a "remarkable woman, and while she looks very frail, and the form hardly able to hold the spirit, her mind is very clear and her memory wonderful."

Almost five months after Charity Eliot reached 100 years of age, she, who was born in 1795, died at the home of her daughter, Mrs. Moody. Mrs. Eliot is buried in Mount Moriah cemetery. A special marker, erected by the Black Hills Chapter of the Daughters of the American Revolution indicates that she is the daughter of a Revolutionary soldier.

The Times concluded her obituary with this verse:

Two pale hands upon the breast
   And labors done,
Two tired feet crossed in rest
   The race is won.

Arrangements have been made for a memorial service to be held for Mrs. Charity Eliot, a real daughter of a Revolutionary soldier, and a marker will be placed on her grave in Mount Moriah cemetery on Sunday. The Black Hills chapter of the Daughters of the American Revolution will place a marker for Mrs. Eliot, whose father was Charles Warner, who fought in the American Revolution. Circuit Judge Charles Hayes will give the memorial address. **Deadwood Pioneer-Times,** October 9, 1940

IRENE CUSHMAN WILSON
DIARIST AND CULTURAL LEADER

The talented Cushman sisters, Irene, on the right, kept a diary before her marriage describing her romances and recording life in Deadwood. 1890-1891. Charlotte, the younger girl, did not begin writing her memoirs until she was in her 80's and going blind.

Photo courtesy of South Dakota Historical Society.

Irene Cushman Wilson kept a delightful and lengthy diary for about a year and a half (Feb. 8, 1890 to Sept. 29, 1891) when she was a 23-year-old young lady of Deadwood. Despite the relatively short period of time that she recorded her thoughts, she conveyed a sense of "you-are-there-ness" about the social life and happenings in Deadwood in the late 19th century. Irene spoke directly to her diary in endearing terms: "book dear," "book of mine," and "dear old book."

Her favorite subject was analyzing her reactions to being courted by two eligible young men; she identified all young men by the abbreviation "ym." "When I am away from Norman T., I like him best, and when I am with Albert D., I like him best," she wrote. Engineer Albert D. Wilson was the successful suitor who eventually won Irene's hand in marriage.

Several pages are torn out of Irene's diary, and the reader can surmise

that these were about the other suitor, a "ym" with the initials, N.M.

On Sundays, Irene played the organ for the services held at the Congregational Church where her Papa was in charge of the music. During the week Irene participated in the busy social life of Deadwood: church socials, dances until three a.m., card and game parties of progressive anagrams and euchre. Along with other Deadwood-ites interested in the arts, she attended performances of grand opera, like "The Mikado" in the elegant opera house, and theater productions presented by the traveling acting troupes.

There were horse and buggy rides "around the belt" to visit the mining towns of Pluma, Lead, and Central City; train rides on the narrow gauge to Piedmont, and to Hot Springs in the southern Hills for swimming; and sleigh rides and skating in the winter. Irene mentions playing tennis, hiking, and climbing Mount Moriah, White Rocks, and Terry Peak; these were all popular outdoor activities for natives who never tired of exploring the mountainous region that was their home.

Irene's best friend was Estelline Bennett, and the two talented young ladies graduated in Deadwood's first high school class. Estelline, who later wrote **Old Deadwood Days,** mentions "my chum, Irene," 11 times in her book; she described how the girls confided in each other about their boy friends and how they "held long and frequent naive discussions concerning the Badlands and their careless, mysterious inhabitants." The wicked Gem Theater and all the other dives and saloons were of course off-limits to all respectable females. But nothing dispelled their curiosity.

Although Irene did not become a professional author like "Es," she probably could have been a successful writer too; her diary displays literary ability, an eye for colorful detail and the trenchant observation like her comments on Susan B. Anthony's speech to a packed house in Deadwood's city hall. Irene labeled this early women's rights leader as a "tiresome old lady."

Irene described a visit to Mount Moriah on the way back from a climb to White Rocks, the glittering pinnacle and historic landmark above Deadwood Gulch from which the climber is rewarded with spectacular views of the Black Hills panorama.

Two couples made the climb on a warm summer's day, and Irene was with N. M., the unlucky suitor. She wrote about how much fun they had

I'll try to take up the thread of my romance, going back to March 9th. Mr. Wilson, as I said before, was quiet, seeming much occupied with his thoughts. After a few commonplace remarks about anything in general, he said, 'I have fallen in love with you, Miss Cushman.' . . . I was so amazed at the suddenness of it that I looked up thinking it to be one of his jokes . . . He said that I should not commit myself at all but to think it over and 'in a few months I'll ask you again.' Diary of Irene Cushman

I went down to Estelline's and spent the afternoon. We had a good long talk and made up our plans as to how we'd fix some people who think the earth is their own and all the young men thereon. She also gave me some more news and advice and that sort of thing. We gossiped some. April 24, 1890. Diary of Irene Cushman

scrambling down among the bushes and rocks and how Mr. M. held her arm so tightly that she protested.

Irene confided to her diary, "We drank out of the trough by the cemetery, wandered among the graves, and called upon the ghosts" while holding solemn conversations befitting the place and time while the other "ym" quoted tragic poetry to his lady friend.

When it was getting dark in the cemetery, Irene and Mr. M. sat on the outcropping called Brown Rocks. She commented on how pretty the streets below looked with their well-lighted stores "and the eight electric lights helped out." Later, the foursome went to Vienna Restaurant where a complete lunch cost twenty-five cents.

But it was Mr. Albert D. Wilson, not N.M. who eventually persuaded Irene to become his bride, and she recorded the proposal scene at length. At another point in her diary, Irene wrote "while Mr. W. begged to see you, little book," she would not permit it. However, Mr. W. allowed Miss Cushman to see his diary, but she was disgusted to discover that it was written entirely in Spanish.

Irene confessed to her diary how she gave her first "maiden kiss" to Mr. Wilson, and how, in true Victorian tradition, he asked Papa for her hand and how Papa had at first refused.

Irene married A. D. Wilson on October 8, 1891; but before her marriage, she wrote, "This entry will probably be Irene Cushman's last, and I pray, dear old book that Irene Wilson may never have to come to you in her unhappiness."

She never did. Irene Wilson wrote a few more sporadic entries, occa-

Irene Cushman Wilson (Mrs. A. D.) and the sons who kept her too busy to write in her diary. Williams Street, Jan. 1898.

sionally the time elapsing between entries being four years and even 10 years apart. In these short and infrequent entries she commented glowingly on her happy married life as Mrs. Wilson and eventually as the mother of two sons. She was a charter member of The Round Table Club, the first woman's club in Deadwood; and she was chairman of the committee that selected the first books for the Carnegie Library which opened Nov. 8, 1905. After her marriage, Irene played the organ for many years at her husband's church, the Episcopal, instead of at the Congregational.

Irene Cushman Wilson was born in the mining town of Central City, Colorado, in 1867; and when she was 11 years old, she came on the stagecoach with her parents to Deadwood in 1878. Her father Samuel Cushman, a graduate of Brown University in Rhode Island, was at various times superintendent of schools in Lawrence County and Dean of the School of Mines at Rapid City. Her mother, Indiana Sopris Cushman, also a diarist, was the first woman schoolteacher in Denver. Her younger sister Charlotte or Sharly became Mrs. Horace Clark, "the last pioneer" who lived to be 102 and died in 1978. An illustrious family.

Irene herself attended a women's seminary in Massachusetts. Her husband Albert D. Wilson, a Yale civil engineering graduate, was superintendent of the Deadwood Central Railway when she married him. He also surveyed the track for the narrow gauge railway from Deadwood to Lead.

Irene Wilson is buried in the family lot with her husband and sons in Mount Moriah where long ago she and her friends "wandered among the graves and called upon the ghosts." The date of her death was incorrectly recorded in the Record Book as July 3, 1923; the correct date, Dec. 28, 1922, is on her tombstone.

Long after Irene's death from uremia, her relatives decided that her diary would be of interest to patrons of the Deadwood Carnegie Library and had a typewritten copy placed in the Centennial Archives.

Long after Irene was married, she came across her diary in the bottom of a trunk and then penned this farewell entry: "Have to smile in spots at my own great conceit, April 23, 1908."

Irene Wilson need not have apologized for Irene Cushman. Her "dear diary" does not make her sound conceited, only charming and female and perceptive. More than that, it provides a colorful account of a brief span in her own life and chronicles the social and cultural activities of Deadwood in the 1890-1891 era.

———————————————————————————————————————

To the east of the city, and but a short distance away, the celebrated White Rocks, like 'Guardian Angels' rear their heads above all surrounding objects. To visit Deadwood and not climb the summit of the peak, is to go to Egypt and not visit the pyramids. "The Black Hills of South Dakota," Deadwood Board of Trade, 1881

Wonder if people never think of their journals excepting when unhappy or uncertain in love affairs. Jan. 29, 1891, Diary of Irene Cushman

Married—Wilson-Cushman: The wedding was one of the season's notable events . . . in the beautifully decorated parlors of Mr. and Mrs. Cushman's comfortable Williams Street home . . . Mr. Wilson is well-known and deservedly popular . . . His bride is one of the most valued ornaments of metropolitan society, and Mr. Wilson has indeed reason to be proud for having won her. **Black Hills Daily Times,** October 10, 1891

Once when I was 14, I went to a dance with Norman Mason, a prominent young lawyer and a good friend of Irene's and she was out of town. Estelline Bennett didn't get invited to the dance, and she was indignant that Norman took me when she was available. However, he had quite a case on Irene and he liked me, too. Memoirs of Charlotte Cushman Clark.

The Merchants' Carnival was given by the women of the Congregational Church to raise money. I don't know how they could have done it without Irene and me . . . Irene represented the Merchants National Bank and wore a pink surrah silk gown with high-powered bills all over it. She looked as though she owned the United States Treasury. **Old Deadwood Days,** Bennett

And in the midst of life there is death. Diary of Irene Cushman, June 3, 1890

Funeral services were held for Mrs. A. D. Wilson at St. John's Episcopal Church yester-day afternoon . . . Rev. Flockhart officiated, extolling the beautiful and kind deeds of Mrs. Wilson's living moments . . . Many beautiful floral offerings illustrated the large circle of friends of the deceased . . . The remains will be held at Schultes undertaking parlors until the road to Mount Moriah is placed in such condition that the remains can be interred. **The Deadwood Pioneer-Times,** Dec. 31, 1922

Mr. A. D. Wilson was a partner in the Lundberg, Dorr and Wilson Mine and Mill. After his wife Irene died, he went to Florida. He died there in a traffic accident. Memoirs of Charlotte Cushman Clark

HORACE CLARK
AN HORATIO ALGER HERO

The story of Horace Clark's life resembles a Horatio Alger tale of "Rags to Riches." When he was nine years old, in 1878, he came with his family by stage-coach from Denver to Deadwood. When Horace was 14 years old, his father became one of Deadwood's murder victims as the result of an altercation over a saddle. Then Horace, the oldest, took over the responsibility of supporting his mother and three brothers and sisters.

He peddled newspapers, operated a candy and peanut stand, did all kinds of odd jobs after school, which along with selling papers, often neces-sitated his walking back and forth on the rugged climbs between Deadwood and Lead. Soon his reputation as a reliable worker and an unusually mature adolescent became the talk of both towns, and he was able to persuade even skeptical bankers to loan him money for his initial investments.

When Horace was a boy of 14, he bought a cabin on City Creek, from that time on he began to accumulate more and more property in both Dead-wood and Lead. Eventually, he became known as Mr. Real Estate of the Twin Cities, freely admitting that he didn't know how many tenants he had renting apartments and houses or how many pieces of property he owned.

Photo courtesy of Cushman Clark.

Horace Clark, Mr. Real Estate of Deadwood-Lead, who sponsored free tours of the Black Hills for the public school faculty of Lead.

He became the largest individual taxpayer in Lawrence County.

But before he reached the stage of earning a large income and coping with a huge income tax, he had to work and work hard. He dropped out of high school to take a full-time position, but throughout his life he continued to educate himself by omnivorous reading.

When he worked for a freighting company between Deadwood and Sturgis, he customarily walked back and forth beside the loaded horse-drawn wagons up and down Boulder Canyon; and in the cold months he wore long underwear to keep warm, refusing rides because he would get too cold without the exercise.

With a remarkable head for figures, Horace was able to do accounting when he was 12; later he worked 17 years in the general office of the Homestake Mining Company. For the next 17 years he was a Ford dealer; and the last years of his life he devoted mainly to his real estate interests.

Horace married Charlotte Cushman, the "Sharly" often mentioned in her older sister, Irene's diary. Although the Clarks lived for 60 years in the

same house in Lead, yet they were an integral part of both the social and business life in Deadwood, too.

In her memoirs, Charlotte wrote often about the dynamic character she had married, calling him a "self-made man who was aggressive and determined to make good." She explained his reason for acquiring so much property was that he wanted to leave his children and grandchildren well provided for and to assure their all getting college educations.

Horace Clark bought the second automobile in Lead; it was an Oldsmobile with no top or windshield, and passengers entered by a rear door. He loved automobiles: selling them, driving them, and taking anyone who would come along for hair-raising rides on the bumpy trails that passed for roads in the early part of the 20th century. "Every ride with Horace was sort of an adventure," his wife recalled. One time he got carried away and took his sister, Lillie Ayers and her very pregnant friend on an impromptu jaunt to Casper, Wyoming, without taking time to tell anyone their plans or to pack a suitcase for an overnight stay.

Mrs. Clark described an outing when the whole family, including the baby, went in their open car. Horace wanted to go to Hot Springs, but Mrs. Clark and the children, after the long trip in an open car on the dirt roads with high bumps in the middle, persuaded him that Rapid City was far enough and to stop there to rest up before the return trip.

Although Horace was tight-fisted about money in some situations, he was fantastically generous to innumerable people. He believed that the new teachers in Lead should get acquainted with the Black Hills, thus every year he invited the Lead faculty and their families to go on a free sight-seeing trip, with Horace furnishing the cars, paying for gasoline, food, and hotel accommodations. On several occasions he also had a large truck outfitted for camping and took a load of high school and college-age girls on chaperoned expeditions.

Children fascinated Horace Clark, and he thought they should be constantly supplied with candy. He never smoked nor drank and had such an obsession against cigarette smoking that he stopped smokers on the street to give them anti-smoking lectures, whether he knew them or not.

Travel, whether in the Black Hills or around the world appealed to Horace. Even though he developed a wanderlust when the children were too

The number of bicycles in and around Deadwood is surprisingly large, when the rough, hilly nature of the country is taken into consideration. There are between 75 and 100 wheels in the city and there is not a perfectly level street in the city ... . Some ambitious drivers make Hot Springs, a little over 100 miles. This last trip was made by Horace Clark and A. Mochon, two of the best riders in this section, who made the trip in 10 hours, over heavy roads and the latter part of the trip in drenching rain. **The Minneapolis Times,** June, 1895

Dear Sharley and Horace were married about 18 months ago, October 1, 1896, and are living in Lead in their nice home, very happily. They went to Chicago and Denver on their wedding trips, also. Horace makes money all the time and has none on hand—all invested. March, 1898, Diary of Irene Cushman

small for Mrs. Clark to leave them, she encouraged him to go alone and go he did.

When he was in his 50's and didn't feel too well, he was afraid he might die without seeing more of the world, so he took a Mediterranean cruise. In Rome, where he had lost his pass for an audience with the pope and was wearing a gray suit instead of the recommended dark-colored one, he managed to talk his way past the guards.

During his audience with the pope, when the pontiff held out his hand for Horace to kiss the ring, he just shook the pope's hand. Horace, who liked to tell that story, said that the pope smiled but the cardinals all glared at the Congregationalist from the Black Hills of South Dakota.

Horace sold many Fords in the area, but the company objected to Horace's doing his own financing, and he finally quit his Ford dealership. Never did he lose interest in automobiles and in sharing their benefits with others.

Surely there are other measures of success than the money and property one accumulates in a lifetime. Then Horace Clark may be counted as an all-around successful man with carloads of friends who remember a variety of anecdotes about him which illustrate his driving personality, his Santa Claus-like generosity, his sense of humor (especially about himself), and his delightful idiosyncrasies.

Camille Yuill, longtime Deadwood journalist, tells the story that Horace enjoyed telling on himself: one day Horace was riding around the Twin Cities with his sons Cushman and Rogers who eventually went into the real estate business with him. Horace noticed an old house that had possibilities. The trio stopped to inspect it and decided it needed fixing up before it was worth buying. By further checking, Horace discovered that he already owned the decrepit house himself.

A janitor in one of Horace's apartment buildings became critically ill. Horace insisted on paying the man's medical expenses at the Mayo Clinic, the expenses of the sick man's wife to accompany her husband; and when the janitor died, this generous employer paid the funeral expenses.

No wonder people still tell wonderful stories about Horace Clark.

When he died at age 93 on May 17, 1962, the tributes were many. Camille Yuill in her newspaper column wrote: "Horace Clark was one of our most colorful characters and he served his fellow man. As a landlord, he attempted to provide good quarters at reasonable prices. He was stern but lenient . . . He was interested in preserving history and was past presi-

An excited and happy crowd of about 55 people from Lead and Deadwood boarded two passenger automobiles and two large trucks converted into comfortable passenger vehicles at 7 o'clock this morning and left for a two-week trip to the west coast, the guests of Horace Clark, pioneer Northern Hills real estate man. The caravan is headed for San Francisco and the Golden Gate Exposition. The trip is the most lavish thing of its kind Mr. Clark has ever done, although he has been host to many parties of tenants and friends on interesting trips over the Black Hills and nearby country in the years past. **Deadwood Pioneer-Times**, Aug. 16, 1939

dent of the Society of Black Hills Pioneers. . . Horace Clark left a legacy of service and of love.''

Mr. and Mrs. Horace Clark of Lead were host and hostess to a party of 56 Lead people most of them members of the Lead school faculty on the annual trip to the southern Hills. The party went to Sylvan Lake and Camp Galena, where they enjoyed a picnic lunch, going from there to Hot Springs where dinner was served them in the Brown Hotel. The return trip was made Sunday afternoon. **Black Hills Weekly,** Oct. 17, 1939

A fellow from Lead who thought he had some auto tried to throw dust in Horace Clark's eyes. Horace forgot all about that 15-mile-an-hour speed limit on main street and proceeded to show the Ford gait. It cost him $5 when called before the justice, but he paid it without murmuring. It was worth the price to show what the Ford can do. **Deadwood Daily Telegram,** June, 1915

CHARLOTTE CUSHMAN CLARK
THE LAST PIONEER

Photo courtesy of Cushman Clark.

Charlotte Cushman Clark who believed too much attention was paid to the ''wild and woolly side of Deadwood.'' In her memoirs she emphasized that ''there was a good-sized population of educated solid citizens in the early days.''

Charlotte Clark, called ''The Last Pioneer,'' lived to be 102 years old. She grew up with the gold camps of Deadwood and Lead, and her lifetime

spanned travel from stagecoach to 747 super-jet of the space age.

When she was three years old, in 1878, she arrived in Deadwood with her parents, riding the stage-coach from Sidney, Nebraska, to Deadwood when it took "four days and three nights to make the trip, stopping every 20 miles for a change of horses and for meals."

The stage-coach, an imposing cradle on wheels, always made a grand entrance into Deadwood, rumbling and swaying down the steep hill with the driver on his high and mighty seat whipping the horses into a fast gallop,

Photo courtesy of Centennial Archives, Deadwood Public Library.

Passengers piled on McClintock's stages. Many pilgrims, especially women and children, first arrived in the gold camp after an exhausting and often frightening journey by stage-coach. One of the rules for men riding a stage was this: "Gents guilty of unchivalrous behavior toward lady passengers will be put off the stage. It's a long walk back. A word to the wise is sufficient."

then whoaing them up in front of a hotel. People interrupted their dreams of gold to run out of the buildings and rush down the streets to crowd around the frothing horses delivering this magnificent visitor from the outside world. Always, the stage-coach was bursting with news and mail and fresh arrivals to the gold camp—like the Cushman family that October day in 1878.

Charlotte's father, Samuel Cushman, a descendant of the Pilgrims, had come west for his health, first to Denver and the Colorado gold camps before trying his luck in the Black Hills.

Charlotte's older sister Irene called her "Sharly" and frequently mentioned the activities of the two girls: their hikes on the Deadwood board-walks, dances, roller skating, mountain climbing, and strolls on Williams Street, high above Main Street, where the girls could enjoy the band music played on the balcony of the Gem Theater and wonder at the goings-on in that forbidden den of iniquity.

The literate Cushmans were a writing family who believed in preserving their memories and in recording significant moments in their lives which often turned out to have historical interest. Mrs. Cushman had kept a diary

of her days in Colorado. Irene kept a detailed diary of her life in the two years before she was married. Charlotte, in her 80's, began writing her memoirs chronicling her well-remembered life in Deadwood and Lead.

In her memoirs, Charlotte explained that young people didn't often go steady, but went first with one member of the opposite sex and then with another to the varied social activities. When she was 15 or 16 years old, she was allowed to attend public dances sponsored by hose companies which the best young men of the town attended.

Charlotte married Horace Clark, the hard-working young man who presented her with flowers when she graduated from high school. Horace, who had been too busy supporting his family to be able to finish high school, had built a brand new home in Lead for his bride.

In her memoirs, Charlotte explained how she happened to marry Horace: "I suppose it was partly a case of propinquity. Both the Clark and Cushman families attended the Congregational Church. And when we were older, we all went to Christian Endeavor, and at night we had to carry lanterns to see our way."

Keeping up with Horace was a challenge—and sometimes it was a tiring one. Charlotte wrote that she frequently refused to go along on some of the calvacades and camping-out junkets which Horace subsidized for the teachers and other fortunate people because she did not always feel up to doing the cooking and chaperoning.

However, tolerant Charlotte did not try to restrain her energetic husband from carrying out his remarkable travel projects nor from his seeing as much of the world as possible. She was often content to stay home and take care of her family.

During her married life, Charlotte, much interested in women's club work, was a charter member of the Thursday Club in Deadwood. She was also a member of the P.E.O. Sisterhood in Lead. She reported that the highlight of her life as a clubwoman was when she learned that she was not only the oldest living member of the Lead Women's Club, but she was also the oldest clubwoman in South Dakota, having been a member of a Federated women's club for 83 years.

Sharly is at a "C" party tonight at Lenore's where everything they are to eat begins with "C" and everything they play begins with "C", as did also each work on the invitation Lenore sent to the Aurora Borealis Club, Diary of Irene Cushman, April 17, 1893

Once after I was engaged to Horace we went to a big dancing party at the Blackstones who lived in Gayville. The Northwestern train ran a special train up the gulch to take guests up and back. Memoirs of Charlotte Clark

Teaching English to the Chinese was a project of the Congregational Church about 1885-1886. My sister Irene had as her pupil Yu Chung Mark who was very bright and became one of the best penmen using Spencerian copy books. My sister received gifts from her Chinese pupils: a handsome large white silk handkerchief with embroidery all around the hem, a pink crepe shawl with embroidered fringe, and a carved ivory Chinese junk and sandalwood fan. Memoirs of Charlotte Clark

When Horace Clark had a stroke and was severely disabled, Charlotte took care of him at home until he died in 1962. When she herself was unable to live alone, she moved to the Dorset Nursing Home in Spearfish where she lived for one year until her death.

Her son-in-law John Barstow, married to her daughter Veronica, frequently taped conversations with his mother-in-law through the years. In the published excerpts he reported how vivid her recollections were about the history of the Homestake Mine, the strikes, and the dangerous situations when the main street of Lead began caving into the mine workings. Fires and cyclones and floods were still clear in her mind. In 1964, Charlotte Clark, when she was only 89, was honored as the Gold Queen in the Labor Day Parade at Lead.

Alert and energetic in her 80's, Charlotte, at the suggestion of her family, began writing down recollections of her early life. She wrote in large notebooks, but because she was going blind, her writing was often slanted down the page; however, it is still readable and provides much interesting information about her own family and about Deadwood-Lead in general. She often expressed regret that she was unable to edit these memoirs herself.

When Charlotte Clark died in February, 1978, at age 102, she was truly "the last pioneer" because she had been the lone survivor among the pioneers who had come to the Black Hills before the Deadwood fire of September, 1879. Even those Black Hillers who did not know her felt a sense of loss, for she was the last link to the historic days of early Deadwood and Lead.

Rev. Stephen Doughty of the Presbyterian Church of Lead was in charge of the simple services the family had requested for Charlotte Clark, who had 5 children, 14 grandchildren, and 22 great-grandchildren. The text was from Proverbs 31: "Who can find a virtuous woman? For her price is far above rubies . . . Strength and dignity are her clothing; and she shall rejoice in the time to come . . . She looketh well to the ways of her household and eateth not the bread of idleness. Her children rise up and call her blessed; her husband also, and he praiseth her."

The day of Charlotte Clark's funeral was a cold, overcast day. Rev. Doughty recalled: "The occasion at Mount Moriah cemetery impressed me deeply. A few miles to the south of us, gigantic dim forms, a tower and a building of the Homestake Gold Mine arose from the top of a hill. So many in Charlotte's lifetime had come for the gold. We passed the graves of Wild Bill Hickok and Calamity Jane. So many had come to this cemetery for the 'notables.' On this particular winter day, though, we had come for a life lived out in many years of quiet goodness, for one who had been handsome, keen, and loving even into great old age. The gold and the 'notables' would continue to receive the most attention, but somehow it seemed, that in the long sweep of time, the life of quiet goodness mattered most."

Although Mrs. Clark enjoyed remarkably good health, her failing eyesight has limited her activities. However, after she was 90 years of age she flew by plane from Denver to Rapid City. This took about an hour whereas she recalled that by stage-coach from Cheyenne to Deadwood it took 'four days and three nights.' Barstow "The Last Pioneer," **Black Hills Nuggets**

I attended the Columbia Exposition in Chicago for graduation from high school in 1893. I heard much classical music and took vocal lessons . . . I often visited relatives in Denver and saw Pavlova dance and heard fine musicians in concert—Lawrence Tibbett, Rachmaninoff, Itirbi. I saw the operas 'La Boheme' and "Aida." I also heard many artists at Lead and Rapid City who later became famous. Memoirs of Charlotte Clark

It seems to many old timers that so much stress is put on exploiting the wild and woolly side of Deadwood that they lose sight of the fact that there was a good-sized population of educated solid citizens in the early days. Of course, Wild Bill, Calamity Jane, Poker Alice—are of more interest to the tourist, but the present-day citizens of Deadwood should know more about the ones who really made Deadwood a town that has been lived in since 1876. Memoirs of Charlotte Clark

FREEMAN KNOWLES
SOCIALIST CONGRESSMAN AND
RADICAL EDITOR

Sinner or saint, devil or god, criminal or martyr—Freeman Knowles was undoubtedly the most controversial man in Deadwood's history of contradictions; this tall, slender dynamo was a lawyer, newspaper editor, socialist leader, and a United States Congressman. There are many venerable natives in Deadwood with long memories; some claim Knowles was a deceitful rabble-rouser, deserving of every dirty name; others revere his memory as a champion of the poor and oppressed, comparable to Abraham Lincoln.

Born in Maine into a family of 11 children, the young boy, when not yet 16 years old joined the Union Army, served for three years during the Civil War, was captured and became a prisoner of war in a southern prison for seven months.

After the Civil War, Knowles studied for the law in Iowa and was admitted to the bar. He came to the Black Hills in 1888 and started the first newspaper in Tilford, a few miles south of Sturgis. Here he began using his caustic printing press to expose injustice and political corruption as he saw it.

To Deadwood he came in 1890, where illegal gambling and prostitution were entrenched, bringing his explosive printer's ink and established the **Evening Independent,** the recognized organ of the Populists (or Socialists), of the Federation of Miners, and of other labor organizations. By the advent of the 20th century, he was also publishing two other newspapers: **The Equality** and **The Lantern,** in which he vigorously promoted the cause of the laboring man, supporting the struggling unions against the Homestake Mining Company. He often quoted the doctrines of his mentor Eugene Debs, the national socialist leader.

Describing Knowles' venture into politics, a biographical source wrote that his nomination for Congress "was the spontaneous desire of the elements which he represents and which predominate in this section." A member of the Populist party, in 1896, he won over the Republican by only 700 votes. Knowles served as Representative-at-large for the Black Hills region for one term in Congress, the first and only political position he ever held.

But he apparently preferred trying to influence society by the power of the press rather than the power of Congress. With his inflammatory editorial pen, Knowles, a daring radical, did battle with the rich and mighty of the Black Hills.

Perhaps Knowles' most famous editorial and one which had the most repercussions was a restrained discussion of a respectable young woman who had died of an abortion. He wrote in part: "A good illustration of the beauties of our social system was recently given when 'society' in Lead and Deadwood was convulsed by the news that a sweet and amiable young woman died at Denver from the effects of an operation performed upon her to hide what society calls her 'shame.' Why—simply that an unmarried girl having disregarded the sanctions of some priest or magistrate had made the discovery that God had worked in her the wonderful miracle of motherhood. Love had its way and God blessed the union with the most stupendous fruit of the universe, a human child, and society steps in and cries 'shame' and causes the mother to kill both herself and the baby."

For this editorial in **The Lantern,** May 30, 1908, Freeman Knowles was indicted and convicted in the Federal Court of sending "lewd, obscene and lascivious matter through the mail" with Nathan Franklin, son of millionaire Harris Franklin, as the complainant.

For his views, which many interpreted as recommending free love and illigitimacy, Knowles was imprisoned in the Pennington County jail for 23 days, refusing to allow his friends to pay the $500 fine. Later, the case was appealed in the Court of Appeals where the conviction was upheld, the fine eventually paid.

From his jail cell, Knowles continued to write editorials reviling the Franklins and requesting his subscribers to send their subscription money to his wife, Alice Knowles. The voice from jail said: "It is hardly necessary for me to tell the people of Lawrence County the animus behind this persecu-

The church people warn sinners of hell after death but some good Christians voted hell for both saints and sinners right here in Deadwood. I wonder if God will interfere to save the children from the damnation of the saloons voted upon by the city of Deadwood last Tuesday. **The Lantern,** April 23, 1908

Union men should beware of anything savoring of violence, and they should keep a close eye upon anyone who talks in that direction. **The Lantern,** Nov. 7, 1909

Oh Yes, men are equal before the law—in a pig's ear!" **The Lantern,** Sept. 9, 1909

We speak of free men—why not free women? **The Lantern,** May 14, 1908

tion. DID THIS ARTICLE SHOCK MR. FRANKLIN'S MODESTY? Great God! His debaucheries could not be published, for they would certainly constitute 'lewd, obscene, and lascivious matter.' Oh, it was not that. It was because I have told of the stealings of the gang of thieves of which Franklin is the local head.''

Because of his vitriolic editorials, Knowles was often sued for libel. One time he was sued because he implied that Judge Quimby of Lead had been "bought" by the Homestake Mining Company. A jury acquitted Knowles of the charge. Always, he fought for higher wages for the miners and improved working conditions.

Especially during the Homestake lockout, Knowles' accusations and implications against the Homestake, largest gold-producer in the western hemisphere, and the controlling economic force in the Black Hills, aroused the wrath of many people, including tempestuous Chambers Kellar, chief counsel for the Homestake Mining Company.

According to the **Deadwood Pioneer-Times,** January 6, 1910, traditionally the anti-Knowles newspaper, the now legendary fight between two prominent adversaries happened this way: "Freeman Knowles was publicly horsewhipped by attorney Chambers Kellar in the office of the county commissioners in the presence of a dozen county officials. According to Kellar's statement the chastisement was administered in retaliation for alleged slanderous articles published recently in **The Lantern.**" With a quirt Kellar "slashed Knowles several times across the face and head" before the aggressor was grabbed by several county officers. Then Knowles gained control of the whip, hitting Kellar in the face with the butt end. Knowles' glasses, which Kellar had earlier asked him to remove, dropped from Knowles' hand during the fight and were broken as they lay on the floor. "The editor of **The Lantern** says he will not ask that a complaint for assault be made."

Right or wrong—or somewhere in between—Knowles was an eloquent writer, a forceful speaker, and a fearless adversary against the Establishment, often expressing viewpoints far ahead of his time.

I promise you that I shall be far happier in my prison cell, sent there because I dared raise my voice to free women from degradation, than Franklin will be in his palatial mansion, built upon the foundations of human skulls, of poor wretches who have filled drunkards' graves. "Why I Went to Jail," Knowles, **The Lantern,** June 4, 1908

They tell me you are in jail. What an outrage! While such men as you live, the cause of humanity, however bitterly assailed or foully betrayed, can never fail. Yours, for the revolution, Eugene V. Debs, **The Lantern,** June 18, 1908

What is the wild and woolly west coming to when a harmless comment on a great moral problem gains the distinction of federal prosecution for its author? "Decadent Deadwood," **The Denver Post,** July, 1908

I understand the pimps and preachers and gamblers are having a general jollification during my imprisonment. **The Lantern,** June, 1908

Freeman Knowles, age 64, died in June, 1910, from pneumonia following an operation. At his funeral in the Deadwood City Hall he was eulogized by Chauncey Wood, the Rapid City lawyer who had defended him in court many times: "He had an abiding faith in the common people and was by nature a reformer. Such thinkers as Mr. Knowles led the world out of the Dark Ages."

The Deadwood Pioneer-Times reported that Knowles' funeral was attended by the largest "concourse of people that ever attended a funeral in the Black Hills." Hundreds of miners followed the cortege to Mount Moriah, and there were delegates from all the labor organizations of the Black Hills.

In Mount Moriah the grave of Freeman Knowles is in the corner of a

The lonely grave of editor Freeman Knowles who fought for miners' rights and was jailed for writing an anti-abortion, anti-society editorial.

large plot, enclosed by a wrought-iron fence and shaded by a tall ponderosa pine. The inscription on the faded white Civil War marker is: "Corporal F.T. Knowles, Co. A 16, Me Inf."

A view of Mount Moriah from road in front of Brown Rocks overlook. In the middle of the picture the ponderosa pine is growing in the corner of the Freeman Knowles burial lot surrounded by a wrought-iron fence.

There is nothing to identify him as a Congressman or an editor or an influential leader.

The Record Book lists Mrs. Knowles and several of the eight children as being interred in Mount Moriah, including the child Bee and Olive, a popular teacher in the local schools. However, there are no markers identifying individual members of the family.

Knowles had once written, "Let no man write my epitaph." And none did. But some of his own lines sound as they belong on the tombstone of Freeman Knowles: "I am ready to die, but while I live I will defend the poor and oppressed and expose villainy and injustice."

I most sincerely believe in the teachings of the Great Socialist, Jesus. **The Lantern,** July 11, 1908

I express my abhorrence over the veil of secrecy which is thrown by society over the sex life when the young are taught that certain parts of their bodies are 'indecent.' What should be openly and freely discussed, is sternly suppressed and forbidden. But this cannot keep the young from making discoveries. **The Lantern,** May 28, 1908

I was just a little girl when, along with my mother and a large group of people, I watched the long funeral procession for Freeman Knowles from the Brown Rocks overlook in Mount Moriah. When the first crowd of mourners in buggies and on foot had reached his grave, we could look across town and see people still pouring out of the city hall. I remember that it was said Jack Gray's Wasp No. 2 mine about closed down that day because so many miners were determined to attend the funeral of their champion. The Knowles were a wonderful family— all brilliant. They probably couldn't afford to put up stone markers for each one in the family plot. Recollection of Marie Lawler, daughter of James Lawler, Black Hills Pioneer of 1876

DR. FLORA HAYWARD STANFORD
FIRST WOMAN DOCTOR

Flora Hayward Stanford was a pioneer woman doctor in Deadwood in an era when few women took up the medical profession. She received her degree from Boston University School of Medicine in 1878, then practiced medicine in Washington, D.C. for 10 years. She was separated from her husband, Valentine Stanford, and their son Victor stayed with his father in Pennsylvania.

Dr. Stanford decided to come west with her 16-year-old tubercular daughter Emma; in Deadwood, Dr. Stanford's maternal instincts combined with her medical knowledge made her hopeful that the dry climate would improve Emma's health.

Fifty years old when she began practicing in Deadwood in 1888, Dr. Stanford bought a home on Williams Street which also served as her medical office. She and Emma entered the social and cultural life of the busy community which was by then outgrowing the wild gold rush days.

The only lady doctor who ever practiced in Deadwood, this calm and efficient woman went on calls by horse and buggy, and on horseback, dis-

Photo courtesy of Centennial Archives, Deadwood Public Library.

Dr. Flora Stanford and her ailing daughter, Emma, in front of their home on Williams Street which doubled as an office.

pensing medical care to whoever needed it and not expecting much payment for her services.

Among her famous patients were Calamity Jane, Buffalo Bill Cody, and whoever was then impersonating Deadwood Dick. The nature of her medical services to them is not known—unfortunately for the curious.

In a letter to her son Victor, she wrote about an unidentified man "badly shot up" who burst into her office for help. Dr. Stanford removed three bullets from his body, dressed his wounds, and "permitted him to leave via the rear door to her office."

Soon after, the County Sheriff appeared, interrogated her, and was able to describe perfectly the man she had just treated. The sheriff told her who he was, then left her office to track down this notorious gunfighter. Dr. Stanford reported to her son, "On several occasions I had removed one bullet from a man, but this was the first time I had ever removed three at one time."

Despite the loving and expert care Emma received, the girl's health did not improve. Dr. Stanford gave up her practice and took Emma to southern California in hopes her daughter might improve in a warmer climate. Emma

died in California in 1893 and was buried there. Sad and alone, Dr. Stanford returned by train and stage-coach to Deadwood, the place she called home.

Even before Emma died, Dr. Stanford had begun practicing medicine in Sundance, Wyoming, a distance of 50 miles from Deadwood. After her return from California, she resumed her practice in both places. She traveled back and forth by horseback and by horse and buggy over the wilderness trails to visit her patients, upholding the best traditions of the country doctor.

In 1897, she took up a claim near Sundance and homesteaded on the Double-D ranch. Her strenuous life on the ranch combined with the physical effort expended by her practicing medicine in two localities probably contributed to the deterioration of her own health.

Dr. Stanford died February 1, 1901, at age 62 of heart trouble and is buried somewhere in Mount Moriah in an unidentified grave.

At the time of her death, her son Victor came to Deadwood, but authorities were unable to contact an adopted son, Frank Daly-Stanford.

Dr. Stanford had requested that she did not want funeral services held in a church. As she had specified, simple last rites of the Episcopal Church were conducted at her flower-bedecked grave. **The Deadwood Pioneer-Times** described the ceremony at Mount Moriah: "Tenderly the last offices were performed, and the form of her who had been mother, friend, and medical advisor to numbers of struggling and benighted souls was lowered into its narrow home amid a flood of silent tears."

Dr. Stanford, whom the newspapers usually called "Mrs. Dr. Stanford," was a highly regarded professional in Deadwood during her 12 years there and was apparently accepted by the other physicians—all men—who were her colleagues.

Sixty-eight years after Dr. Stanford's death, her granddaughter and her husband, Mr. and Mrs. Albert S. Hidy of Portland, Oregon, made a special trip to Deadwood to present a geneological record of Dr. Flora Stanford and her family to the Deadwood Carnegie Library. The Hidys also presented a bronze plaque honoring Dr. Stanford which now hangs in the main reading room of the library.

In the last letter Victor Stanford received from his mother, she sent this verse, which he always regarded as the motto of Dr. Flora Stanford:

> Let every moment as it flies
> Record thee good as well as wise,
> They who improve life's shortest day
> Will not regret its parting ray.

One night two weeks ago I went to a choir rehearsal with Allie for his choir at Emma Stanfords. They are practicing Easter music. Diary of Irene Cushman, Jan. 13, 1891

Dr. Stanford visited Mr. Inman at the mouth of Nevada Gulch yesterday, and today she again went to visit Mr. Inman, who was very low. Dr. Stanford has hopes of his pulling through if he can hang on for a few days. **Black Hills Daily Times**, August, 1893

Dr. Flora H. Stanford—Homeopathist. Office and Residence, Williams Street between Lee and Gold Streets. Hours: 10 to 12 a.m., 5 to 7 p.m. Advertisement in **Black Hills Daily Times,** May 1, 1895

Notwithstanding that she has busied herself with her profession and domestic life, yet she has taken a lively interest in public affairs, she has been prominent in the work of the churches and societies, and her name has been associated in one way or another with almost every laudable enterprise in the city where her assistance was welcome. She was for a number of years a member of the Board of Education of Deadwood, and in that capacity she rendered valuable service. **The Deadwood-Pioneer Times,** Feb. 3, 1901

DIFFERENT STAR
AN OGLALA SIOUX SUICIDE

"Another Good Indian" was the customary headline in the early Deadwood newspapers announcing the death of an Indian.

A variation, "Good Injun Now," heralded the suicide of a Sioux Indian jailed in Deadwood: "Different Star, a full blood Oglala Sioux from

Photo courtesy of South Dakota Historical Society.

Deadwood, SD. Scaffold on which the first Indian was hanged.

Pine Ridge, committed suicide in his cell in the county jail Sunday by choking himself to death with a cord. Different Star was committed to jail five weeks ago on a charge of horse-stealing . . . Since that time he has shown evidences of remorse and not being able to speak a word of English, showed on numerous occasions that his heart was bad and that he meant violence

sooner or later. His actions were interpreted to mean that William David-son, confined in jail, waiting a new trial for the murder of Giles was offen-sive to him and that it was Different Star's intention to kill Davidson and destroy his own life. Although Sheriff Plunkett had no apprehensions of the Indian doing any harm, he deemed it advisable to remove him to another part of the jail. . . . Different Star was about 26 years of age, single, and we

Indians performing in "Days of '76" celebration in Deadwood.

Photo courtesy of South Dakota Historical Society.

understand his parents are well-to-do stock owners and farmers on the Pine Ridge reservation. . . . Full instructions have not been received with refer-ence to disposition of the remains but they will doubtless be buried here," concluded the **Deadwood Pioneer-Times,** January 18, 1898.

Different Star—Indian—Suicide—Jan. 18, 1895. Record Book of the Deadwood Ceme-tery Association

General Phil Sheridan uttered the immortal words: 'The only good Indians I ever saw were dead.' A lieutenant who was present remembered the words and passed them on, until in time they were honed into an American aphorism: THE ONLY GOOD INDIAN IS A DEAD IN-DIAN. **Bury My Heart at Wounded Knee,** Brown

The members of the expedition for the most part, had but small confidence in the good faith of their savage neighbors, believing the old saying that there are "no good Indians but dead Indians." **The Black Hills,** Tallent

"A Good Indian—Cha Nopa Uhah, Alias Two Sticks, Paid the Death Penalty Yester-day." Two hundred people with tickets stood inside the gallows area and heard Chief Two Sticks Sing his Death Song and watched him Hang. Two Sticks said in a loud clear voice: 'My heart is not bad; I did not kill the cowboys—the Indian boys killed them. I have killed many In-dians but never killed a white man. The Great Father and the men under him should talk to me and I would show them that I was innocent . . . My heart knows I am not guilty and I am happy.'

A grating sound, a bang, a thud, tell the story which were almost simultaneous, and Two Sticks changed in the twinkling of an eye from an amiable being full of energy and powerful, in the world beyond the chasm that is inpenetrable to those he left behind. **Black Hills Weekly,** Jan. 5, 1895

Photo courtesy of Centennial Archives, Deadwood Public Library.

Chief Two Sticks who was hanged for murder in Deadwood, Jan. 4, 1894. On the gallows he said: "My heart knows I am not guilty and I am happy."

One of two Indians listed in the Record Book, Different Star, like hundreds of others, is buried in an unknown grave in Potter's Field, the wooded area overgrown with underbrush which surrounds the visible part of Mount Moriah. The wooden headboards used in Potter's Field soon disappeared because of the ravages of weather and vandals.

(Chief Two Sticks is buried in an unmarked grave outside the fence in St. Ambrose Catholic Cemetery, Deadwood)

DORA DUFRAN
BROTHEL MADAM AND AUTHOR

Dora DuFran was a noted madam in red light districts throughout the Black Hills: in Deadwood, Lead, Belle Fourche, and Rapid City. She was

also a confidante and occasional employer of Calamity Jane, about whom she wrote a booklet entitled, **Low-Down on Calamity Jane.** Calling herself D. Dee, the bashful authoress, whose identity was well-known despite the pseudonym, identified herself only as "Written by one who knew her for many years and who was intimately associated with her in the early days of the Hills."

Dora married Joseph DuFran, a Black Hills Pioneer of 1876, who died 25 years before she did. Dora also had children, but her biggest family was composed of the prostitutes who worked in her various brothels through the years. These females were important contributors to the financial success of what was called the sporting fraternity, which included operators of brothels, gambling dens, saloons, and dance halls.

Traditionally, the terms "prostitutes" and "whores" have not been generally used by Black Hillers—especially not in indulgent Deadwood—to describe the professionals of the red light districts, called the Bad Lands in the old days of the gold camp. The early newspapers established the custom

Photo courtesy of South Dakota State Historical Society.

The Gem Theater, the most famous or infamous den of iniquity in the Bad Lands of lower main street. According to Madam DuFran, the Gem band played from the balcony when "the ladies of the night came forth to dance, drink, and hustle."

of using kinder-sounding terms: girls, upstairs girls, soiled doves, ladies of the night, sisters of sin, and demi-reps.

One point on which all historians and the oldest Deadwood natives agree is that the Gem Theater was the worst den of iniquity in Sin City, and it combined gambling, drinking, dancing, and prostitution with its bawdy

stage shows. Historian John McClintock damned the Gem as a "vicious institution." Both he and Dora DuFran described how Al Swearingen, the infamous manager of The Gem, lured innocent girls from the East out to Deadwood with promises of acting jobs on his stage. Instead he forced them into "white slavery," said McClintock.

Estelline Bennett, the Judge's daughter, wrote in her book that a county official looking over old records of Undertaker Smith "was appalled by the number of girls in The Gem and houses of like repute who had committed suicide in those hard, early 80's. No one knew how many they were."

Whether or not Dora DuFran was ever involved with the Gem Theater is unknown, but she wrote authoritatively about its activities and could certainly be classified as an expert on the dives of lower main street. According to Dora, in 1886, when Deadwood's population was about 3,000, 1,000 of these residents were members of the sporting fraternity, and at least half (500) of these were women. She described how the Gem band played every night from the balcony "when the ladies of the night came forth to dance, drink and hustle." And this was the excitement that brought out the curious young people to promenade and to speculate from their vantage point on lofty Forest Hill.

Dora explained that the girls received ten cents for every dance, twenty cents for every bottle of beer sold, and one dollar for every bottle of wine. But she did not reveal how much a girl earned for turning a trick or what percentage the madams received from the house take.

Dora's name is mentioned by many authors in histories and reminiscenses about the Black Hills. Robert Casey, a Rapid City native, in his entertaining book, **The Black Hills and Their Incredible Characters,** mentions

---

Almost simultaneously yesterday, two cases of suicide were reported from the Bad Lands, the first to occur victimizing Etta Lindenbower. . . . Etta has for years led a fast life with all of its evil features, including opium and gambling. . . . To make assurance doubly sure, the poor creature first swallowed laundanum poison, then repairing to the bed, spread the covering over her face, and pressing the pistol to her breast—knew no more. Deceased was about 23 years of age.

Brief announcement of the foregoing had scarcely reached the street, when word passed from mouth to mouth that Hazel Kirke had suicided with morphine. "Hazel Kirke" was an assumed name. As Julia Laundy the unfortunate girl was christened about 19 years ago. Julia was a comely girl, with a bright, cheerful disposition, and was a great favorite with associates. . . . She resolved to escape the sea of trouble with which her young life was so woefully beset. "Two of a Kind," **Black Hills Daily Times,** May, 1888

The death yesterday of Olga Armstrong, aged 20, known here as Minnie Morris, is but a repetition of one more unfortunate going to her death. The deceased suffered from consumption. . . . Nothing whatever is known here of her antecedents and it is probably just as well that such be buried with her to save from sorrow and shame loving parents and brothers and sisters. **Black Hills Daily Times,** July, 1893

Thomas Jones was shot by a young woman whose name is given as Jess Taylor, better known as "Big Jess," an inmate of Dora DuFran's bagnio in West Bleeker street in Lead. **Deadwood Daily Telegram,** July, 1913

The inside of the Gem Theater where male patrons cheered the stage shows, drank, gambled, and danced with the "ladies of the night" who entertained men privately in the small curtained rooms on the left.

Dora five times, although he spells her last name "DeFranne" instead of DuFran, as it is on her tombstone in Mount Moriah. When Dora marched in and out of the saloons in Rapid City looking for her drunken piano player, "You couldn't ignore her anymore than you could ignore a brass band." Although Casey wrote that she lacked the elegance of another madam called Black Nell, he commended Dora for "a certain amount of silent popularity" and for being a good business woman.

Carl Leedy, another Rapid Citian, in his reminiscences recalled that during prohibition days when the amusement parlors were closed, he asked Dora if she were going to start up a new sporting house. "Kid," she replied, "you can't run a sporting house on creek water."

The dates of Dora's whereabouts are muddled but she certainly got around, operating houses at one time or another in four Black Hills towns. In Belle Fourche, her brothel was called the Three D's—Drinking, Dining, and Dancing. A newspaper ad announced, "A place where you can bring your mother." At the bottom of the ad, a sheep-herder comments, "I wouldn't want my mother to know I had been there." In a faded ledger in the Tri-State Museum in Belle Fourche, there is a 1908 entry about Dora DuFran's being fined $200 for selling liquor without a license.

In Belle Fourche, Deadwood, Lead, and Rapid City, a good number of

A man named Johnnie Moore felt sorry for a girl who had come from Milwaukee in response to an ad: "Actresses, dancers wanted. Good Pay." It nearly broke her heart when she found what kind of den of iniquity she was supposed to sing and dance in. Moore went into the gambling dens and appealed to the faro players for a contribution to send this innocent young girl back home again. He collected a total of $442 and presented it to the girl with a speech, saying 'You are not obligated to the donors—and remember that although this is called a tough town our people as a rule have the largest and most generous hearts to be found on earth.' "Early Day Charity in Deadwood," Handlin, **Deadwood Pioneer-Times,** Aug. 12, 1939

graybeards still remember Dora. "Yup," exclaimed a retired cowboy, chuckling wickedly, "She was a tough old bag but mighty good looking!" Another ancient with dreamy eyes recalled, "She was a real woman I'll tell you and she ran a clean house." Not one of Dora's faithful admirers wanted his name used.

The grave-site of Madam DuFran with its four decorative urns is one of the most ornate in Mount Moriah.

Dora DuFran died in Rapid City in 1934, aged 60. Her death is reported by many area newspapers, except no obituary identified her as a madam. Both **The Rapid City Journal** and the **Deadwood Pioneer-Times** published brief notices. **The Belle Fourche Bee,** August 10, 1934, identified her as a former resident of Belle Fourche, then wrote glowingly about her as an outstanding charity and social worker in Rapid City for the preceding 15 years, stating that "She nursed the sick, bought food and clothing and paid for the rent for the poverty-stricken."

Sounds as though Dora must have been the legendary scarlet woman with a heart of gold—and what else could a heart be made of in the Black Hills?

Dora DuFran is buried in Mount Moriah just across the flagstone walk

Joseph DuFran, one of the pioneers of the Black Hills, and a popular and generous fellow, passed away at Hot Springs. **Deadwood Pioneer-Times,** August 5, 1909

At a late hour last night, Gertie, a red-headed siren at the Gem Theater, in a fit of jealousy sailed into Dutch Anne with a knife and carved her all about the head and face. It is thought one of Anne's eyes are gone, and there are two desperate gashes in the back of her head and neck. The victim was carried off covered with blood and the carver was escorted by the police to jail. "Thirty Years Ago", **Deadwood Pioneer-Times,** April, 1914

A new girl from Cheyenne shaped like she had been warped over a barrel, face downwards, was drunk on the streets yesterday. **Black Hills Daily Times,** May 28, 1878

from the grave of her friend, Calamity Jane. On each corner of the imposing DuFran lot where both Father and Mother are buried is an urn adorned
with a grinning gargoyle. Engraved on Dora's tombstone are the words,
"Gone But Not Forgotten." And that's an accurate epitaph.

FOUR BROTHELS THRIVE IN DOWNTOWN DEADWOOD, Headline in **Deadwood
Pioneer-Times,** August 6, 1979

EDWARD SENN
CRUSADING JOURNALIST
AND PROHIBITIONIST

"For has not Deadwood gloried for many years in its 'tough' reputation? Have not leading businessmen maintained that the more prostitutes
and pimps and gamblers that could be attracted to the city, the greater
would be its prosperity? Until Deadwood cleans out the rubbish of pioneer
days, it must pay the penalty for being one of the few cities within the confines of civilization which welcomes that class of people, licenses houses of
prostitution, permits gambling resorts to operate under flimsy cover and
violates other state laws, with the approval of its chief executive." So wrote
Edward Senn, the crusading and fearless editor of **The Deadwood Daily
Telegram** in June, 1915.

The ambition of this fiesty little bald-headed man was to clean up
Deadwood—and that was a superhuman job.

But before Senn took on the lawless sporting fraternity and its many

supporters in Deadwood, he had plenty of in-service training doing battle against wickedness wherever he found it.

Senn, who always did his best to prove that the pen was mightier than the sword—or six-shooter—started a newspaper in a one-room shack in Lyman County, South Dakota, just west of the Missouri River. There he determined to break up a gang of cattle rustlers by the power of his printed words.

When a leader of the cattle rustlers came into the newspaper office with a gun and kicked over the ink bucket, wiry little Senn grabbed the six-shooter and said, "Get your cattle rustlers out of here, or I'll smear this whole country with printer's ink. I'm backing a decent judge and he'll put you all in jail."

The rustlers set fire to Senn's home, his barn, his newspaper office—even his fences—and the fires killed many of his horses. Fortunately, his wife and children were staying with a neighbor, and he had just moved his printing equipment to a safer location during the much-publicized vendetta to "get Senn."

Senn's tiny newspaper office became a rendezvous for the law—United States marshals and sheriffs who finally broke up the cattle-rustling ring and killed Jack Sully, one of the West's most notorious badmen. But the lawmen couldn't have done it without the power of Senn's press behind them.

Senn's wife, Christie, who had been one of his pupils when he had taught a one-room country school, supported her husband all the way, despite threats to life and property. This brave woman encouraged him to follow his conscience wherever it led him, next to Dirkstown in Lyman County where his newspaper wielded even more influence.

During the homesteading era in the early 20th century, newspapers in South Dakota supported themselves by publishing final proof notices, a requirement of the United States Land Office involved in the process of issuing deeds to settlers for their claims. Senn used his newspaper columns for

Almost any man of normal disposition, who had been handed the lesson that E. L. Senn received in the municipal election yesterday would conclude that he was persona non grata in the community. But it is not likely that it will have the slightest influence on him. He has nothing to lose and the satisfaction he derives from saying mean things about Deadwood and its people more than repays him for the labor of filling his editorial page with slurs, innuendos and slander. Six hundred and fifty voters showed by their secret ballot that they wanted Nathan Franklin for mayor and were glad for the opportunity to repudiate Senn. **Deadwood Pioneer-Times,** April 23, 1914

Edward L. Senn of the Deadwood **Telegram** and formerly publisher of about 35 other papers in western South Dakota has been sued for $50,000 damages by George W. Egan of Sioux Falls. Egan claimed Senn libeled him in the last campaign when Egan was independent candidate for governor. Well, Senn is always looking for trouble, apparently, and if Egan had a good case, it should keep the scrappy editor busy for a few days at least. **Belle Fourche Bee,** March 25, 1914

earning a living with this business and his editorial page to combat lawlessness wherever he found it.

When one publishing plant was paid for, Senn mortgaged it to buy another. At one time he owned 35 newspapers in western South Dakota; Senn was known as the Final Proof King and actually had a one-man monopoly going. With his flourishing final proof business and his gutsy editorials against crime, he became a political power in South Dakota.

In 1909, Edward Senn bought **The Daily Telegram** at Deadwood, expecting to make that the headquarters for his extensive operations covering a ready-print business that served some 70 newspapers including his own.

Immediately, Senn became incensed over goings-on in Deadwood which continued to live up to its pioneer-days nickname of "Sin City." He vowed to clean up wide-open Deadwood.

Years later, Senn described the situation as he saw it to a Denver newspaper reporter: "Deadwood has 24 saloons, plus other gambling dens, dance halls, and houses of ill fame running day and night. Lurid ladies parade down the street from which decent women and children were all but barred. Of the 3,000 population, several hundred were connected with the operation of these institutions. They controlled the money from which tradesfolk and even churches and schools were largely dependent."

Senn used his printer's ink, black and bold, to appeal to the law-abiding element in Deadwood to do something—but his enemies were legion. The underworld put pressure on Senn's advertisers, burned down his newspaper office, and wrecked his machinery. Even when he was beaten up on the street, the courageous little man would not cease his attacks on the sporting fraternity. For five years he kept up the battle; at one time 300 soiled doves were run out of Deadwood—temporarily.

People often reminded Edward Senn that he was fighting a one-man battle. He replied confidently, "Yes, but one man and God make a majority in any fight."

Mainly because of his fanatical dedication to routing the underworld in Deadwood, no matter what it cost him in advertising business, he eventually lost his large string of newspapers. His loyal wife Christie encouraged him to sell the farm to pull him through a financial crisis. His two older boys helped him run the newspaper which kept going despite fires and vandalism. Eventually, Deadwood elected a mayor who stood for law and order, and grand jury indictments broke the underworld's control over Deadwood—for a time.

The motto for Senn's last newspaper in Deadwood, **The Forum,** was "Uncompromising hostility to liquor business whether legal or not."

President Calvin Coolidge appointed Edward Senn Prohibition Administrator for South Dakota in 1925 with 15 deputies to help him enforce

State Deputy Prohibition Officer E. L. Senn led a series of raids last week, making 11 arrests in Aberdeen on Brown County violators. **Black Hills Weekly,** October 28, 1929

the law and with headquarters in Sioux Falls, SD.

Senn was vitally interested in preserving an accurate history of Deadwood—whether good or bad. It was he who encouraged '76 pioneer John S. McClintock to write his history book for which Senn acted as editor.

Senn wrote and published three small booklets about early-day characters: Wild Bill Hickok, Preacher Smith, Calamity Jane, and the last Deadwood Dick (Deadwood Dick was the name adopted by several opportunists through the years). These were the result of meticulous research and many interviews with pioneers who had actually known the legendary four. This versatile journalist also began to write a book about frontier history which he never completed.

When Edward Senn was an old man, he was poor but undefeated. Although he had been reviled and persecuted throughout most of his career, he had also been praised and honored. Many well-known writers and historians came to Deadwood to visit this rugged individualist.

A Denver reporter asked Senn if he had any regrets over his free-for-all fights and the subsequent loss of his newspaper kingdom. Edward Senn's eyes lit up, "I would do it all over again. But I could never have done it without my wife Christie."

He survived his beloved wife and died at age 86 in his home at Deadwood in November, 1951. He is buried in Mount Moriah.

Whatever he was—evangelist or hypocrite, impartial judge or prej-

The burial place of the "firebrand of South Dakota journalism" who hoped people would make pilgrimages to his grave which is on the right side of the main entrance road into the cemetery.

udiced observer—people who knew this firebrand of South Dakota journalism would probably agree on one point: Edward Senn was a man who had
the strength of his convictions.

"Let him who is without sin cast the first stone." No, please, dear kind Mr. Senn, don't
accuse the Pioneer-Times of disloyalty to any of its candidates. Remember that you are occupying a false position, that of a traitor within the Republican party. We know you are more of
a mugwump than you are a conscientious supporter of any party, principle or cause. **Deadwood Pioneer-Times,** Feb. 5, 1914

Yes, Edward Senn was my father-in-law. His campaigns against gambling and prostitution and alcohol and his subsequent unpopularity in Deadwood were very hard on his family.
When it came to business dealings, he was a child. Although he was a fanatical ego-maniac, he
had some good points. At least he never lectured to me about prohibition while I was having a
drink. He envisioned that after his death, faithful followers would make pilgrimages to his
grave in Mount Moriah. Recollection of Rogers Clark, son of Horace and Charlotte Clark,
Black Hills Pioneers of 1877

SIDNEY JACOBS
COMEDIAN, PRACTICAL JOKER,
AND MERCHANT

"I wish all my friends a Happy and Prosperous New Year, signed
Sidney B. Jacobs." This greeting appeared in the **Deadwood Pioneer-
Times,** January 1, 1914, and was probably the only way the author could
think of to greet his many friends. For friends were one of Sidney's most
cherished assets.

Today, almost half a century since his death in 1934, an extraordinary
number of the older residents of Deadwood, when asked for their recollections of Sidney Jacobs, smile first, then recall how much they liked him, re-
lating some story illustrating his generosity, his practical jokes, his love of
humanity.

Sidney Jacobs was born in Rogova, Germany, immigrated to America
when a young man and took up an acting career; he went on the stage in
New York City with three men who became world-famous vaudeville come-
dians at the turn of the century: Lou Fields, Joe Weber, and Sam Bernard.
Sidney was also a personal friend of Irving Berlin's.

While on tour with the vaudeville troupe in Kansas City, Mo., Sidney
met a young lady having the same last name as his, Jennie Jacobs. He
promptly fell in love with her and proposed within two days of their
meeting.

Jennie, a petite darling, said, "I'll marry you if you'll leave the stage
and come to Deadwood to live." Jennie's parents, Simon and Dora Jacobs,
had settled in Deadwood in 1886. Her father operated a candy and card
shop, sold diamonds, and managed a junk yard. Jennie, a graduate of
Deadwood High School, was devoted to her hometown and refused to
leave.

Photo courtesy of Centennial Archives, Deadwood Public Library.

Sidney Jacobs—Master of Ceremonies for the side-show on Deadwood's main street.

Sidney and Jennie were married within two weeks of their first meeting. Thus, Sidney did give up his successful stage career for love and settled down in Deadwood, which was a long way from New York and the big-time vaudeville circuit. Soon, he opened up The Hub, a men's clothing store.

Eventually, Sidney Jacobs also owned clothing stores in Lead, Sturgis, Edgemont, Mobridge—all in South Dakota—and Sheridan in Wyoming.

He became a highly successful merchant, typical of many Jewish business-men in Deadwood.

At one time, around 1915, on just one side of main street, there were at least nine business establishments owned by Jews; and many other Jews who were not merchants also lived in Deadwood. Although this Jewish group preserved their religion and customs, they mingled freely with people from the varied ethnic backgrounds in Deadwood, and were a respected and integral segment of Deadwood life, contributing much to the development of the community.

Sidney Jacobs was a short, fat man who weighed 265 pounds, had a 52-inch waist, and ate five square meals a day, plus the innumerable candy bars he always carried. His son Berthald recalled how his father invariably had dinner with the family at five o'clock, then went downtown and ordered a second dinner at a restaurant.

When Sidney, at the urging of his family, went to the Mayo Clinic for a check-up, the doctors immediately put him on a strict diet. As an out-patient he stayed at a hotel but conscientiously ate his three low-calorie meals in the diet kitchen of the famed clinic. Just as faithfully, after con-suming each skimpy meal, he went out to public restaurants for the hearty meals he relished. The Mayo doctors could never understand why this pa-tient never lost any weight.

Sidney Jacobs may have left the stage but the stage never left him. He told stories on himself, and he was an entertaining comic whose tales of life on the stage and in hair-raising Deadwood delighted the ever-present au-diences that gathered around him.

He often settled his rotund body in a commodious chair at the rear of his store to hold court while supervising the clerks. When a customer came in and asked for some drawers, Sidney sent a young clerk up on the movable ladder attached to the high shelves packed with boxes. Sidney, with his three chins shaking, called out, "Take down your drawers and show the man vot you've got!" The audience roared—even the red-faced straight man on the ladder.

This man who must have believed in the adage, "Laugh and be fat," loved practical jokes. In the Broken Arch club, named in his honor, where many plans for the community were formulated over coffee and where many card games took place, Sidney played the card game called solo for hours with his cronies.

When a stranger dropped in to kibitz, Sidney and his friend Ray Walker, would go into their act, yelling and throwing cards, swearing in language not heard since Calamity Jane's reign in Deadwood. When the threats of death and destruction became unbearably violent, the panic-

Berthald Jacobs was among the Northwestern arrivals and will remain in the city for a few days with his parents, Mr. and Mrs. Sidney Jacobs. **Deadwood Pioneer-Times**, August 9, 1922

Sidney B. Jacobs, proprietor of The Hub, writing from Chicago says: 'They can't beat Harding with an ox—impossible.' **Deadwood Pioneer-Times**, October, 1920

stricken stranger would often run with the bait, rush out, and bring back a lawman to stop the fight. By that time, the two quarrelsome card players were serenely playing a quiet game of cards. That performance always rated lots of laughs—if not from the hoodwinked bystander and the policeman.

From the front door of The Hub, Sidney would yell at a friend, "Come on over here, you son of a bitch, and buy a suit." He got by with the outrageous language, perhaps, because he was never cruel—and he genuinely liked people. Many recall his generosity: the jewel box he presented to his competitors which they treasured forever; the party dress for a little girl who had none; the food baskets for the needy. But he could not resist a chance to tease and trick and show off. In turn, his friends delighted in putting one over on him, like the time they framed him by planting silverware in his pocket in a cafe. The victim, a practical joker expert, knew immediately what had happened. Legend has it that Sidney swore for 10 minutes in both Hebrew and English without repeating himself.

There was no synagogue in Deadwood, and like other Jewish leaders, Sidney Jacobs often donned the skull cap and shawl to play the part of rabbi for Jewish services held in the Elks Lodge or City Hall. On Yom Kipper Day, he could quote long passages of Hebrew about the Day of Atonement.

Despite some of his salty outbursts, Sidney was always a diplomat. His son Berthald can't count the number of occasions when old-timers reminiscing about his father have said: "Your dad was a great old Republican," or "Your father was a dyed-in-the-wool Democrat." Even his son did not know which party his father favored. Perhaps it was Sidney's diplomacy and fabulous memory for names which motivated Governor Frank Byrne to appoint this clothing merchant to represent South Dakota at the National Mining Congress.

Sidney Jacobs operated The Hub in Deadwood for 32 years. After a long period of failing health and consequent decline in business, he died in November, 1934, at age 62. The funeral services were held at the Elks Lodge with some prayers read in Hebrew. **The Deadwood Pioneer-Times** reported that "Sidney Jacobs was widely known throughout the Black Hills and his passing will be deeply regretted by all with whom he came in contact. John Heffron, past exalted ruler, delivered a beautiful eulogy on the life and character of the deceased."

He is buried beside his wife Jennie in the Jewish section, high up in

An open-faced silver case watch was found in front of The Hub last night. Owner may recover it by applying to Sidney Jacobs and paying for the time and trouble which the finder expended in defending the time-piece from two bandits who attempted to wrest it from him. **Deadwood Pioneer-Times,** March 7, 1914

Remember, this is not a fake or a humbug sale, but will be conducted absolutely on the square. Extra! Extra! At The Hub. Five Hundred Men's Suits—$15—Why pay $25, $30, and $35 for a suit when you can buy a better suit at The Hub for $15? ALL WE ASK YOU TO DO IS TO SEE FOR YOURSELF. SALE NOW GOING ON AT THE HUB. Advertisement in **Deadwood Pioneer-Times,** April 30, 1914

Photo courtesy of Al Gunther.

In the Jewish section is the Jacobs family marker engraved with the Star of David, the symbol of Judaism. The Hebrew Society in 1890 was the first organization to purchase burial ground for its members.

Mount Moriah. Also buried in the same lot are his in-laws, Simon and Dora Jacobs.

Sidney Jacobs, veteran performer that he was, kept the laughs echoing up and down the main street of Deadwood for many years. The mention of his name brings both a smile and a tear to the faces of his old friends. What man could ask for more?

My grandparents, the Simon Jacobs, first came to Deadwood in 1886. Then in 1902, my father, Sidney B. Jacobs, founded the original Hub Clothing Store. Since his death in 1934 I have strived unceasingly to bring HIS customers nothing but the finest merchandise. I have diligently maintained HIS standards ever since. Signed, Berthald Jacobs. Advertisement in **Deadwood Pioneer-Times,** 75th Anniversary Edition, June, 1951

In 1934, following the death of Bert's father, Bert and Ruth Jacobs took over the men's wear store he had operated for 32 years in this small Black Hills mining community; the year before, sales at the once-flourishing establishment had shrunk to just $12,000 and debt had mounted dangerously. "The Jacobs Brothers Opt Not to go Home to Deadwood, SD" (Article explaining why Sidney's grandsons did not want to take over his old Deadwood store), **Wall Street Journal,** July 26, 1973

MARY PHILLIPS
ENGLISH TEACHER

Miss Mary Phillips of Deadwood, a member of the Lead Public School Faculty for 32 years and widely-known throughout the Black Hills country, passed away after a lengthy illness. The daughter of Lee and Harriet Phillips, she was born in Illinois, but lived in Deadwood most of her life.

She attended the Deadwood Public School, then attended college at Jacksonville College, Ill.

When she resigned from teaching two years ago, the Lead high school paid her a very fine tribute. This tribute to her character as well as her teaching would also be the expression of a large circle of intimate friends: 'Miss Phillips' teaching was characterized by a keenness of understanding of the intellectual aspects of her subject and by a depth of appreciation for the meaning and beauty of literature. She will be missed by pupils, teachers, and those connected with the administration of the schools.'

She had a beautiful sentiment for all the fine things in life. Burial will be in Mount Moriah cemetery. **Deadwood Pioneer-Times,** July 13, 1940

Mrs. Minnie Callison, who was murdered last night, taught the first school in the Hills. **Black Hills Daily Times,** August 20, 1878

Twelve school marms have made application to our school board for the primary department to be created and they are just only beginning to come in. There seems to be lots of book larnin' among the girls of the Hills. **Black Hills Daily Times,** June 19, 1878

Mary Phillips taught fourth and fifth grades and later high school English in Lead. She dyed her hair red and had the temperament to match. She was a super teacher although very tough and strict. Her students learned a lot although we didn't always appreciate her at the time. We memorized poetry like "Thanatopsis" and "Flower in the Crannied Wall" which many of her students can still recite when we reminisce. She was a dedicated teacher who expected the best from her classes.

Recollections of Jack Morcom and Richard Morcom, long-time residents of Lead

MATILDA HILL
CHERISHED NEGRO COOK

Matilda Hill was one of the best-known and most popular of the 28 Negroes buried in Mount Moriah, identified in the Record Book as "col-

Photo courtesy of Centennial Archives, Deadwood Public Library.

Matilda Hill, popular gourmet cook and housekeeper. The Black Hills reminded her of the Blue Ridge Mountains of Virginia where she was born.

ored.'' The black race was well-represented in cosmopolitan Deadwood in the late 19th and early 20th centuries.

Matilda Hill was also known as Auntie Hill, Mattie Hill, and Mammy Hill. In 1870 she was born in the Shenandoah Valley of Virginia to parents who had been freed from slavery five years before by the Emancipation Proclamation.

Matilda was well-educated. Her mother taught her to read and write before the child went to elementary school. Matilda eventually attended Whalen Seminary and Harshore Memorial College, both in Washington, D.C.

While attending college in the nation's capital, she earned tuition money by working in the household of an army officer, Charles Fenton. When he and his young wife were transferred to Fort Meade near Sturgis, SD, the couple first asked another of their servants to accompany them to their new post, but the girl refused, being afraid of Indian attacks. Next, the Fentons asked Matilda, who was adventurous and who knew that the Indian wars were over by the year 1900. Matilda agreed to come West, and she

worked several years for the Fentons at Fort Meade, acquiring a reputation as an excellent cook.

When Matilda was 32 years old, she married Isaac Hill, a Negro laborer from the area. During their brief honeymoon, Isaac had to drive a team of horses to Whitewood and thus leave his bride alone. That night, the neighbors gave the newly-married couple an old-fashioned salute, what the Germans called a belling and the French called a chivareee. The neighbors serenaded the newly-marrieds with horns and bells and by beating on pots and pans—not knowing that the lonesome and frightened bride was all alone.

The Hills homesteaded on a ranch in Crook County, Wyoming, where their two children, Amy and James, were born. In a few years the Hills moved to Deadwood so their children could attend school. Auntie Hill, as she was most commonly called, wanted her children to like school as much as she had. She hoped they would enjoy **Uncle Remus** and **Brer Rabbit** and **Mrs. Wiggs of the Cabbage Patch.** And when they reached high school age, she hoped they would study Latin.

Auntie was the first cook for the Tomahawk Country Club south of Deadwood. Many praised her culinary skills, saying that she frequently prepared elegant recipes from an old southern cookbook. According to Marie Auguspurger who wrote an unpublished character sketch about her in 1959, Auntie loved working and being with all kinds of people. However, she would never sit at a table with whites, saying it was "not proper."

Many of the older lady golfers remember how Auntie used to boss them around like a group of kids, telling them to put on their sweaters and rubbers "or you'll catch your death playing that silly game."

After her husband Isaac died in 1938, Auntie Hill continued living alone in her little house in Pluma and doing cleaning and catering company meals for many families.

She often told friends, "I think I'll wind up the ball right here." She lived in the same house for half a century, and she died there at age 85 with her Bible in her hand, on May 11, 1954.

According to the **Deadwood Pioneer-Times,** the soloist at her funeral services sang two of Auntie Hill's favorites, "He'll Understand" and "Beautiful Isle of Somewhere." Matilda is buried beside her husband Isaac in Mount Moriah; his grave is marked with a tombstone, but the name on her temporary marker has been obliterated. She no doubt Rests in Peace on the beautiful hilltop cemetery overlooking the green valleys and peaks of the Black Hills which always reminded her of her first home in the Blue Ridge Mountains of Virginia.

Isaac Hill, 73, a resident of the Black Hills for more than 40 years, died at his home near old McDonald park of failing health. Deceased lived for many years on a ranch he owned west of Savoy in Spearfish Canyon. He was well-known among the older residents as one of the most highly respected colored men in the Black Hills. He is survived by his wife Matilda, one son James, and a daughter Amy. **Deadwood Pioneer-Times,** Sept 8, 1937

Old Mattie Hill has gone her way.
God bless her kindly heart I say.
Many the child her goodness knew.
Many the neighbor her help found, too
God bless her smiling face I say
It shines in glory I'm sure today.

"Letter to the Editor" by Imogene Baggaley, **Deadwood Pioneer-Times,** May 12, 1954

GEORGE M. BUTLER
CREATIVE JEWELER

The black-bearded man is George M. Butler. The white-bearded man is his father S. T. Butler, founder of the jewelry manufacturing business on Lee Street. In the flood of 1883, this building floated down the current like a chip of wood.

George M. Butler was born in New York and came to Deadwood in 1881 and began working for his father, S. T. Butler, who had established the first jewelry-manufacturing business in 1878.

George Butler learned from his father how to use a kerosene torch for soldering handmade punches to fashion a grape leaf. The colors of the finished jewelry were red gold, green gold, and yellow gold; these were then assembled into grape leaves, grape bunches, grape vines, and tendrils—all made from alloys of gold, copper, and silver to produce a certain color.

In the devastating flood of May, 1883, the first Butler jewelry building was sent "floating down the current like a chip of wood."

The jewelry business begun by S. T. Butler is carried on today by a fifth generation of Butlers under the company name of F. L. Thorpe.

George Butler, son of the first jeweler, carried on his father's business. He also filled many original and interesting orders for jewelry in various forms, preparing the gold cards of invitation sent Theodore Roosevelt and President William Taft when they were in Deadwood for a celebration in 1901.

George Butler was also a musician. He played the violin and alto sax in the Deadwood band which played in many funeral processions and performed in parades and celebrations. He also played for dances in the Gem Theater and had many tales to tell of what he observed in that well-known den of iniquity.

George Butler, son of the first George Butler, now lives in St. Joseph's Nursing Home in Deadwood. He recalled that his father "was a jolly old fellow with a long beard. When I was a boy, he would never spank me even if my mother asked him to. He was also patient at teaching me how to make jewelry, but I liked the business of cooking better."

The second George Butler recalled that a man who sold his father gold was accused of stealing it from the Homestake Mine, and his father was accused of complicity. The case went to court. The gold-seller was convicted but George Butler, Sr., was exonerated of any wrong-doing.

George Butler died in November, 1932, of general disability at age 81 and is buried beside the main road in Mount Moriah cemetery. There are no grape vines marking his grave to remind visitors of the legend associated with Black Hills Gold jewelry.

Two young pioneers on the Pierre trail became lost from their wagon train while out hunting. When about ready to succumb to starvation, they saw grapes hanging on a vine and ate them, thus assuaging both their hunger and thirst. One of these young men was a jeweler and found work in a jewelry shop. One day he showed his employer the result of his experimentation saying: 'The original of that saved my life on my way to the Hills.' The jeweler was delighted with the design. It was a gold ring embellished with grapes and grape leaves, in colors as are to be seen now on the beautiful jewelry, the pride of the Hills, and the prized souvenir of visitors to this section. "The Story of Black Hills Gold Jewelry," Gossage, **Black Hills Trails,** Brown and Willard

LARS SHOSTROM
MASTER MASON AND BUILDER

Lars (Pete) Shostrom was born in Sweden and immigrated to the United States in 1883 when he was 19 years old. He took one of the first trains out of New York City bound for Des Moines, Iowa. Then he came on to Newcastle, Wyoming, on the western edge of the Black Hills where he worked in the coal mines of Cambria.

Photo courtesy of A. H. Shostrom.

Lars Shostrom, a Swedish immigrant who built the first side-walks in Deadwood. A talented grandfather, he showed his grandchildren how to stand on their heads.

In 1886, Lars walked all the way through the woods of beautiful Ice-Box Canyon to Deadwood and liked the town so well he stayed the rest of his life. He first got a job at the mill of the Golden Reward Mining Company in lower Deadwood.

Later, he went into the cement and masonry business and built the first side-walks in Deadwood, which were welcome improvements over the boardwalks and dirt trails throughout the city. This Swedish immigrant took great pride in his work; and many of his side-walks, with his name on them, have withstood the hard use and weather of many years.

Lars Shostrom was a man who loved the role of father and grandfather. He enjoyed teaching his children and grandchildren how to fish and how to go out into the forest and cut down the perfect Christmas tree. He was always in charge of arranging the special Christmas decorations for his grandchildren. When he was 76 years old, he taught his little granddaughter, by example, how to stand on her head.

A Chinese Baptist friend of Lars Shostrom gave this Swedish Baptist a Chinese Bible. His son, A. H. Shostrom, retired banker and city employee, still has the Bible. A. H. Shostrom is an avid Deadwood historian who recalls the excitement and color of the Chinese funerals and of exotic old Chinatown in Deadwood. He also cherishes many warm memories of his father who loved all children and how much they loved him in return.

Lars was a member of the city council for 12 years, a member of the school board, and was active in the Independent Order of Odd Fellows, being Past Patriarch of the Grand Encampment of South Dakota.

In the fall of 1941, Lars and Clara Shostrom celebrated their 50th wedding anniversary among a great crowd of friends who gathered to wish them well. Not many weeks later, in Dec. 1941, Lars Shostrom died. **The Black Hills Weekly** wrote: "He was a man diligent in his calling. The sudden smile that lighted his face always warmed his friends. Tuesday he went quietly to sleep." His wife Clara died in August, 1965.

Lars Shostrom, his wife Clara, and their infant son Arthur all lie on a pretty slope under a handsome concrete cover in Mount Moriah. The workmanship is professional enough to please even that master craftsman and builder of memories, Lars Shostrom.

Funeral services are scheduled Monday for Mrs. Stelline Shostrom, 79, who died Thursday morning at her home in the Smith Apartments in Deadwood. The rites will be held at United Methodist Church. . . . Interment will be in Mount Moriah Cemetery. . . . She is survived by her husband, A. H. (Lex) Shostrom; a son, Keith of New Delhi, India; two daughters, Jeannette Thacker of Deadwood, and Joyce Wilkinson of Las Vegas, Nevada. Also surviving are six grandchildren and three great-grandchildren. . . . A memorial has been established for the Sioux Falls Crippled Children's School and Hospital. **Deadwood Pioneer-Times,** Oct. 13, 1979

DOROTHY KUBLER
RENAISSANCE WOMAN

Dorothy Kubler was a Renaissance woman: she was a talented organist, pianist, and music teacher; she was an actress with verve who played the

role of Calamity Jane in the local melodrama "The Trial of Jack McCall"; she was an accomplished duplicate bridge player; she was a skilled horsewoman; she was a wizard at using and servicing typewriters. Most important of all, this tall, stately, and vivacious woman had many friends of both sexes.

In teaching piano and organ, Dorothy, who had studios in both Deadwood and Rapid City, used what was known as the Miracle system of instruction and had an excellent reputation as a teacher. She was organist for St. John's Episcopal Church in Deadwood. A graduate of Deadwood High School, she also attended both Oberlin College and the American Conservatory of Music in Chicago.

Dorothy, who came to Deadwood as a baby with her parents, was a grand-daughter of Joseph Kubler, a Black Hills Pioneer of 1876. He was an employee of the first newspaper in the region, **The Black Hills Pioneer**, running a hand press in a tent. Later he moved to Custer, and in 1880 established **The Custer Chronicle**, which he published for half a century.

Dorothy and her mother Erma Kubler were very active in the Order of the Eastern Star, and her father Carl Kubler was a prominent Mason. Dorothy was past worthy matron of the Eastern Star in Deadwood and was also past grand organist of the South Dakota Eastern Star.

On April 1, 1953, when Dorothy was giving a music lesson in her Rapid City studio, she was stricken with a cerebral hemorrhage and rushed to the hospital. Her parents were summoned and drove at breakneck speed to the Rapid City hospital, but Dorothy was dead by the time they arrived.

Her sudden death at age 46 was a dreadful shock to her parents, her many friends, and her music students. Today, over a quarter of a century later, several of her faithful friends say they still mourn her death and often bring flowers to decorate her grave in Mount Moriah.

Services for Dorothy Kubler were held in the Masonic Temple and were

conducted by her mother, Mrs. Erma Kubler, a strong, disciplined woman who had also conducted Eastern Star funeral services for her mother and her sister.

In a traditional ceremony, Eastern Star members, representing the five points of the star, arranged carnations in star-point colors upon the casket, signifying fidelity, constancy, purity, light, joy, nature's life and beauty, fervency, and zeal—all of these qualities describing the character and personality of Dorothy Kubler.

Erma Kubler read the final prayer over the bier of her beloved daughter: "Grant that we may find comfort in Him who is the great Comforter of us all."

The myriad melodies of Dorothy Kubler still echo in the hearts of her many friends.

The annual installation of officers in Deadwood Chapter No. 23, Order of Eastern Star, was held Wednesday in the Masonic Temple. Mrs. Erma Kubler, past grand matron, acted as installing officer and installed her daughter, Dorothy Kubler, as worthy matron. Carl H. Kubler, past grand patron, acted as escort for his daughter during the ceremony. **Deadwood Pioneer-Times,** Dec. 20. 1940

BLANCHE COLMAN
FIRST WOMAN LAWYER
IN SOUTH DAKOTA

Blanche Colman, who became the first woman lawyer admitted to the South Dakota Bar, was born in 1884 in Deadwood to Nathan and Amalia Colman.

According to the unanimous verdict of Deadwood oldsters, the Colmans, both emigrants from Germany, became the most prominent of the many Jewish pioneers in Deadwood. Mr. Colman frequently acted as rabbi at Jewish religious ceremonies. In 1878, he was elected Justice of the Peace in lawless Deadwood, a position he held the rest of his life. **The Black Hills Daily Times,** Nov. 4, 1879, promoted his re-election by writing: "If you want a man to settle your little difficulties in an honest and comprehensible manner, elect Judge Colman . . . familiar with the practice in this territory. In fact he is no slouch of a lawyer himself . . . and he is a western man."

Nathan Colman did not arrive in Deadwood until early in the second year of the riotous gold camp's existence, in February, 1877. Not until April, 1877, did his wife and little daughter Anne finally arrive by stagecoach from Sidney, Nebraska. And much to the relief of Nathan; for when the stage was late, rumors flew that it had been attacked by Indians, although the rumor was unfounded.

However, the Colmans, as pioneers in Deadwood, had a multitude of tragedies to face. Eventually, the Colmans had seven children; two died in a diphtheria epidemic in January, 1891; and two died of other diseases, incur-

Attorney Blanche Colman in the Franklin Hotel, her home for many years. When the weather was bad, she often managed her daily constitutional by striding up and down the halls of the hotel—even after she reached age ninety.

able at that time. Three girls survived to adulthood: Anne, Blanche, and Theresa.

In the great Deadwood fire of 1879 which destroyed much of the town, the Colmans lost their home and their tobacco-grocery store. Like so many stalwart victims of this holocaust, the Colmans rebuilt and started over. Again in 1894, in another fire that ravaged Deadwood, the Colmans lost both their home and their business. What courage and perseverance they must have had to begin rebuilding their home, their business, and their lives for the second time.

On that wild morning in 1894 when the second fire attacked the Colman home, 10-year-old Blanche, wearing a skimpy combination of clothes she had rescued from her room, still made it to school on time: she hadn't

As a relief to his sufferings, Nathan Colman, 56, one of the first settlers breathed his last at his Williams street residence. He had been confined to his home for many weeks with Brights' disease. He was a patient sufferer and had courage. . . . He asked for no flowers. . . . He has been Justice of the Peace since 1878, a sterling tribute to his honesty and popularity. Few men possessed a kinder heart. He was a man who searched out the right path and followed it even to his own detriment. **Deadwood Pioneer-Times,** June 5, 1906

The chapter in our history which encompassed the Colmans and other Jews who settled in the Black Hills is perhaps dimming. But it remains a proud one—certainly for me and for my family. Article written by Al Alsehuler, great-grandson of Nathan Colman, Deadwood Centennial Archives

wanted to spoil her perfect record for promptness and attendance, fire or no fire. Surely that incident suggests a significant aspect of Blanche Colman's character which showed up early in her girlhood.

Blanche, an outstanding student, graduated in 1902 from Deadwood High School. Newly-elected Congressman William Parker of Deadwood took her to Washington, D.C. as his secretary. Although Blanche was a whiz as a secretary, she didn't like the big city and was lonesome for the Black Hills.

She returned home in time for her older sister's wedding. In December, 1903, Anne Colman married Maurice Niederman of Lead in the elegant new Franklin Hotel, its parlors and restaurant decorated with potted palms and cut flowers. Blanche, a tiny dark-eyed brunette, carrying pink roses and wearing an embroidered chiffon dress, was maid of honor, rivaling the beauty of the bride. Performing the marriage ceremony was Nathan Colman, father of the bride. First, as Justice of the Peace, he read the civil service; then, as acting rabbi, he read the Jewish marriage service in Hebrew. The **Deadwood Pioneer-Times** reported that "it was one of the most beautiful and unique services ever observed in this city."

Blanche got a job working as a clerk in the law office of Chambers

Photo courtesy of South Dakota Historical Society.

Homestake Mine—largest gold mine in western hemisphere. Its operations cover a 400 square-mile empire. Blanche Colman worked forty years in the law office of the chief counsel for the Homestake.

Kellar, chief counsel for the Homestake Mining Company in Lead, three miles from Deadwood. Although she never attended law school or college, this enterprising girl began studying law in her spare time. In 1911, when she was 27 years old, she passed the state bar examination, thus becoming the first woman admitted to the South Dakota bar and one of the few women lawyers in the United States at that time.

During World War I Blanche volunteered her services as secretary of

the Red Cross Chapter during the devastating flu epidemic of 1918 when more than one hundred lost their lives and emergency hospital facilities had to be set up in the Homestake Recreation Center.

Blanche Colman continued to work for Kellar for 40 years and spent long hours studying law books to assist him in litigation over water rights and labor problems involving the Homestake Mine, the largest gold-producing mine in the western hemisphere.

"Chambers Kellar was a colorful and sagacious lawyer," recalled Clinton Richards, a long-time Deadwood attorney. "We all envied his having a top-notch legal expert doing the homework back stage—Blanche Colman. She was especially good in probate and handled all of that business for Kellar in probate court. When she pushed her glasses back on her forehead and got that look in her sharp eyes, you knew she was solving a knotty legal problem."

Richards reminisced about the Talbot versus Guider estate case, May, 1935, on which Blanche Colman had done most of the research. This probate case went all the way to the Supreme Court of South Dakota, the judge upholding the interpretation of the law developed by Blanche for the firm of Kellar and Kellar, the Lead attorneys. This case set a legal precedent.

During their long lives Blanche and her sister Theresa (Tess) would never join the Society of Black Hills Pioneers because their father Nathan had refused to join. Although in the early days he had very much wanted to join the elite group, he could not meet the original membership requirement of having arrived in the Black Hills before January 1, 1877—and this greatly upset him. Nathan Colman had arrived in February, 1877. Even though in later years the membership requirements were changed to admit all those who came before the great fire of 1879, Colman refused to join. And so did his loyal daughters when they became eligible.

Blanche and her sister Tess lived for many years in apartments at the Franklin Hotel on main street. When Tess, who had been the county

Photo courtesy of Centennial Archives, Deadwood Public Library.

The Franklin Hotel in Deadwood about 1925. Blanche Colman lived here for 46 years, 1932-1978.

auditor, died in 1972 at age 81, the flag at the court house flew at half-mast. Although Blanche mourned her younger sister, she was philosophical about death, saying "My turn will be next."

During her retirement Blanche continued living at the Franklin where she had many friends, ranging from the bell-hop to a Supreme Court judge. Her friends characterize her with a variety of adjectives: calm, dignified, demanding, appreciative, lady-like, honest, strong-willed, reserved, brilliant, fastidious, close-mouthed. Intensely interested in other people and their problems, she remembered to send birthday cards to hundreds of friends. All her life she had loved to walk, and people still remember seeing her petite figure marching to work up and down the hills between Deadwood and Lead.

Blanche wasn't much of a talker, but when she did enter into a conversation, she did not dwell on the past, on the weather, or on other people's business. Instead, she preferred to discuss current events and topics of the day on local and national levels. An avid Republican, she absolved President Nixon of any blame in the Watergate affair. Her favorite reading material was the **Wall Street Journal** and **US News and World Report.**

Although she didn't have an especially good voice, she loved to sing just for her own pleasure. According to Edna Beshara who did housework for her beloved Blanche, she often sang "Auld Lang Syne" and other popular tunes of the thirties and forties like "It's a Sin to Tell a Lie." She would often walk around the apartment reciting verse after verse of poetry she had learned in school, never to be forgotten.

Blanche was rumored to have bought only two winter coats in her entire life. Although she was generous in big things, she watched her pennies. When the Franklin dining room raised its price for dinners, Blanche ignored the increase and refused to pay the new price until Orville Bryan, one of the hotel's owners, sat down with her to explain the management's reasons for the price change. "She had a gracious manner of getting her own way," smiled Bryan, "and we usually pampered her because we loved her but this time I was firm." Bryan recalled that despite her accomplishments Blanche was a tremendous example of humility.

In the Bicentennial year of 1976, NBC interviewed 92-year-old Blanche Colman with the deep, dark eyes for a television program featuring unusual and outstanding people. Her mind remained alert all her life, and people were continually amazed at her sharp intellect, the fluency of her language, and the fact that she never had to grope for a word. And every word counted.

At last it became hard for her to take her daily walks, but if she couldn't go outside, she often walked up and down the halls of the Franklin Hotel. Finally, she had a fall, then a stroke; and like it or not, she had to give in and go to the hospital. Here, the nurses affectionately called this famous little lady, "Miss America," and she loved it. Blanche Colman died in September, 1978, at age ninety-four.

A rabbi from New York City conducted her funeral. One of the mourners was a former bell-hop at the Franklin Hotel. She had sent him through four years of college, and the young man flew from California to be a pall-bearer for his benefactor.

The Myer Jacobs tombstone engraved in Hebrew as are several other markers in the Jewish section of Mount Moriah.

This reticent lady who had always lived so economically and invested wisely in common stocks left an estate valued at $826,000, to be divided equally among two nieces and a nephew, all children of her sister Anne.

About forty-four Jewish people are buried in Mount Moriah, most of them in the Jewish section, often called Hebrew Hill. Several tombstone inscriptions are in both English and Hebrew.

Photo courtesy of Al Gunther.

The Colman family lot including the individual marker for Blanche is high up in the Jewish section. About forty-four Jews are buried in Mount Moriah, not all of them in this special section.

Of the Jewish people buried high above Deadwood, the city to which they contributed so much while building an unforgettable heritage, none is more illustrious than Blanche Colman who sleeps with her family in the large Colman lot.

Her favorite poem was Whittier's "Barbara Frietchie" and the last lines are appropriate for Blanche Colman herself:

"Over Barbara Frietchie's grave,
Flag of Freedom and Union, wave!

Peace and order and beauty draw
Round thy symbol of light and law;

And ever the stars above look down
On the stars below in Frederick town."

The first woman to receive a 50-year award as a practicing attorney in South Dakota is a native of Deadwood, Blanche Colman. The State Bar of South Dakota will accord special recognition to eight attorneys who have practiced law in the state for 50 years, including Miss Colman. Each will receive a solid gold lapel button, indicative of the fact at the annual meeting in Yankton on June 30. **Deadwood Pioneer-Times,** June 28, 1961

Blanche Colman, Deadwood, was complimented on the occasion of her 76th birthday. She is the first woman in South Dakota to take the bar examination. A three-tiered cake, topped with miniature scales of justice was presented to Miss Colman by the hosts, Mr. and Mrs. Kenneth Kellar. Kellar also gave her a Black Hills Gold pen on behalf of the firm of Kellar and Kellar and Driscoll. She became associated with the law office of Chambers Kellar around 1902 until her retirement. **Lead Daily Call,** Dec. 31, 1960

IV
EPITAPHS

Ester
Margaret
Peterson
1895
1901

A sleep in Jesus
Soon to rise
When the last trump
Shall rend the skies

Peter Campbell
died
July 1, 1886
aged
32 years

MARY A. WILSON
DIED MAY 25, 1893
AGE 43
Rest, mother, rest in
        quiet sleep
While friends in sorrow
        o'er thee weep

After fleshly weakness
And after this world's
night. And after storm
and whirl-wind, Are calm
and joy and light.

Richard
Gibson Anderson
born 1852 - died 1878

Little hands
at rest forevermore
Dimpled cheeks
whose blossoming
is o'er
Sealed eyes no
more to smile
or weep
We know our
little Ella has
only gone
to sleep

ELLA CARTER
DIED NOV 4, 1888
AGED 6 YRS. 2 MOS.

Ere sin could harm
 or sorrow fade
Death came with friendly care
The opening bud to heaven
                  conveyeth
And bade to blossom there

VIRGIL VAUGHN - MAR 8, 1883
     7 yrs. old

How we loved our darling
              little boy

Ralph Harold Gilman
 Born May 3, 1909, died Dec 5, 1910

Scott Martin Carter
"Barney"
A Good Guy to Have ALong
1876 — 1949

Vera La Rue - Pawn
of a gambler's game
Queen of a dance
hall floor.

Put away his pick and shovel,
He will never prospect more;
Death has sluiced him from
                his trouble,
Panned him on the other shore.

Miner's epitaph
Black Hills Daily Times
July 18, 1877

Weep not for me my parents dear
I'm not Died but sleeping here

I was not yours but God's alone
Who came and took me to his home.

In memory of
Otto Grantz
Aug. 27, 1880
MASON

ACKNOWLEDGMENTS

Gratefully, I acknowledge the generous assistance of many people. Special thanks to Margaret Howe Clark for permission to quote **Deadwood Doctor,** written by her father, Dr. F. S. Howe; to Rogers Clark for permission to quote **Deadwood Dick and Calamity Jane, Preacher Smith—Martyr of the Cross, Wild Bill Hickok—Prince of Pistoleers,** all three booklets written by his father-in-law, Edward L. Senn; to Cushman Clark for permission to quote the unpublished memoirs of his mother, Charlotte Cushman Clark; to Camille Yuill for permission to quote excerpts from her "Backlog" columns in the **Deadwood Pioneer-Times;** to Rev. Stephen Doughty for permission to quote from his funeral sermon for Charlotte Clark; to Larry C. Nelson for permission to quote his complete poem, "Dramatis Personae"; to Don Clowser for permission to quote from Thomas Russell's **The Russell-Collins 1874 Gold Expedition to the Black Hills of Dakota;** to the Centennial Archives at the Deadwood Public Library for permission to quote "The Diary of Irene Cushman"; and to the Deadwood Public Library for preserving files of numerous Deadwood newspapers from which I have freely quoted.

I am indebted to innumerable people who contributed historical information and reminiscences and those who helped in a variety of ways: Marie Lawler, Albro and Agnes Ayres, George and Mayme Hunter, Rogers Clark, Cushman and Helen Clark, A. H. Shostrom, Mary Adams Balmat, John and Sylvia Baggaley, Bert and Ruth Jacobs, Melvin and Dorothy Hoherz, Stan and Wynnifred Lindstrom, George Butler, Helen Scotvold, Joe Sulentic, Jeff Moye, Katherine Thornby, Gilbert "Rosie" Davis, Edna Beshara, Lucille Tucker, Alan and Margaret Clark, Fred Borsch, Ora and Toni Horsfall, Hank Sordahl, David Ruth, Don and Rose Fletcher, Orville and Taffy Bryan, Marlene Straub and the Deadwood Chamber of Commerce, Marjorie Price, Jo Brotsky, Sharon Hagerty, Don Derosier, Meri Clason, Mike and Brenda O'Connell, Helen Hayes, Clinton Richards, Clyde Mitchell, Francis and Hilda Parker, Rose Gorder, Cecile Roberts, Nettie Johnson, Winona Sparks, Camille Yuill, James Dunn, Mary Frances Frederickson, Paul Cross, Irma Klock, Jack Morcom, Richard Morcom, May Picore, Henry and Loree Volk, Helen Morganti, Ralph Hoggatt, Marian Hersrud, Lois Stokes, Bob and Dolores Lee, Lucy Goodson, Maxine Ward, Betty Martz. And finally thanks to adventurous Juanita Ordahl for guiding me on many expeditions to Mount Moriah and elsewhere; and to Don Clowser for sharing his maps and expertise on early Deadwood; and to two flatlanders who helped, J. B. Graham and Maureen Westbrook.

I wish to thank the staff of these libraries for their cooperation: Dayton Canady and Bonnie Gardner, South Dakota Historical Resource Center, Pierre, SD; Thelma Sanito, Phoebe Apperson Hearst Free Library, Lead, SD; Pat Engebretson, Belle Fourche Public Library, SD; Carol Davis, Sturgis Public Library, SD; Jean Diggins, South Dakota Collections, Rapid City Public Library, SD; Dora Jones, Leland D. Case Library, and Doris Phillips, E. Y. Berry Library-Learning Center, Black Hills State College, Spearfish, SD; Philip McCauley, South Dakota Collections, Devereaux Library, School of Mines, Rapid City, SD; Jennewein Western Library, Layne Library, Dakota Wesleyan University, Mitchell, SD; and Western Collection, Denver Public Library, Colo. Special thanks to Helen Clark for her beautiful organization of the Centennial Archives, Deadwood Public Library, SD.

Heartfelt appreciation to Marjorie Pontius of the Deadwood Public Library whose contributions to this book are of inestimable value. How skillful she is at going up and down ladders while carrying heavy volumes. She is equally skillful at locating hard-to-find sources. Her patience and interest are inexhaustible.

I am indebted to the William Over Museum, University of South Dakota, Vermillion, SD; Martha Castle, Tri-State Museum, Belle Fourche; Martha Behrendt, Minnelusa Museum, Rapid City; and especially to Pauline Rankin, curator of the Adams Memorial Museum at Deadwood, who gave me generous and expert assistance.

I thank Al Gunther for his talents both as a photographer and as an editor. I thank Rose Mary Goodson for her creative art-work—the cover, the maps, the sketches—and for her publishing know-how. I greatly appreciate the excellent suggestions from both co-workers on this book project.

Finally, I am most grateful to my husband John L. Rezatto for his help and support in innumerable ways. Not only has he been tolerant about uncooked meals and an unkept house, he has also been cheerful (usually) about taking over many household chores himself to give me more time for writing. His library research and indexing work have been invaluable. He has good-naturedly accompanied me on many researching trips throughout South Dakota, especially to Mount Moriah, even though he would rather have been playing golf. Without his able assistance, unfailing interest, and wonderful understanding, I could never have completed this book.

BIBLIOGRAPHY

Adams Memorial Hall Museum, Deadwood, South Dakota. Scrapbooks (unpublished): Obituaries, Deeds and Reports, Local Celebrities.

Andreas, A. T. **Andreas' Historical Atlas of Dakota.** Chicago: Donnelly & Sons, 1884.

Alsehuler, Al. A short history of the Jews in the Black Hills (unpublished). Centennial Archives, Deadwood Public Library, Deadwood, South Dakota.

Auguspurger, Marie M. A sketch of Matilda Hill (unpublished). Deadwood Public Library, Deadwood, South Dakota.

Ayres, George V. Diary, 1876 (unpublished). Deadwood, South Dakota.

Barstow, John. "The Last Pioneer," **Black Hills Nuggets,** Commemorative Edition, Rapid City, SD: Rapid City Society for Geneological Research, Inc., 1975.

Belle Fourche (South Dakota) **Bee,** 1895, 1914, 1934.

Bennett, Estelline. **Old Deadwood Days.** New York: Charles Scribner's Sons, 1935.

Bourke, John G. **On the Border with Crook.** New York: Scribners, 1891.

Brown, Dee. **Bury My Heart at Wounded Knee.** New York: Holt, Rinehart, and Winston, 1970.

Brown, Dee. **The Gentle Tamers.** Lincoln: University of Nebraska Press, 1958.

Brown, Jesse, and A. M. Willard. **The Black Hills Trails.** Rapid City: Rapid City Journal Company, 1924.

Bryan, Jerry. **An Illinois Gold Hunter in the Black Hills: The Diary of Jerry Bryan, March 13 to August 20, 1876.** Clyde Walton, ed. Springfield: Illinois State Historial Society, 1960.

Bullock, Seth. "An Account of Deadwood and the Northern Black Hills in 1876." Harry Anderson, ed. **South Dakota Historical Collections,** Vol. XXXI. Pierre, South Dakota, 1924.

Bullock, Seth, Chairman. **The Black Hills of Dakota.** Deadwood: Board of Trade, 1881.

Buel, J. W. **Heroes of the Plains.** Philadelphia: Standard Publishing Company, 1886.

Canary, Martha Jane. **Life and Adventures of Calamity Jane** by Herself. Privately printed, about 1896.

Case, Leland D. **Preacher Smith—Martyr.** Mitchell, SD: Friends of the Middle Border, 1929.

Case, Leland D. "History Catches Up," **The Black Hills,** Roderick Peattie, ed. New York: The Vanguard Press, 1952.

Casey, Robert J. **The Black Hills and Their Incredible Characters.** New York: The Bobbs-Merrill Company, 1949.

Cheyenne (Wyoming) **Leader,** 1878.

Clark, Charlotte. Memoirs (unpublished), Deadwood, South Dakota.

Clowser, Don. **Deadwood—the Historic City.** Fenwyn Press Books, 1969.

Coursey, O. W. **Literature of South Dakota.** Mitchell, SD: The Educator Supply Company, 1916-1917.

Curley, Edwin. **Curley's Guide to the Black Hills.** Facsimile. Mitchell, SD: Dakota Wesleyan Press, 1973.

Cushman, Irene. Diary, 1890-1891. (unpublished). Centennial Archives, Deadwood Public Library, Deadwood, South Dakota.

Custer, Elizabeth B. **Following the Guidon.** New York: Harper & Brothers, 1890.

Custer, General George A. **My Life on the Plains.** Lincoln: University of Nebraska Press, 1971.

Deadwood, South Dakota **Black Hills Daily Times,** 1877-1897.

Deadwood, South Dakota **Black Hills Pioneer,** 1876-1891.

Deadwood, South Dakota Council Proceedings, No. 7, City of Deadwood.

Deadwood, South Dakota **The Lantern,** 1905-1910.

Deadwood, South Dakota **The Daily Telegram,** 1908-1927.

Deadwood, South Dakota **Deadwood Pioneer-Times,** 1897-1979.

The Denver (Colorado) **Post,** 1908.

Driscoll, R. E. **Seventy Years of Banking in the Black Hills.** Rapid City, SD: Gate City Guide, 1948.

DuFran, Dora (D. Dee) **Low Down on Calamity Jane.** Rapid City, SD: Gate City Guide, 1932.

Fielder, Mildred. **A Guide to Black Hills Ghost Mines.** Aberdeen, SD: North Plains Press, 1972.

Fielder, Mildred. **Potato Creek Johnny.** Lead, SD: Bonanza Trails Publishers, 1973.

Fielder, Mildred. **The Chinese in the Black Hills.** Lead, SD: Bonanza Trails Publishers, 1972.

Fielder, Mildred. **Silver is the Fortune.** Aberdeen, SD: North Plains Press, 1978.

Fielder, Mildred. **Wild Bill and Deadwood.** Seattle: Superior Publishing Company, 1964.

Hagedorn, Hermann, ed. **The Theodore Roosevelt Treasury**—A Self Portrait from His Writings. New York: G. P. Putnam's Sons, 1957.

Hot Springs (South Dakota) **Star,** 1895.

Hot Springs (South Dakota) **Weekly,** 1882.

Hidy, Albert S. Sr. A Memorial History of Flora Hayward Stanford (unpublished), Portland, Oregon, 1968. Deadwood Public Library, Deadwood, South Dakota.

Howe, F. S., M.D. **Deadwood Doctor,** 1951.

Hughes, Richard B. **Pioneer Years in the Black Hills.** Glendale, CA: Arthur H. Clark Company, 1957.

Jennewein, J. Leonard. **Black Hills Booktrails.** Dakota Territory Centennial Commission, 1962.

Jennewein, J. Leonard. **Calamity Jane of the Western Trails.** Huron, SD: Dakota Books, 1953.

Kellar, Kenneth. **Seth Bullock—Frontier Marshal,** Aberdeen, SD: North Plains Press, 1972.

Kingsbury, George. **History of Dakota Territory.** Vol. IV, Chicago: S. J. Clark Company, 1915.

Klock, Irma H. **All Roads Lead to Deadwood.** Aberdeen, SD: North Plains Press, 1979.

Klock, Irma H. **Here Comes Calamity Jane,** Deadwood, SD: Dakota Graphics, 1979.

Klock, Irma H. **Yesterday's Gold Camps and Mines in the Northern Black Hills.** Lead, SD: Seaton Publishing Company, 1975.

Lead (South Dakota) **Daily Call.** 1914, 1919, 1960, 1964.

Lee, Bob, ed. **Gold-Gals-Guns-Guts.** Deadwood-Lead '76 Centennial Inc., 1976.

Leedy, Carl. **Golden Days of the Black Hills.** Rapid City, SD: Holmgrens, Inc., 1967.

Mechling, Patricia, ed. "Mount Moriah Cemetery," **Black Hills Nuggets,** Commemorative Edition. Rapid City, SD: Rapid City Society for Geneological Research, Inc., 1976.

McClintock, John S. **Pioneer Days in the Black Hills.** New York: J. J. Little & Ives, 1939.

Memorial Biographical Record, The Black Hills Region. Chicago: George A. Ogle & Company, 1889.

Milton, John R. **South Dakota,** A History. New York: W. W. Norton & Co., Inc., 1977.

Minneapolis (Minnesota) **Times,** 1895.

Minnelusa Museum, Rapid City, South Dakota. C. Irwin Leedy Historical Collection.

Mumey, Nolie. **Calamity Jane.** Denver: The Range Press, 1950.

Nelson, Bruce. **Land of the Dacotahs.** Minneapolis: University of Minnesota Press, 1947.

Nelson, Larry C. "Dramatis Personae," The Hills Aren't Black, A Collection of Black Hills Poetry. (unpublished) Lead, South Dakota.

Paine, Clarence, "Wild Bill Hickok and Calamity Jane," **The Black Hills,** ed. Roderick Peattie. New York: Vanguard Press, 1980.

Parker, Watson. **Gold in the Black Hills.** Norman: University of Oklahoma Press, 1966.

Prospector John. **Gold Panning with Prospector John.** Skagway, Alaska: The Author, 1973.

Queen City Mail, Spearfish, South Dakota, 1933.

Rapid City (South Dakota) **Journal,** 1892, 1928, 1929, 1934.

Rapid City Public Library, South Dakota. Rapid City Scrapbooks (unpublished).

Record Book of the Deadwood Cemetery Association, 1878-1979. (unpublished) City Finance

Office, Deadwood, South Dakota.

Riordan, Kay, ed. **Historical Cooking of the Black Hills,** Yes! But What Did They Eat? Keystone, SD: Mountain Co., Inc., 1971.

Roosevelt, Theodore. **Theodore Roosevelt—An Autobiography.** New York: The MacMillan Company, 1919.

Rosa, Joseph G. **They Called Him Wild Bill.** Norman: University of Oklahoma Press, 1964.

Russell, Thomas. **The Russell-Collins 1874 Gold Expedition to the Black Hills of Dakota.** Clowser, ed. Deadwood, South Dakota, no date.

Saroyan, William. **Obituaries.** Berkeley, CA.: Creative Arts Book Company, 1979.

Senn, Edward L. **Deadwood Dick and Calamity Jane.** Deadwood, SD: The Author, 1939.

Senn, Edward L. **Preacher Smith—Martyr of the Cross.** Deadwood, SD: The Author, 1939.

Senn, Edward L. **Wild Bill Hickok—Prince of Pistoleers.** Deadwood, SD: The Author, 1939.

Simmons, Major A. J. "Looking Backwards Fifty-Six Years," **Black Hills Illustrated.** Black Hills Mining Men's Association. Chicago: Blakely Printing Company, 1904.

Sollid, Roberta B. **Calamity Jane.** The Western Press, 1958.

A South Dakota Guide. Compiled by the Works Progress Administration. Pierre, SD: State Publishing Company, 1938.

South Dakota Place Names. South Dakota Writers' Project. University of South Dakota, Vermillion, 1941.

Spring, Agnes Wright. **The Cheyenne and Black Hills Stage and Express Routes.** Lincoln: University of Nebraska Press, 1948.

Sulentic, Joe. **Deadwood Gulch—The Last Chinatown.** Deadwood, South Dakota, 1975.

Tallent, Annie D. **The Black Hills or The Last Hunting Grounds of the Dakotahs.** Sioux Falls, SD: Brevet Press, 1974.

Wall Street Journal, 1973.

Wilstach, Frank J. **Wild Bill Hickok.** Garden City, NY: Garden City Publishing Company, 1926.

Wheeler, Edward. **The Minor Sport.** New York: Beadle and Adams Pocket Library, 1895.

Yuill, Camille. **Deadwood in the Black Hills of South Dakota.** Deadwood, SD: Seaton Publishing Company, 1968.

INDEX

(Listings omitted because of their frequent use are Mount Moriah, Deadwood, Deadwood Gulch, Lead, Black Hills Gold Rush; and three newspapers—*Black Hills Pioneer, Black Hills Daily* and *Weekly Times,* and *Deadwood-Pioneer Times.)*

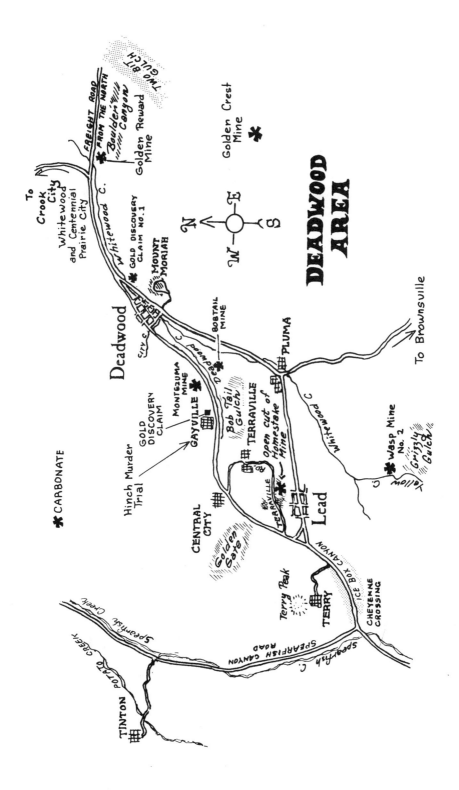

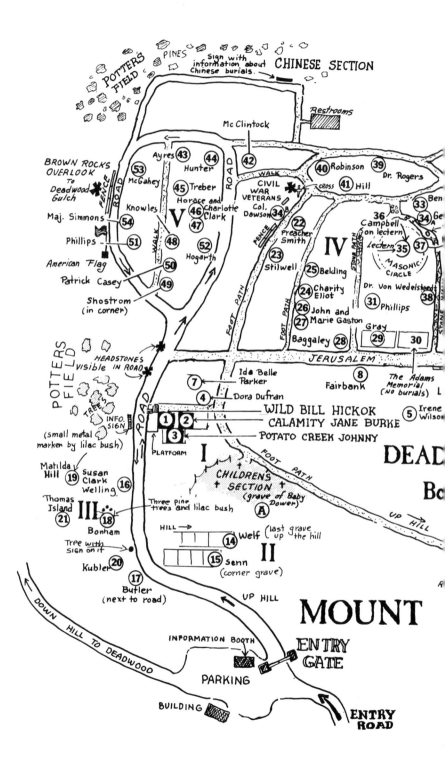

POTTER'S FIELD

PINES

Sign with information about Chinese burials

CHINESE SECTION

Restrooms

McClintock

BROWN ROCKS OVERLOOK To Deadwood Gulch

㊸ Ayres
㊼ Hunter
㊸ McGahey
㊹ Treber
Horace and Charlotte Clark
Knowles
㊷
㊸
㊹
Hogarth

ROAD

WALK

㊷ McClintock

㊸ ㊷ Robinson ㊸ Dr. Rogers

CIVIL WAR VETERANS
Col. Dawson ㉞

㊵ CROSS ㊶ Hill

Maj. Simmons ㊴
Phillips ㊿
American Flag
Patrick Casey ㊾
Shostrom (in corner)

V

WALK

㉒ Preacher Smith

㉓ Stilwell

㉕ Belding

㉔ Charity Eliot

㉖ John and
㉗ Marie Gaston

Baggaley ㉘

IV

㉝ Ben
㉞ Ge
36 Campbell on lectern
Lectern ㉟ ㊲
MASONIC CIRCLE
Dr. Von Wedelstedt
31 Phillips ㊳

Gray
㉙ 30

STONE PATH

JERUSALEM

The Adams Memorial (No burials) L

POTTER'S FIELD

HEADSTONES visible in road

TREES

ROAD

INFO. SIGN

(small metal marker by lilac bush)

⑦ Ida Belle Parker

④ Dora Dufran

① ② WILD BILL HICKOK
CALAMITY JANE BURKE
③ POTATO CREEK JOHNNY

PLATFORM

I

⑧ Fairbank

⑤ Irene Wilson

DEAD
Bo

Matilda Hill ⑲ Susan Clark Welling ⑯

Thomas Island ㉑ III ⑱ Bonham

Three pine trees and lilac bush

CHILDREN'S SECTION (grave of Baby Dower) Ⓐ

FOOT PATH

UP HILL

Tree with sign on it

Kubler ⑳

⑰ Butler (next to road)

HILL →

⑭ Welf (last grave up the hill)

⑮ Senn (corner grave)

II

UP HILL

MOUNT

DOWN HILL TO DEADWOOD

INFORMATION BOOTH

PARKING

ENTRY GATE

BUILDING

ENTRY ROAD

SECTION I — "Big Three" — Wild Bill, Calamity Jane and Potato Creek "Johnny" — on main road in front with flagstone steps and terrace. More graves up hill including Hebrew section at top — plus Seth Bullock. Includes children's section.

(1) WILL BILL HICKOK — Unofficial Black Hills Pioneer – 1876 – Prince of Pistoleers – Frontier Marshal — Gambler.

(2) CALAMITY JANE BURKE — Unofficial Pioneer – 1875 – Prostitute – Scout – Bullwhacker – Nurse – Markswoman – Most liberated female of the frontier.

(3) POTATO CREEK JOHNNY — Tiny prospector who found large gold nugget.

(4) DORA DUFRAN — Brothel Madam with heart of gold — Author of Calamity Jane biography

(5) IRENE CUSHMAN WILSON — Unofficial Black Hills Pioneer – 1877 – Romantic Diarist and Cultural Leader.

*(6) WILLIAM LARDNER — Unofficial Black Hills Pioneer – 1875 — Early Prospector – Discovered gold at Gayville in Deadwood Gulch.

*(7) IDA BELLE PARKER — Black Hills Pioneer – 1876 Art Shop Owner — oldest pioneer woman at death, age 95.

*(8) MAJOR JOHN FAIRBANK — Black Hills Pioneer – 1876 – Mining Interests — Popular Speaker at schools and ceremonies — Civil War Veteran.

(A) CHILDREN'S SECTION — (identified by sign) graves of many children who died in small pox, scarlet fever, and diphtheria epidemics — 1878 – 1880.

HEBREW HILL

(9) HARRIS FRANKLIN — Black Hills Pioneer – 1878 Millionaire Banker — Cattleman – Golden Reward mine — Franklin Hotel.

(10) SIDNEY JACOBS — Clothing Store Founder — Unofficial Rabbi — Prince of practical Jokers.

*(11) SAMUEL SCHWARZWALD — Black Hills Pioneer 1876 — Furniture Store Founder

(12) BLANCHE COLMAN — Daughter of Jewish leader, Nathan Colman — first woman lawyer in South Dakota.

(13) SETH BULLOCK — Black Hills Pioneer – 1876 – Deadwood's first sheriff — U.S. Marshal Forest Supervisor — friend of Theodore Roosevelt. (turn left at pump house — his grave is half-way up road to White Rocks)

SECTION II Right hand side of main road, inside gate — before "Big Three"

(14) EDWARD SENN — Historian – Controversial Newspaper Editor — Prohibition Officer.

*(15) ARTHUR WELF — Wholesale Mercantile — Civic Leader.

orical

Williams

EN'S A

Blanche Colman — (12)

Sidney Jacobs — (10)

Samuel Schwarzwald

(11)

Jacobs HEBREW INSCRIPTIONS

The Franklin Monument is largest stone in cemetery

Harris Franklin

(9)

HEBREW HILL ROAD

Seth Bullock's grave about ¼ mile walk. Stay to the left.

Pump House

OD'S

1

tery

RIAH

ROAD

To Seth Bullock's grave and White Rocks

(13)

SECTION III

Left hand side of main road inside gate.

(16) SUSAN CLARKE WELLING — Black Hills Pioneer — 1876 - Walked to the Black Hills.

(17) GEORGE BUTLER — Jeweler — Manfactured Black Hills gold Jewelry — City Band member.

(18) W. H. BONHAM — Black Hills Pioneer 1877 — 50-year-editor of DEADWOOD PIONEER TIMES — Chief of Deadwood Fire Dept.

(19) MATILDA HILL — Popular Negro Woman — first cook at Tomahawk Country Club.

(20) DOROTHY KUBLER — Musician and Teacher.

*(21) THOMAS ISLAND — Rancher — Store-Keeper, Log Cabin Builder.

SECTION IV

Largest section — in the middle — to the left and across uphill road from "Big Three." Includes Preacher Smith, Civil War Vets, Masonic Circle, and Mass Grave of 11 burned in fire.

(22) REV. HENRY WESTON SMITH — Preacher Smith — Unofficial Black Hills Pioneer — 1876 Killed by Indians.

*(23) LUCIEN W. STILWELL — Black Hills Pioneer 1879 — Bookkeeper and Curio Shop.

(24) CHARITY ELIOT — Died at age 100 — Daughter of Revolutionary Soldier.

*(25) JOHN BELDING — Black Hills Pioneer 1876 — Miner — Locator of Water Rights — Sheriff.

(26) JOHN GASTON — Black Hills Pioneer — 1876 — Storekeeper — sold firearms.

(27) MARIE GASTON — Black Hills Pioneer — 1879 — First Librarian of Deadwood.

(28) JOHN BAGGALEY — Black Hills Pioneer 1877 — Mine Broker — Real Estate — Curios.

(29) JOHN GRAY — Black Hills Pioneer — 1876 — Mine Owner of Wasp No 2.

(30) W. E. ADAMS FAMILY MEMORIAL MARKER No member of Adams family buried here. Erected by W.E. Adams — long-time mayor and Black Hills Pioneer 1877 — Donor of Adams Museum.

*(31) KIRK PHILLIPS — Black Hills Pioneer — 1877 Contractor for Boulder Ditch — Druggist — State Treasurer.

(32) J.J. WILLIAMS — Black Hills Pioneer — 1874 Member of illegal Gordon Party — Miner — Laid out Deadwood Townsite — Member of Deadwood Pioneer Hook and Ladder Company.

(33) GRANVILLE G BENNETT — Black Hills Pioneer 1877 First District Court Judge — Father of Estelline, author of OLD DEADWOOD DAYS.

(34) GENERAL ANDREW R. Z. DAWSON — Black Hills Pioneer — 1876 — has two tombstones: Large one for General in G. Bennett plot; small marker of Civil War Veterans for Colonel. First collector of internal revenue — Popular Orator.

(35) MASONIC CIRCLE WITH STONE LECTERN — Open Bible atop — names engraved on sides of lectern of those buried within twenty feet of marker.

*(36) HUGH O CAMPBELL — Unofficial Black Hills Pioneer — telegrapher killed in Canyon Springs stagecoach robbery of 1878 — grave unidentified — name on lectern.

(37) CHAMBERS C. DAVIS — Unofficial Black Hills Pioneer — 1877 — Assayer — name on lectern and on nearby tombstone for Davis and wife.

(38) DR. H. L. VON WEDELSTAEDT — Unofficial Black Hills Pioneer — 1877 — Physician — Only white member of Chinese Masonic Order.

(39) DR. MORRIS ROGERS — Unofficial Black Hills Pioneer — 1877 Physician.

*(40) C. H ROBINSON — Black Hills Pioneer — 1876 — Undertaker.

*(41) HENRY HILL — Black Hills Pioneer — 1877 — Attorney — Justice of Peace.

(42) JOHN McCLINTOCK — Black Hills Pioneer 1876 — Miner — livery stable — stagecoach line — historian — author of PIONEER DAYS IN THE BLACK HILLS.

SECTION V

Two levels with walk between — Near overlook and flag.

(43) GEORGE AYRES — Black Hills Pioneer — 1876 — Witty Hardware Merchant — Civic and Masonic leader — walked to Black Hills from Cheyenne, Wyo.

(44) JOHN HUNTER — Black Hills Pioneer — 1877 — brought saw mill to Hills by stage coach — lumber and mercantile business.

(45) JOHN TREBER — Black Hills Pioneer — 1877 — Wholesale Liquor Business — State Legislator.

(46) HORACE CLARK — Black Hills Pioneer — 1877 Automobile Dealer — Real Estate.

(47) CHARLOTTE CUSHMAN CLARK — Black Hills Pioneer — 1878 — Last Pioneer at death — age 102 — wrote memoirs.

(48) FREEMAN KNOWLES — Congressman — Radical Newspaper Editor for Populist Party — Civil War Veteran.

(49) LARS SHOSTROM — Mason and Cement Business — built Deadwood's first sidewalks.

(50) PATRICK CASEY — Black Hills Pioneer — 1876 — Saloon-keeper — bizarre suicide victim.

(51) MARY PHILLIPS — Lead High School English Teacher.

*(52) MARY JANE HOGARTH — English Immigrant with tragic death — 1893.

*(53) DAVID McGAHEY — First Curator of Adams Museum. Immigrant from Ireland.

(54) MAJOR ANDREW JACKSON SIMMONS — Unoffical Black Hills Pioneer — 1878 — Special Indian Agent — Negotiated with Sitting Bull for railroad right of way — Philanthropist — Educational Leader.

GRAVES NOT LOCATED

*DICK COSTELLO — Deadwood Chief of Police — died 1947.

DR. FLORA STANFORD — First and only woman doctor in Deadwood — died 1901.

KITTY LeROY — Unofficial Black Hills Pioneer. Prostitute murdered by husband, Sam Curley who committed suicide — originally buried in double grave with him at Ingleside — died 1877.

DIFFERENT STAR — Sioux Indian accused of stealing horses — committed suicide in Deadwood Jail — died 1895.

*JOHN HINCH — first murder victim in Deadwood Gulch — body moved from Ingleside. died 1876.

JOHN LAWRENCE — Unofficial Black Hills Pioneer — County Treasurer — Territorial Legislator — Politician for whom Lawrence County was named — died 1889.

YUNG SET — unknown Chinese man who had elaborate Chinese funeral — died 1878.

CHINESE SECTION

Down slopes to right of main part of cemetery near sign explaining about Chinese section. Includes several well-marked graves of white people.

* No Vignette